Edexcel GCSE (9-1)

History

The USA, 1954–1975: conflict at home and abroad

Series Editor: Angela Leonard   Author: Margaret Hudson

ALWAYS LEARNING

PEARSON

Published by Pearson Education Limited, 80 Strand, London, WC2R 0RL.

www.pearsonschoolsandfecolleges.co.uk

Copies of official specifications for all Edexcel qualifications may be found on the website: www.edexcel.com

Text © Pearson Education Limited 2016

Series editor: Angela Leonard
Designed by Colin Tilley Loughrey, Pearson Education Limited
Typeset by Phoenix Photosetting, Chatham, Kent
Original illustrations © Pearson Education Limited
Illustrated by KJA Artists Illustration Agency and Phoenix Photosetting, Chatham, Kent.

Cover design by Colin Tilley Loughrey
Picture research by Ewout Buckens
Cover photo © Bridgeman Art Library Ltd: Private Collection

The right of Margaret Hudson to be identified as author of this work has been asserted by her in accordance with the Copyright, Designs and Patents Act 1988.

First published 2016

23
10 9 8 7 6

British Library Cataloguing in Publication Data
A catalogue record for this book is available from the British Library.
ISBN 978 1 292 12732 3

A note from the publisher
In order to ensure that this resource offers high-quality support for the associated Pearson qualification, it has been through a review process by the awarding body. This process confirms that this resource fully covers the teaching and learning content of the specification or part of a specification at which it is aimed. It also confirms that it demonstrates an appropriate balance between the development of subject skills, knowledge and understanding, in addition to preparation for assessment.

Endorsement does not cover any guidance on assessment activities or processes (e.g. practice questions or advice on how to answer assessment questions), included in the resource nor does it prescribe any particular approach to the teaching or delivery of a related course.

While the publishers have made every attempt to ensure that advice on the qualification and its assessment is accurate, the official specification and associated assessment guidance materials are the only authoritative source of information and should always be referred to for definitive guidance.

Pearson examiners have not contributed to any sections in this resource relevant to examination papers for which they have responsibility.

Examiners will not use endorsed resources as a source of material for any assessment set by Pearson.

Endorsement of a resource does not mean that the resource is required to achieve this Pearson qualification, nor does it mean that it is the only suitable material available to support the qualification, and any resource lists produced by the awarding body shall include this and other appropriate resources.

Websites
Pearson Education Limited is not responsible for the content of any external internet sites. It is essential for tutors to preview each website before using it in class so as to ensure that the URL is still accurate, relevant and appropriate. We suggest that tutors bookmark useful websites and consider enabling students to access them through the school/college intranet.

Contents

How to use this book

What's covered?

This book covers the Modern Depth study on The USA, 1954–1975: conflict at home and abroad. This unit makes up 30% of your GCSE course, and will be examined in Paper 2.

Modern depth studies cover a short period of time, and require you to know about a society or historical situation in detail. You need to understand different aspects within this period, such as social, economic, political, cultural and military, and how they interact with each other. This book also explains the different types of exam questions you will need to answer, and includes advice and example answers to help you improve.

Features

As well as a clear, detailed explanation of the key knowledge you will need, you will also find a number of features in the book:

Key terms

Where you see a word followed by an asterisk, like this: Civil rights activist*, you will be able to find a Key Terms box on that page that explains what the word means.

> **Key term**
>
> **Civil rights activist***
> Someone who campaigns for equal rights and tries to persuade others to do the same.

Activities

Every few pages, you'll find a box containing some activities designed to help check and embed knowledge and get you to really think about what you've studied. The activities start simple, but might get more challenging as you work through them.

Summaries and Checkpoints

At the end of each chunk of learning, the main points are summarised in a series of bullet points – great for embedding the core knowledge, and handy for revision.

Checkpoints help you to check and reflect on your learning. The Strengthen section helps you to consolidate knowledge and understanding, and check that you've grasped the basic ideas and skills. The Challenge questions push you to go beyond just understanding the information, and into evaluation and analysis of what you've studied.

Sources and Interpretations

This book contains numerous contemporary pictorial and text sources that show what people from the period, said, thought or created.

The book also includes extracts from the work of historians, showing how experts have interpreted the events you've been studying.

You will need to be comfortable examining both sources AND interpretations to answer questions in your Paper 3 exam.

Source A

A photograph showing Rosa Parks being fingerprinted on 1 December 1955.

Interpretation 1

From 'To Walk in Dignity: the Montgomery Bus Boycott' in the *Organisation of American Historians Magazine of History* (2005) by Clayborne Carson.

The ultimate success of the boycott resulted not only from the perseverance of MIA members but also from the determination of the lawyers who challenged segregated bus seating in the courts. Clifford Durr worked closely with black attorney Fred Gray to provide legal defence for Parks and later advised NAACP attorneys involved in the *Browder v. Gayle* (1956) case that struck down the legal basis for segregation on Montgomery's buses, achieving the boycott's objective.

Extend your knowledge

These features contain useful additional information that adds depth to your knowledge, and to your answers. The information is closely related to the key issues in the unit, and questions are sometimes included, helping you to link the new details to the main content.

> **Extend your knowledge**
>
> **Earlier sit-ins**
> In August 1958, in Oklahoma City, a 15-year-old black girl, Barbara Posey, organised a sit-in at a lunch counter. She was a member of the local NAACP. About 85 black children took part in the sit-in. Barbara organised more demonstrations in Oklahoma, the largest of which involved about 500 students. Most stores desegregated after one or two days of protest.

Exam-style questions and tips

The book also includes extra exam-style questions you can use to practise. These appear in the chapters and are accompanied by a tip to help you get started on an answer.

Exam-style question, Section B

Study Sources D and E. How useful are Sources D and E for an enquiry into the aims of the Black Panthers? Explain your answer, using Sources D and E and your knowledge of the historical context. **8 marks**

Exam tip

When considering how useful sources are, think about how the type of source (e.g. interview, pamphlet, photograph) might affect its usefulness.

Recap pages

At the end of each chapter, you'll find a page designed to help you to consolidate and reflect on the chapter as a whole. Each recap page includes a recall quiz, ideal for quickly checking your knowledge or for revision. Recap pages also include activities designed to help you summarise and analyse what you've learned, and also reflect on how each chapter links to other parts of the unit.

These activities are designed to help you develop a better understanding of how history is constructed, and are focused on the key areas of Evidence, Interpretations, Cause & Consequence and Change & Continuity. In the Modern Depth Study, you will come across activities on Cause & Consequence, Evidence and Interpretations as these are key areas of focus for this unit.

The Thinking Historically approach has been developed in conjunction with Dr Arthur Chapman and the Institute of Education, UCL. It is based on research into the misconceptions that can hold students back in history.

THINKING HISTORICALLY ▶ Cause and consequence (6a) — conceptual map reference

The Thinking Historically conceptual map can be found at: www.pearsonschools.co.uk/thinkinghistoricallygcse

At the end of most chapters is a spread dedicated to helping you improve your writing skills. These include simple techniques you can use in your writing to make your answers clearer, more precise and better focused on the question you're answering.

The Writing Historically approach is based on the *Grammar for Writing* pedagogy developed by a team at the University of Exeter and popular in many English departments. Each spread uses examples from the preceding chapter, so it's relevant to what you've just been studying.

Preparing for your exams

At the back of the book, you'll find a special section dedicated to explaining and exemplifying the new Edexcel GCSE History exams. Advice on the demands of this paper, written by Angela Leonard, helps you prepare for and approach the exam with confidence. Each question type is explained through annotated sample answers at two levels, showing clearly how answers can be improved.

Pearson Progression Scale: This icon indicates the Step that a sample answer has been graded at on the Pearson Progression Scale.

This book is also available as an online ActiveBook, which can be licensed for your whole institution.

There is also an ActiveLearn Digital Service available to support delivery of this book, featuring a front-of-class version of the book, lesson plans, worksheets, exam practice PowerPoints, assessments, notes on Thinking Historically and Writing Historically, and more.

ActiveLearn
Digital Service

Timeline: Conflict at home and abroad, 1954–75

Events at home

1954
The *Brown v. Topeka* case

1955
Emmett Till murdered

1955
Rosa Parks arrested for refusing to move from her seat on a segregated bus

1955
Beginning of Montgomery Bus Boycott

1956
Supreme Court upholds decision of *Browder v. Gayle* case that buses should be desegregated

1957
Founding of the SCLC

1957
Little Rock High School crisis

1957
Civil Rights Act

1960
First Greensboro sit-in

1960
SNCC set up

1961
Kennedy becomes US president

1961
'Freedom Rides' test desegregation on buses

1962
James Meredith enrols at the University of Mississippi

1963
Campaign 'C' launched in Birmingham, Alabama

1963
Martin Luther King makes his famous 'I have a dream…' speech in Washington, DC

1963
President Kennedy assassinated – Johnson becomes US president

1964
Freedom Summer in Mississippi

1964
Civil Rights Act

1965
Assassination of Malcolm X

1965
Selma to Montgomery protest march

1965
Voting Rights Act

1954	1956	1958	1960	1962	1964

Events abroad

1954
Defeat at Dien Bien Phu leads to French withdrawal from Vietnam

1956
Ngo Dinh Diem refuses to hold elections

1959
Ho Chi Minh begins sending troops and weapons into the south of Vietnam

1961
President Kennedy increases US involvement in Vietnam

1963
Quang Duc, a Buddhist monk, sets fire to himself in Saigon

1964
Gulf of Tonkin incident

1965
Operation Rolling Thunder launched

1965
Major increase in US troop numbers in Vietnam

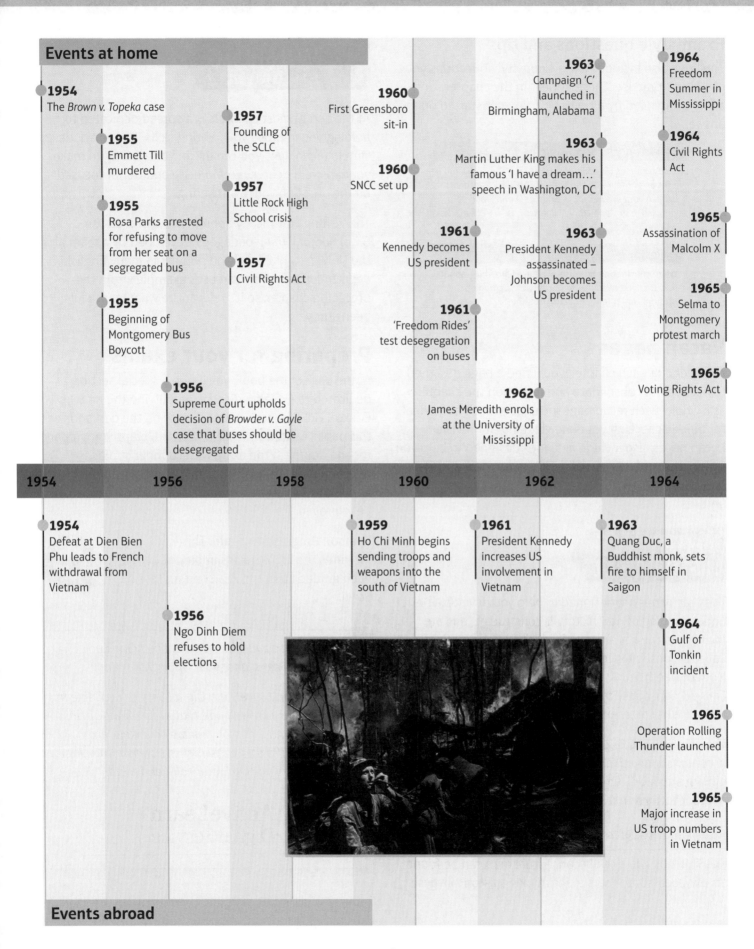

1966
James Meredith leads the March Against Fear

1968
Assassination of Martin Luther King

1970
Kent State shootings during protest against the Vietnam War

1966
Black Panthers set up

1968
Kerner Report on riots

1971
Lieutenant Calley found guilty of murdering civilians at My Lai, Vietnam

1969
Nixon becomes US president

1969
Nixon appeals for support from the 'silent majority'

1969
President Nixon outlines the Nixon Doctrine

| 1966 | 1968 | 1970 | 1972 | 1974 | 1976 |

1968
Battle for Khe Sanh and Tet Offensive

1970
US and South Vietnamese forces briefly invade Cambodia

1973
Paris Peace Accords

1968
My Lai massacre

1971
US and South Vietnamese forces attack Laos

1968
Tommie Smith and John Carlos give Black Power salute at Mexico Olympics

1972
North Vietnamese Easter Offensive

1969
US opens secret peace talks with North Vietnam

1972
US launch Operation Linebacker

1972
Formal peace negotiations commence

1975
Saigon falls to the North Vietnamese Army

01 | The development of the civil rights movement, 1954–60

By the early 1950s, slavery had long been abolished and, by law, black Americans were equal to white Americans and had the same rights. However, black Americans were not actually treated as equal. All over the USA, most black Americans lived in the worst parts of towns and cities, with the worst hospitals, schools and other facilities. They did the least desirable jobs and were often 'last hired, first fired'. Many jobs were beyond their reach because training for these jobs was not given to black people.

The situation was worse in the South. In most southern states, local laws meant that black Americans could not use the same toilets as white people, swim in the same swimming pools, ride in the same part of the train or eat in the same restaurants. This system of segregation kept black and white communities separate. Black Americans had the right to vote, but were stopped from doing so by a system that deliberately discriminated against them. They were also stopped by threats and violence.

How could this happen? How did black Americans react?

Their reaction depended on where they lived and what their circumstances were. Some black Americans, especially in the South, tried to improve their lives inside the system enforced by white people. Others joined civil rights organisations to campaign for equality. This chapter will look at how they campaigned and whether their campaigns were successful.

Learning outcomes

In this chapter, you will study:

- the position in society of black Americans in the early 1950s
- the *Brown v. Topeka* case (1954) and its significance
- the Montgomery Bus Boycott and its impact, 1955–60
- opposition to the civil rights movement, 1954–60.

Segregation and discrimination

All across the USA, black Americans faced segregation* and discrimination* every day. However, there was a significant difference. Segregation in the North was produced by discrimination. Black people usually had the worst-paid jobs, so had to live in the poorest parts of towns and cities, called 'ghettos'. Here, people were crowded together in buildings that were not well maintained and had poor facilities. Workers in schools and hospitals, for example, had to cope with run-down buildings, old equipment and shortages of supplies. Most of the people living in ghettos were black.

Segregation in the South was different. Racist state laws, often called 'Jim Crow' laws*, enforced segregation. Black Americans could not eat in 'white' restaurants. They could be thrown off buses, or even arrested, if they did not sit in the 'colored' section of the bus. Cinemas, theatres and churches were either just for white or black Americans or had separate seating. Black children could not go to the nearest school if it was a 'white' school. They had to walk or catch a bus to the nearest 'black' school which, because far less state money was spent on it, might have no heating or textbooks. Southern states could pass laws enforcing this because in the USA there were two levels of government and law-making (see page 10).

Key terms

Segregation*

Separating groups of people, usually by race or religion.

Discrimination*

Treating people unfairly because of their race or religion.

Jim Crow laws*

Jim Crow was a (supposedly funny) lazy, stupid black character, played by a white comedian. 'Black code' laws enforcing segregation were given the nickname 'Jim Crow'. The laws varied from state to state, but they all separated black and white people.

Source A

A photograph showing black and white Americans on a segregated bus in Florida in April 1956. The black Americans have, by law, to sit at the back of the bus.

Exam-style question, Section A

Give **two** things you can infer from Source A about segregation in 1956. Give the detail in the source that tells you this.

4 marks

Exam tip

You infer something from a source by working out something the source does not actually tell you directly. In this case, you could look at where people are sitting and their behaviour.

Figure 1.1 The Southern states are the blue and green states on the map above. The blue states are the 'Deep South'.

Federal laws are laws which cover the whole country. State laws only affect one state. A state can pass its own laws, but the Supreme Court can overrule them. In the USA, a bill is a proposed law. A bill has to be passed in the House of Representatives and the Senate, and also has to be approved by the president before it becomes a law. When passed, a bill becomes an Act.

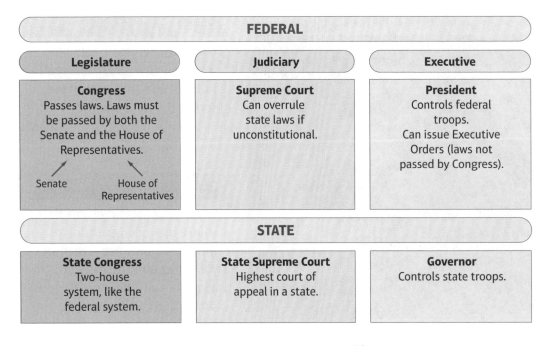

FEDERAL		
Legislature	**Judiciary**	**Executive**
Congress Passes laws. Laws must be passed by both the Senate and the House of Representatives. Senate ← → House of Representatives	**Supreme Court** Can overrule state laws if unconstitutional.	**President** Controls federal troops. Can issue Executive Orders (laws not passed by Congress).

STATE		
State Congress Two-house system, like the federal system.	**State Supreme Court** Highest court of appeal in a state.	**Governor** Controls state troops.

Figure 1.2 The government of the USA, created by the United States Constitution of 1787, had federal and state government. It split both of them into a legislature (to make laws), a judiciary (to interpret laws) and an executive (to carry out laws).

Extend your knowledge

North and South

Before and after the Second World War, many black Americans moved north. For example, James Roberson and his mother moved from Birmingham, Alabama, to Cincinnati, Ohio, in the North in the early 1950s, when James was about ten. The railway company James' father worked for had promised him a transfer to Cincinnati. James and his mother lived in Cincinnati for about six months, but his father was told he could not transfer, so they had to go back to Alabama. When their train stopped in a small Southern town, James went into the station building to get something to eat. Everyone looked at him in horror. One woman said 'get out of here, nigger!' and everyone looked at him with hate. He ran back to the train.

Attitudes in the South

Many Southern white people were brought up to see black people as racially inferior: 'childlike', lazy and unintelligent. Most black people worked on farms or as domestic servants. Few black people in Southern towns could find work in factories, even in the lowest-paid jobs. White people called black people by their first names, or 'boy' or 'girl', even if talking to adults. White Southerners were unlikely to shake hands with black people because that was a sign of equality. The few white Southerners who objected to discrimination were called 'white niggers' and faced the same violence that black Americans faced.

The police and the law courts in the South were full of racist white officials who did not support complaints by black people. This was especially true in the Deep South, where many policemen and judges were members of the Ku Klux Klan*. Black people were regularly beaten up to get them to confess to crimes they did not commit. They were imprisoned for no reason and often represented in court by white lawyers who made no effort to defend them. Black people could not sit on juries either, and if a black person murdered another black person it was dismissed as 'a Negro crime' and often was not investigated. One of the frightening things for black people was knowing that the officials who were meant to protect them might well belong to the racist white groups that were threatening them.

Key term

Ku Klux Klan (KKK)*

A group who persecuted Jews, Catholics, communists, and anyone who was not white, especially black people. They put burning crosses in front of houses, blew up homes and murdered people.

The effect of the Second World War

Over a million black Americans fought in the Second World War, in segregated units. Millions more worked in factories, making weapons or doing the jobs of those who had gone to fight. They hoped for more equality when the war ended and some white people, even in the South, were more open to civil rights after the war. This was especially true for white Americans who had worked with black people for the first time.

Also, racial inequality was a political embarrassment for the USA. The USA had gone to war in 1941 to fight for democracy and freedom. Then, in the Cold War* that developed after the Second World War, the USA was seen as the leader of the 'free world'. However, opponents of the USA used the example of black Americans to show that it did not even give freedom to its own citizens. This put pressure on federal government to improve the situation of black Americans, especially in the South.

Key term

Cold War*

A term which refers to the political tension and military rivalry that developed at the end of the Second World War between the USA and its allies and the USSR (also called the Soviet Union) and its allies. Both sides used political propaganda against each other, to get the support of other countries. The war was 'cold' because it stopped short of a full-scale war between these two states, though each backed opposite sides in other conflicts.

Activity

In groups, discuss white attitudes to black people in the South and how segregation reinforced these attitudes. Decide on one social change that you think would have helped the most to change these attitudes. Write a campaign slogan for this change.

Source B

These photographs show a white school (left) and a black school (right) in Farmville, Virginia, in the early 1950s.

Source C

From a speech by James Eastland, given on 27 May 1954. He was a US senator for Mississippi, and a supporter of segregation.

The southern institution of racial segregation or racial separation was the correct, self-evident truth which arose from the chaos and confusion of the reconstruction period [the period after 1865, when slavery was abolished]. Separation promotes racial harmony. It permits each race to follow its own pursuits, and its own civilization. Segregation is not discrimination. Segregation is not a badge of racial inferiority, and that it is not is recognized by both races in the Southern States. In fact, segregation is desired and supported by the vast majority of the members of both races in the South, who dwell side by side under harmonious conditions.

THINKING HISTORICALLY ▸ Evidence (3b)

It depends on the question

When considering the usefulness of historical sources, people often consider 'reliability' (whether a witness can be trusted). This is important, however some sources are not witnesses – they are simply the remains of the past.

Work in small groups.

1   Imagine you are investigating whether segregation gave black Americans inferior lives. Look at Source B.

   a   Write at least two statements that you can reasonably infer about life for black Americans based solely on Source B.

   b   Which of your statements are you most sure of? Explain your answer.

2   Source C is unreliable testimony – its author had good reason not to tell the truth. Try to think of at least two statements that you can still reasonably infer about life for black Americans using this source.

3   Which source is more useful for investigating life for black Americans? Explain your answer.

In your group, discuss the following question and write down your thoughts: How are reliability and usefulness related?

Voting rights

The right to vote gives people power because politicians need votes to get elected. If enough black people register to vote, then politicians need some policies that black Americans approve of to win their support. This was happening in the North in the 1950s. In some parts of the South there was more acceptance of black Americans voting, especially for their own officials in segregated communities. For example, by 1954, there were 143 Southern towns with black policemen; there had been very few before the Second World War.

In 1956, about 20% of black Americans in the South were registered to vote. This was not a huge percentage, but more than the 3% who were registered before the war. However, in many Southern states, white people stopped black people from voting by both official and unofficial methods.

- White employers threatened to sack black employees if they registered to vote or voted.
- On voting and registration days white gangs gathered outside registration and voting places. They physically stopped black Americans from voting, and often beat them up for trying.
- Black people who went to court to defend their right to vote (and the lawyers and civil rights activists* who helped them) faced beatings or even murder.
- States set their own rules for state elections. Some passed laws making it harder for black people to vote. Others said political parties were 'private organisations' that could choose their members.
- Most states had a literacy qualification to register to vote, which involved either reading a passage of text or passing a written test. A common way of preventing black people from registering to vote was to give them a far harder passage to read, or written test to complete, than they gave to white people.

Source D

From an interview given in 1991 by William Patrick Murphy, a white man who grew up in segregated Tennessee and taught law at the University of South Carolina from 1953 to 1962.

You'd go in the stores, and here was a water fountain with a sign "White Only" or a restroom [toilet], "White Only". And maybe there wouldn't be any water fountain or restroom for black people. And I grew up under that system, and I never gave it much of a thought until long after I became an adult. I guess I first began to think about it, maybe, when I was in the Navy during World War II, and then when I was in law school. And I guess it's fair to say that by the time I started teaching at Ole Miss [the University of Mississippi], I had come to the conclusion in my own mind that segregation was wrong and that something ought to be done about it, and not just segregation but racial injustice across the board. My God, I was thirty years old before I really began to rethink all these things that I had grown up taking for granted.

Activity

In groups, select one person to be a civil rights activist who has to persuade the rest of the group to register to vote in a state. The activist should list the benefits of voting, while the rest of the group pretend to be black Americans and list arguments against voting. Hold a debate. Which arguments concern people most? Did the activist persuade anyone to register?

Key term

Civil rights activist*
Someone who campaigns for equal rights and tries to persuade others to do the same.

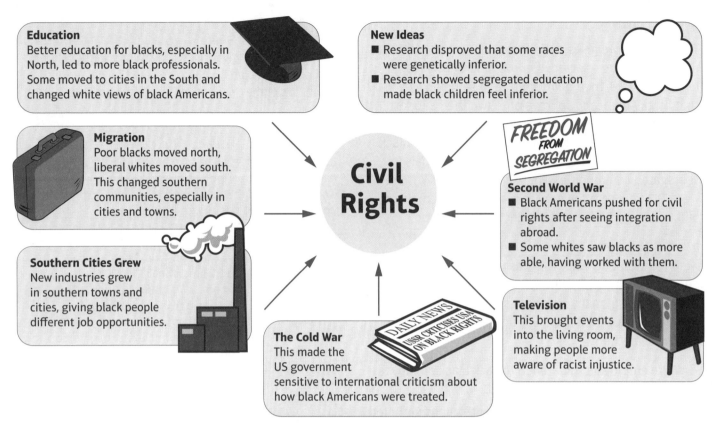

Figure 1.3 Factors that contributed to the growth of the civil rights movement in the 1950s.

After the Second World War there were several factors that helped the growth of the civil rights movement. The USA was changing and so was the way black and white Americans looked at life, including issues such as segregation. Figure 1.3 shows some of these factors. These factors had a greater impact in the North than in the South. Also, while the way some white Americans viewed black Americans was changing this does not mean that the change was immediate or that all whites were affected.

Interpretation 1

From *Grand Expectations: The United States, 1945–1974* (1996) by James T. Patterson.

Black people in the South still struggled in a Jim Crow society that segregated everything from schools and buses to bathrooms, beaches, and drinking fountains. Despite campaigns by black activists for voting rights, only a token few black people in the Deep South states were permitted to register to vote. Daily humiliations continued to remind black people of their third-class status. Whites never addressed black men as "mister" but rather as "boy", "George" or "Jack". African-American women were called "Aunt" or by their first names, never "Miss" or "Mrs". Newspapers rarely reported the names of black people but instead described them as "negro", as in, "a man and a woman were killed, and two Negroes". Whites did not shake hands with blacks or socialise with them on the street.

Source E

A photograph showing a 'whites only' shop in South Carolina in the 1950s.

Activities ?

1 In groups, discuss the factors leading to the growth of the civil rights movement shown in Figure 1.3. Choose the one you think is the most significant and write a slogan for it, using no more than seven words.

2 Does Interpretation 1 support the idea that support for civil rights was growing? Choose one sentence from the interpretation to justify your opinion.

3 Does Source E support the idea that support for civil rights was growing? If not, does it suggest that support was not growing? Write a paragraph to explain your answer.

Civil rights organisations

By 1950, there were many organisations working for civil rights. Some had groups nationwide, such as the National Association for the Advancement of Colored People (NAACP, set up in 1909) and the Congress of Racial Equality (CORE, set up in 1942). These groups had more members in the North and made more progress there, partly because they had more white support there. Both groups had black and white members and campaigned for integration*.

Small local organisations, often church-based, also fought for the rights of black Americans. These groups often had more success in the South, as they were willing to campaign for equality in ways that did not conflict with Southern prejudices. Some were even in favour of separatism: black and white people living separately in segregated communities. They thought black people would face less discrimination (and so have a better life) if they lived separately from white people. Their focus was on winning equal standards of living for segregated black communities. These groups were important in developing the tactics of **non-violent direct action**.

The NAACP

The NAACP focused on fighting for civil rights in the courts. They set up the Legal Defence Fund (LDF) in 1940 to help wrongly-convicted black people appeal against their convictions. In 1950, LDF lawyers decided not to fight cases for equal (but separate) facilities in the South. It wanted to fight segregation in the law courts, not work within it. In the South, it also focused on appeals against wrongful convictions, or prosecuting white people who murdered black people. It also brought cases to enforce voter registration.

The legal fight against segregation faced the problem of the *Plessy v. Ferguson* – '**separate but equal**' – decision of the Supreme Court in 1896. This ruling upheld the Jim Crow laws. It said that segregation was acceptable if the facilities provided were equal. All states had to follow Supreme Court rulings, and it meant that Southern states could use *Plessy* to segregate facilities legally and oppose any attempts at desegregation. If black Americans were to have equality in the South, it was vital for the NAACP to get *Plessy* overthrown.

Key term

Integration*

When black and white people share all facilities. For example, a law enforcing integration in schools would say that all schools had to have black and white pupils sharing classrooms.

Overcoming Plessy

NAACP lawyers used two approaches to overcome *Plessy*. Firstly, they provided evidence that facilities were not equal. Secondly, when they fought to desegregate schools and colleges, they argued that equal facilities were not the same as equal opportunity. They used psychological studies to show that school segregation gave even very young black children a sense of racial inferiority. The NAACP selected the cases they wanted to fight carefully and won nearly every case they took to the Supreme Court in the 1950s.

It is important to remember that winning a legal case was not the same as getting it enforced. After all, the 14th and 15th Amendments of the United States Constitution had made black Americans full US citizens with the same rights as white Americans, but they still did not have those rights in real life. It was not fair, but the fact remained that from 1954 to 1975 black people had to fight for their legal rights, often against violent opposition from white people. Time and time again, black Americans won a legal right to desegregation only to find that local officials found a way to block it.

CORE

CORE had a smaller membership than the NAACP and worked mainly in the North. It was unusual because, in its early years, most members were white and middle-class. CORE campaigns targeted segregation, but not in the courts. CORE used non-violent direct action protests, such as boycotts*, pickets* and 'sit-ins*' of segregated places (e.g. lunch counters* in department stores). These tactics had been used before, but often only by small groups of black people, which were usually ignored. CORE trained its members in non-violent methods such as not reacting if spat at or sworn at. Members were also taught the best position to lie in if they were being physically attacked. Trained members then trained local groups in these techniques. In this way, although CORE had a small membership, they managed to influence a lot of local groups all over the country. Figure 1.4 outlines the key features of CORE's version of non-violent direct protest.

Figure 1.4 The key features of CORE's non-violent direct protests.

Key terms

Boycotts*

To refuse to use a service if you believe it is doing something wrong (e.g. discriminating against black people).

Picket*

Demonstrating outside a place you believe is doing something wrong (e.g. discriminating against black people).

Sit-in*

Sitting down somewhere and refusing to move (e.g. a black person sitting at a 'whites only' lunch counter).

Lunch counters*

A place that served food and drink in a department store. In the South, in the 1950s, black people could shop in department stores, but were not allowed to use the lunch counters.

Church organisations

Black American churches were the centre of most black Southern communities. Black clergymen were often community leaders and organisers, and were involved in the civil rights movement because:

- most were paid by their church, so would not lose their jobs if they spoke out against white racism
- they were educated, effective speakers
- they could negotiate with the white community, because of their status in the black community
- they had their own network of contacts, so they could organise people and events
- they could gain support from black people of all ages and classes, depending on the location of the church.

Black churches were often used for meetings and as gathering points for marches or protests. This made them a target for white violence on a regular basis. Their non-violent direct action protests were similar to those of CORE, but stressed forgiving opponents as well as not fighting back.

White attitudes

White people had conflicting attitudes to the black church organisations. Some whites approved of the church organisations because they urged non-violence, and because many of them also emphasised working within the segregated system. Many white political leaders favoured meetings with black churchmen, if they had to have meetings with members of the black community at all. Black churchmen were educated, polite and, so the white politicians thought, easy to send away with promises of future reform.

Other whites were suspicious of black American church groups. They thought they were too organised, that they could call on too much support. These whites were fearful that the church groups could become a threat. It was from this group of whites that the attacks on black churchmen and churches came.

Extend your knowledge

Why be fearful?

Black churches organised church services. They held prayer meetings and 'socials' where people came together to have picnics, celebrate and pray. They organised charity collections for the poorest in the black community and held Bible study groups, including classes that taught children Christian values such as forgiveness and obedience. So why did some whites fear black church organisations? Black churches provided an organisation that could be used to organise not just picnics, but protest. Black churchmen had authority in the community, so were more effective in calling people to action than other individuals.

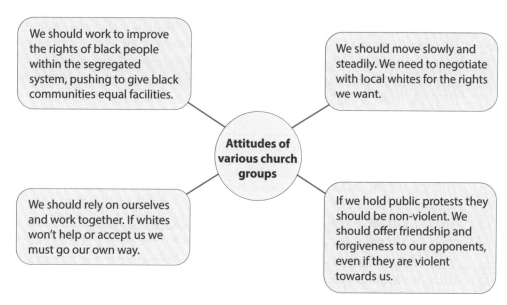

Figure 1.5 The attitudes of various church groups.

Source F

A photograph showing the people who had come to Sharp Street Church, Baltimore, in September 1955, to hear speakers protest at the murder of 14-year-old Emmett Till (see page 19).

Activities ?

1 Make a quiz of five questions about civil rights organisations for your classmates. Write out the questions and answers. You can ask about the types of organisation, tactics and membership.

2 a What can you infer about black church organisations from Source F?

  b How useful is Source F for an enquiry into the involvement of black churches in the civil rights movement?

3 'Mound Bayou was an all-black town. The RCNL were safe to protest there'. Write a paragraph explaining how far you agree with this statement.

Other organisations

Other local organisations included the Regional Council of Negro Leadership (RCNL, set up in Mississippi in 1951). The RCNL leader, T.R.M Howard, lived in Mound Bayou, an all-black town. The RCNL campaigned for black rights within segregation and worked for voter registration. It also campaigned against police brutality against black people in Mississippi. Between 1952 and 1955 it held annual civil rights rallies that attracted speakers from the North and crowds of over 10,000 people.

Many civil rights campaigners in the North met, and organised protests, on desegregated university campuses. Universities in the South, most of them segregated, were also a focus for middle-class black people to organise protests. Black students and academics had the organisational skills and the educated voice that many black groups wanted to represent their campaigns. Educated black Americans were more likely to be listened to by white people. Also, as more black people moved into the towns and cities in the South, black business organisations grew. These organisations campaigned for equality within segregation and also provided work, loans and other help to the black community.

Opposition: the Ku Klux Klan and southern racists

The civil rights movement faced opposition in the South on many different levels. They faced violent opposition from organisations such as the Ku Klux Klan (KKK). Opposition also came from white Southern church organisations which claimed that the Bible said that integration was a sin. Many Southern church-goers were also KKK members.

There was frequent white violence against black people in the South. Registering to vote, or campaigning for civil rights in any way, made black people even more of a target for violence. In Mississippi, in 1955, Reverend George Lee and Lamar Smith were murdered for registering to vote. There was no arrest for either crime – Lee's shooting was written off as a car accident.

The murder of Emmett Till

Emmett Till, a 14-year-old from Chicago, visited relatives in Mississippi in August 1955. He knew about Jim Crow laws. Till told his Southern cousins about life in the North and said he had a white girlfriend. One of them dared him to go into Roy Bryant's store and talk to Carolyn, Roy's wife. Till went in and bought some sweets. His cousin then came in and they left together.

There is conflicting evidence about what happened in the store. Carolyn Bryant said that Till grabbed her and made sexual suggestions. She said she was scared, ran out for a gun from her car for self-defence and Till wolf-whistled as she passed. His cousins admitted the wolf-whistle, but said nothing could have happened in the short time Till and Carolyn Bryant were alone. When Roy Bryant returned from a trip the next day he was told the story. The next night he and his half-brother went to Till's uncle's house, hauled Till into a truck and drove off. They beat Till, shot him and then threw him into the river with a heavy weight attached to his neck with barbed wire. The body was found three days later.

Murders of black Americans were almost 'normal' in Mississippi. What was not normal was what happened next. Till's mother, Mamie Bradley, insisted on having her son's body returned to Chicago and had an open viewing of the body at the funeral home. This led to huge publicity, which in turn led to widespread shock and outrage among black and white people. The trial of Till's killers was reported across the whole country. The jury cleared the defendants after about an hour. The defendants later sold their story (admitting the murder) to a magazine for $3,500. This fuelled further outrage.

Emmett Till did not get justice. Black Americans were still murdered in Mississippi and their murderers still went free. However, the Till case is significant in the history of civil rights. Some historians say it started the rapid growth of the civil rights movement. It showed how public outrage, and publicity, won support for civil rights. Civil rights campaigners used publicity to make it hard for people to ignore outrages and injustice. The NAACP produced a pamphlet called *M is for Mississippi and Murder*, linking the cases of Till, Lee and Smith – all black, all murdered in Mississippi in 1955.

Activities ?

1 List three ways in which the fact that Emmett Till came from the North may have affected events before and after his murder.

2 Write a short paragraph to explain why you think Emmett Till's mother, Mamie Bradley, had an open viewing of his body at the funeral home.

3 List points for and against the statement, 'The murder of Emmett Till created a lot of publicity but made no difference to the position of black Americans'. Notice that the statement gives no timescale and talks about no particular group.

Political opposition: Congress, Dixiecrats and state government

Opposition to civil rights also came from the government (both federal and state). Attempts to produce a civil rights act to enforce the rights of black Americans were constantly blocked by Southern members of both the House of Representatives and the Senate in Congress (which passed the laws). The most significant opponents were nicknamed 'Dixiecrats' after Southern Democrats who had formed their own breakaway party rather than support a civil rights bill put forward by President Truman in 1948. By 1954 they had rejoined the Democrats, but kept their strong views on segregation and the rights of states. There were enough of them in Congress that presidents needed their support, so they had to take their views into account.

Southern governors, local mayors and other state officials also mainly favoured segregation. There were no black judges and black juries were banned. Even if a civil rights group brought a lawsuit and had a sympathetic judge, any ruling he gave would have to be supported by local officials.

Interpretation 2

From *Race and Racism in the United States* (2014) by Charles A. Gallagher and Cameron D. Lippard.

Former Dixiecrats played conspicuous [clearly visible] roles in white resistance to the struggle of African American Southerners to achieve social and political equality. Therefore the Dixiecrats were an important factor in the white South's stubborn refusal to abandon the discriminatory customs and laws of Jim Crow segregation.

Interpretation 3

From *From Jim Crow to Civil Rights* (2004) by Michael J. Klarman.

Rather than viewing the Dixiecrat revolt as evidence of a powerful… racist backlash, a contemporary political scientist concluded from its defeat [its failure to survive as a separate political party] that "the great masses of southerners would no longer be bamboozled by racist appeals".

Exam-style question, Section B

Study Interpretations 2 and 3. They give different views on Dixiecrat influence.

What is the main difference between these views?

Explain your answer, using detail from both interpretations. **4 marks**

Exam tip

When discussing how interpretations differ, quote details from both sources to support what you say, or you will lose marks.

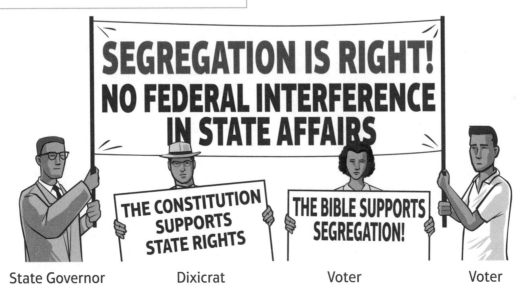

Figure 1.6 Reasons for political opposition to civil rights.

THINKING HISTORICALLY — Cause and consequence (6a)

Seeing things differently

People have different sets of ideas at different times and in different places. Beliefs about how the world works or how society should be governed can all be radically different from our own. It is important for the historian to take into account these different attitudes when examining people's reactions and motivations in the past.

Segregation

Segregation in the South involved keeping black and white Americans separate, providing there were different facilities and schools for black and white people. Segregation was enforced through Jim Crow laws. There were many white Southerners who believed that segregation was good for both black and white people and that most black people wanted it.

1 Imagine the government brought in segregated schools in Britain for white and non-white children.

    a What would be the reaction of parents and children in Britain?

    b What would be the reaction of teachers in Britain?

    c What would be the reaction of the press and the general public?

2 Southern attitudes to segregation were different to current attitudes in Britain.

    a Write one sentence explaining the importance of segregation to the governments of Southern states in the 1950s. Write one sentence explaining how attitudes might differ today.

    b Write one sentence explaining the importance of segregation to ordinary people in the Southern states in the 1950s. Write one sentence explaining how attitudes might differ today.

3 Write a paragraph explaining how attitudes towards segregation in the South in the 1950s contributed to the enforcing of Jim Crow laws. Remember to refer to both the attitude of the state government and the attitude of ordinary people.

Summary

- Black Americans faced segregation and discrimination across the USA, especially in the Southern states where segregation was imposed by Jim Crow laws.
- Voting rights were most restricted in the South.
- Nationwide civil rights organisations, such as the NAACP and CORE, worked to end segregation through legal challenges, protests and boycotts.
- In the South, church organisations were vital for organising black protest. Black civil rights groups in the South were more likely to work to improve conditions for black Americans, rather than to end segregation.
- Attempts at gaining civil rights faced opposition on all levels in the South, especially the Deep South.
- There was also political opposition to civil rights, at both federal and state level.

Checkpoint

Strengthen

S1 Give four examples of the way the lives of black Americans were restricted by segregation.

S2 What kinds of opposition did the civil rights movement face in the South? Give some examples.

Challenge

C1 How did life in the Southern states in the 1950s limit what black Americans in these states tried to achieve and how they tried to achieve it?

If you are not sure that you answered this question well, you could discuss it in a group.

1.2 Progress in education

- Understand the key features of *Brown v. Topeka* (1954) and its significance.
- Understand the significance of the events at Little Rock High School in 1957.

By far the biggest segregation issue for most people in the South was education. In the early 1950s, many Southern states made segregated public schools* more equal, hoping to avoid calls for desegregation. For example, James Byrnes, governor of South Carolina,

Key term

Public schools*

State-funded schools that provide free education. In the UK they are called state schools.

said he would close state schools rather than desegregate them. He then spent over $100m dollars upgrading black schools.

Linda Brown was one of many black children in Topeka, Kansas, who had to pass their local 'white' school and travel further to the nearest 'black' school. In 1951, the Browns and 12 other parents went to court to fight for their children's right to go to their nearest school, which was 'white'. They lost because of the *Plessy* 'separate but equal' ruling, as did four other cases in the South.

Source A

A photograph showing Linda Brown (first desk in second row from right) in her all-black class in 1953.

Key features of the *Brown v. Topeka* case

- In 1952, the NAACP bundled all five school desegregation cases together and took them to the Supreme Court as *Brown v. the Board of Education of Topeka, Kansas*.

- NAACP lawyers argued that separate was not equal in education, even with equal provision, because segregated schooling made black children feel inferior. They argued that the 14th Amendment was being broken, because segregation made black children feel unequal.

- By December 1952, the Supreme Court judges had not made a ruling. They voted to hear more legal advice and try the case again. Before the retrial began, a pro-segregation judge died. His replacement, Earl Warren, was not pro-segregation and became Chief Justice (which meant he led the group).

- On 17 May 1954, the Supreme Court ruled that life had changed since the *Plessy* ruling. A good education was vital to progress. Segregated education made black children feel inferior, so was unconstitutional. 'Separate but equal' had no place in education and schools had to desegregate.

- In 1954, the Supreme Court set no timescale for desegregation. In May 1955, a second Supreme Court case based on *Brown v. Topeka* (called *Brown II*) ruled that desegregation should be carried out 'with all deliberate speed'. This was deliberately vague to allow time to make changes, but the states had to make 'a prompt and reasonable' start.

What about Linda Brown? By the time the Supreme Court reached a decision on *Brown*, it was too late for Linda to go to the white elementary school near her home. She had reached the age to go to a junior high school. Junior high schools had been desegregated in Topeka by this time.

Immediate significance of *Brown*

In terms of civil rights, *Brown* reversed *Plessy*, and so sparked off many more desegregation campaigns. Many of these campaigns won legal victories. *Brown* also had varying effects on the position of black Americans in the South.

Activities	?

1. Draw a concept map (spider diagram) to show the key features of *Brown*, describing each feature in no more than ten words.
2. Write a sentence to explain what civil rights campaigners would most approve of about the Supreme Court decision in *Brown*.
3. Write a sentence to explain what civil rights campaigners would least approve of about the Supreme Court decision in *Brown*.
4. Put yourself in the shoes of an NAACP lawyer going to talk to one of the groups of parents involved in the *Brown* case. You want to convince them to go to court for desegregation, not for more equal provision. What is the main point you will argue, and why?

Changes in the South

The Southern 'border' states (those furthest north) and the District of Colombia desegregated schools in the years immediately following *Brown v. Topeka*. There were protests about federal intervention, and some petitions not to desegregate, but very little violence. By the end of the 1957 school year, 723 school districts had desegregated, paving the way for desegregation in other areas of life.

It was a different story in the Deep South. The day of the *Brown* decision became known as 'Black Monday'. An extreme white backlash began, as shown in the Southern Manifesto (see Source B, page 24). Black children who had previously integrated in 'white' schools were the target of threats and violence (as were their families). So were NAACP members and anyone, black or white, who spoke up for integration. What about school desegregation in the Deep South?

- Many school boards said they were making plans to integrate schools, but did nothing.

- Governors of some states, such as Kansas, did not accept desegregation, but called for calm. Governors of other states, such as Mississippi, made emotional pledges to keep segregation. Senator Harry F. Byrd of Virginia demanded 'massive resistance' to desegregation. He said he would close public schools that tried to desegregate.

- Citizens in Indianola, Mississippi, set up a **White Citizens' Council** (WCC) in July 1954. Its aims included preserving segregation, especially in schools. It spread rapidly and used extreme violence.
- Ku Klux Klan membership grew and its attacks focused on supporters of civil rights.
- Many local groups were set up to fight school desegregation, often started by parents. They protested outside schools and threatened and intimidated people (see Source C).
- Many black people felt in a worse position after *Brown*. They had gained a legal right, but it was clear that it was difficult and dangerous to make it work in practice.

Extend your knowledge

The drawbacks of desegregation

In 1955, the writer Zora Neale Hurston wrote an article as part of the segregation debate started by *Brown*. Her view was that legally enforced desegregation was harmful to black people. Black children going to 'white' schools that were forced to integrate, she said, would be unwelcome. They would be humiliated and threatened. She also felt that integration would mean the loss of black teachers and schools that provided a good, supportive, education for black pupils.

How might going to a well-equipped school with 'white values' be a problem for black children?

Activities

1. In groups, prepare a role-play conversation between the following people on hearing about the *Brown* decision:
   a the mayor of a small town in Mississippi
   b an NAACP member in Mississippi
   c a black mother in Mississippi
   d a white mother in Mississippi.
2. List three types of person you think would approve of the *Brown* ruling and explain why.
3. Write a paragraph to explain why the answer to the previous question is open to debate.

Source B

From the Southern Manifesto, a declaration signed by 11 Southern states and made public on 12 March 1958. It rejected the *Brown* decision as illegal because the states did not accept that segregation was unconstitutional.

This unwarranted exercise of power by the Court, contrary to the Constitution, is creating chaos and confusion in the States principally affected. It is destroying the amicable relations between the white and Negro races that have been created through 90 years of patient effort by the good people of both races. It has planted hatred and suspicion where there has been heretofore friendship and understanding.

Without regard to the consent of the governed, outside agitators are threatening immediate and revolutionary changes in our public-school systems. If done, this is certain to destroy the system of public education in some of the States.

Source C

From the memories of Pat Shuttlesworth Massengill, daughter of the civil rights activist Reverend Shuttlesworth. Here Pat remembers when she and her sister, Ricky, were taken to Phillips Academy in Birmingham, Alabama, in 1958 to be integrated into a 'white' school.

The car pulled up and there were mobs of people saying, "Niggers go home!" and shouting obscenities. All those vicious-looking people saying things you hadn't heard before out loud. It didn't make sense to me to get out of the car with all those people surrounding us. But Daddy was going to try to do it anyway. They started to attack him. Then my mother got out because he was being attacked, and that's when she got stabbed in the hip.

Long-term significance of *Brown*

In the longer term, the significance of *Brown* lay in the constant legal pressure for desegregation in the South and the increased awareness of civil rights issues that it produced. People, then and now, are divided over how much *Brown* helped black Americans.

Integrating schools, especially in the Deep South, was dangerous. Many students, parents and teachers were hostile. Black students often went to school each day through mobs chanting racist taunts. They and their families were threatened at home as well as at school. Their education suffered as well as their home lives. Black schools that had given a good education in a supportive environment were shut and many black teachers lost their jobs. Black teachers in integrated schools often faced trouble from white students.

Interpretation 1

From *From Jim Crow to Civil Rights* (2004) by Michael Klarman.

After both *Brown* rulings, the NAACP urged southern blacks to petition school boards for immediate desegregation on threat of litigation [being taken to court]. Blacks filed such petitions in hundreds of southern localities, including in the Deep South. In a few cities, such as Baton Rouge and Montgomery, blacks even showed up in person to try to register their children at white schools. In the mid-1950s, but for *Brown*, such challenges would have been inconceivable in the Deep South, where race relations had been least affected by broad forces for racial change.

Source D

A cartoon from the *Washington Post* published in 1962, eight years after the *Brown* decision. The school behind the little girl is a segregated school.

A 1962 Herblock Cartoon, © The Herb Block Foundation

Extend your knowledge

On the front line
Education was one of the first big battles of the civil rights movement. They had to face the hate and rage of whites who were against integration. In some ways, the battle for school integration was the easiest battle to win in the Supreme Court, because the inequalities were most obvious. But it was the hardest battle for black Americans to fight, because their children had to fight it.

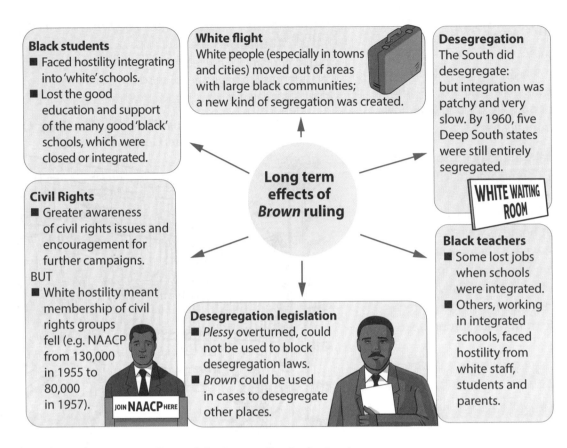

Figure 1.7 Long-term effects of the *Brown* ruling in the South.

The significance of events at Little Rock High School

Little Rock, Arkansas, had already desegregated its parks, library, university and buses. Following *Brown*, a plan was made for gradual school desegregation, starting with Central High School. About 75 black students applied to the school. The school board chose 25. Opponents threatened the families of the black students with the loss of their jobs and with violence. At the start of the 1957 school year, only nine students were still willing to go – they later became known as the Little Rock Nine.

A key opponent of the plan was Orval Faubus, governor of Arkansas. When the school term started on 3 September, Faubus sent 250 state troops to surround the school 'to keep the peace', stopping the black students going in. The school board told the black students to skip the first day of school. Daisy Bates,

the local NAACP organiser, arranged for them to arrive together the next day – but one student, Elizabeth Eckford, missed the message and arrived by bus, alone. The mob of waiting white people, many of them women, was terrifying. She walked up to the state troopers, thinking they would protect her. They turned her back towards the mob that was shouting 'Lynch her! Lynch her!' (see Source E).

The publicity

Many students integrating into schools and colleges faced similar problems. However, on 4 September there were over 250 reporters and photographers outside the school in Little Rock, alerted by the events of the previous day. Photographs of Elizabeth and the mob were in newspapers worldwide. The outrage, inside and outside the USA, was enormous. The Little Rock Nine were famous. The federal government felt the publicity was bad for the USA's image abroad.

Source E

A photograph showing Elizabeth Eckford, one of the Little Rock Nine, trying to get to school at Little Rock High School on 4 September 1957.

Source F

From an interview given in 1991 by Daisy Bates, the NAACP organiser at Little Rock who helped the Little Rock Nine. The interview was for a large oral history project by the University of Carolina. Here Bates was asked if she had the support of the parents of the Little Rock Nine.

Oh, they [the parents] were completely behind us, because I told them that we were taking a great chance, and the kids knew they were taking a great chance, because white people had gotten to where they were killing negroes, you see. This was something entirely new [in Little Rock]. And they had said they'd kill negroes; a child meant nothing. So I told them that one of us might die in this fight. And I said to them, 'If they kill me, you would have to go on. If I die, don't you stop.'

Exam-style question, Section B

Study Sources E and F. How useful are Sources E and F for an enquiry into attitudes to integration in the Deep South? Explain your answer, using Sources E and F and your knowledge of the historical context. **8 marks**

Exam tip

When considering how useful sources are, be sure to focus on the subject of the enquiry. Consider the information the sources provide and think about how the purpose of the source might affect its usefulness. Don't forget to consider the historical context.

The Presidential Order

President Eisenhower did not approve of legally enforcing integration. He thought that it would do more harm than good. By this point, the reaction of white people in the South seemed to be proving him right. He was even less happy about the idea of sending in federal troops to force a state to obey the law. However, as the situation worsened and worldwide publicity increased, he was forced to act. Eisenhower ordered Faubus to remove the state troops from Little Rock.

- On 23 September, Faubus removed his troops, but there was rioting outside the school. The police chief took the black students out of the school, saying the riot was their fault.

- On the evening of 24 September, Eisenhower signed a presidential order (which did not need the approval of Congress) sending over a thousand federal troops to Little Rock. Faubus' state troops were 'federalised': placed under federal control. Eisenhower had to use a presidential order because he wanted to move quickly and he knew Congress would not agree to his plan.

- Eisenhower's action was so controversial that he went on television to explain himself.

The outcome

The troops (under federal control) stayed until the end of term, making sure the Little Rock Nine got to and from school and moved between classes in safety. However, the troops could not stop the threats and taunts of white teachers and students. They did not guard the black students' homes and could not stop hate mail and threatening phone calls.

The school year ended in May 1958. Faubus then closed every Little Rock school for the next school year, putting off integration yet again. White parents forced him to open the schools (integrated) in September 1959.

Interpretation 3

From *We Ain't What We Ought To Be* (2010) by Stephen Tuck.

Over 250 reporters and photographers descended on the city like a flock of vultures, sensing a kill. Above all, though, Little Rock stood out because it led to federal action. On September 24 Eisenhower ordered one thousand paratroopers to enable the nine black students to go to school. It was the first time a president had sent troops to defend African Americans since Reconstruction [the period after 1865, when slavery abolished]. Little Rock became a pincer movement against segregationists – an assault by black southern protesters on one side and by the federal government on the other.

Interpretation 4

From 'The Little Rock Desegregation Case in Historic Perspective' in *PS: Political Science and Politics Journal* (1997) by David L. Kirp.

What had seemed so simple in Little Rock in 1957 – that nine intrepid black adolescents should not be turned away from a public high school because of their race – had become more complicated by the 1970s. In both the South and the North, residential segregation [segregated housing] had increased, making school desegregation logistically harder to accomplish. Nor was it so clear that, in terms of educational outcomes, busing [taking students to integrated schools by bus] was worth the political and social price. New black voices were being heard, many of them unsympathetic to the desegregation project.

White Citizens' Councils grow

White Citizens' Councils (WCC), set up after *Brown* ruling (see page 23), grew rapidly. WCCs and other groups petitioned and campaigned against desegregation. They also threatened the families of children who were signed up to desegregate schools, and they even bombed schools.

The Ku Klux Klan also carried out bombings and other intimidation, such as threatening phone calls. White violence against black Americans escalated after *Brown* because desegregating schools was such a big issue. There were acts of violence that, while not directly connected to *Brown*, were probably a result of the anger it produced.

Political opposition

On 25 February 1956, Senator Harry F. Byrd of Virginia demanded 'massive resistance' to desegregation. He said he would close public schools in his state that tried to desegregate. No school did.

'Massive resistance' was ruled illegal in 1959 by state Supreme Court judges and areas began slow, partial, integration. Only Prince Edward County in Virginia closed all its public schools. They did not reopen until 1964.

Byrd's resistance was obvious. Many school boards resisted in less obvious ways.

- They drew up plans for gradual desegregation, a school year at a time.
- They allowed only a few black children into each year group.
- They put black and white students in the same school, but segregated within the school.
- They introduced 'testing' and 'psychological testing' that was supposed to decide which children went to which schools. The tests were then skewed against black pupils.
- They used the examples of violent resistance, such as mobs and riots outside of schools, as a reason to exclude black students from schools, claiming it was 'for their own safety'.
- They desegregated one or two schools in each area, but left the rest segregated.

Coping with opposition

The NAACP and CORE sent representatives to work with the families of children involved in the desegregating of schools. They talked about the hostility the children would face and explained that they would be under constant scrutiny. CORE produced a leaflet that applied the rules they had developed for non-violent protest to school integration.

All the advice in the world was not enough to prepare the families for what they had to face. One of the worst things about the opposition was that it was everywhere: state governors, the school board, the local police and local white people. Students often had to be escorted to school by police or state troops (see Source G). Black Americans felt there were few white people they could rely on. Many white people who supported desegregation were afraid to give the black students open support.

INTEGRATION RULES

- BE CLEAN AND NEAT AT ALL TIMES
- BE POLITE TO THE TEACHERS AND OTHER STUDENTS
- DON'T SHOUT AT, OR FIGHT WITH ANYONE, NO MATTER HOW PROVOKED YOU ARE
- STICK TOGETHER

Figure 1.8 CORE's school integration rules.

Source G

A photograph showing police escorting black American children and their parents into Caldwell School, Nashville, Tennessee, in September 1957.

Activities

1. Make a flow chart of the events at Little Rock, starting with 'Brown decision to desegregate schools' and ending with 'Governor Faubus closes Central High School'.

2. Write the headline for a 1957 article on the benefits of integration for black students. Underneath, list the three main points you would want to make in the article.

3. List the points you would make in a speech addressing the question: 'Were the problems black children faced integrating into schools worth it?' Consider the children, their families and the students who followed them.

Summary

- In the *Brown v. Topeka* case, the Supreme Court ruled that schools should be desegregated. No timetable was set for desegregation.
- *Brown II*, in 1955, ruled that schools should be desegregated 'with all deliberate speed'.
- White Americans in many Southern states, especially in the Deep South, reacted badly to *Brown*. White Citizens' Councils were set up and Ku Klux Klan membership rose.
- Schools in some states desegregated with little trouble and within a few years. However, at Little Rock, federal troops had to be brought in to protect black pupils from intimidation and violence.
- The violent reactions to attempts at school desegregation were publicised worldwide, causing government concern about the image of the USA abroad.
- Many school boards in the South found ways to delay desegregation or avoid it altogether.
- Civil rights groups became more aware of the power of the media to help their cause.

Checkpoint

Strengthen

S1 List the key features of the *Brown v. Topeka* case.

S2 Explain what made the *Brown* decision so significant for the civil rights movement.

S3 Give one social, one cultural and one political reason to explain why some white people in the South opposed desegregation.

S4 Give one social, one cultural and one political reason to explain why some black people in the South opposed desegregation.

S5 Explain what made the Little Rock crisis so significant for the civil rights movement.

Challenge

C1 How did social, cultural and political factors combine to produce such extreme reactions to school integration in the South?

C2 Make a table of the various ways that school boards resisted desegregation under the headings 'obvious resistance' and 'less obvious resistance'.

How confident do you feel about your answers to these questions? If you are not sure that you answered them well, think about what you have learned about the way people grew up in the Deep South and how segregation was maintained.

1.3 The Montgomery Bus Boycott and its impact, 1955–60

Learning outcomes

- Understand the causes and events of the Montgomery Bus Boycott and the significance of Rosa Parks.
- Understand the reasons for the success of the boycott and the Supreme Court ruling.
- Understand the importance of Martin Luther King's leadership.
- Understand the 1957 Civil Rights Act and opposition to it.

On 1 December 1955, in Montgomery, Alabama, Rosa Parks got on a bus to go home after work. Montgomery buses were segregated. She sat in the first row of 'colored' seating. The bus filled with white people. One white man was standing. The bus driver told Parks and the three other black people in her row of seats to move. The whole row had to move for him to sit, as there could not be a mixed race row. The others moved. Rosa Parks refused. The driver called the police and the police arrested her.

Other black people did occasionally refuse to move on segregated buses in the South, including in Montgomery, although it did not happen every day. Drivers had a system to deal with refusals. They drove to the nearest pay phone, told everyone to stay seated and rang the police. When the person was taken off the bus the drivers returned to their route. What happened after Parks was arrested, however, was not normal. A bus boycott began. It lasted 381 days and almost all of the black people of Montgomery took part. The boycott only ended when buses were desegregated.

Source A

A photograph showing Rosa Parks being fingerprinted on 1 December 1955.

Extend your knowledge

The Montgomery bus system

Most Southern towns had a system of seating similar to that used by the Montgomery bus company. Black people sat at the back and white people sat at the front, with the sections clearly labelled 'whites' and 'coloreds'. Montgomery did not employ black drivers, but that was not unusual.

Two significant things led to the breakout of the boycott in Montgomery rather than elsewhere. Firstly, the white bus drivers were a problem. They bullied black passengers, especially the women. They took black passengers' fares at the front of the bus, then made them get off the bus and board in the middle (rather than walk through the white seating). Sometimes they closed the doors and drove off when a black passenger got off to re-board. They were also quick to call the police if a black passenger refused to move for a white passenger. Secondly, there were several active civil rights groups in Montgomery (the NAACP and local groups). There was already an awareness of the need to fight for civil rights and a structure in place to allow a quick and efficient campaign.

The causes of the boycott

The immediate cause of the boycott was the arrest of Parks, but there were also longer-term causes. The Women's Political Council (WPC), set up in Montgomery in 1946 to fight discrimination, had focused on bus reform since Jo Ann Robinson became president in 1950. The WPC were asking for changes to the issues of drivers and empty seats (see Figure 1.9).

The significance of Rosa Parks

Rosa Parks was not the first woman in Montgomery to be arrested for refusing to move on a segregated bus – in fact she was the sixth in 1955 alone. However, it was Parks who became the figurehead of the boycott. Why?

- Appeals to bus company officials for change were being ignored. More and more people were being arrested for not giving up their seats. The WPC had warned Montgomery's mayor, Mayor Gayle, that there would be a boycott if bus policy did not change. Parks' arrest was the last straw.

- Parks was a respectable, middle-aged, married woman who was well regarded within the black community. There was nothing disreputable about her that opponents could use to make her look bad and cast doubt on what she said.

- She was the secretary of the Montgomery NAACP and the leader of its Youth Council. She had been trained in how to behave in non-violent protest, and was involved in voter registration.

- She would look good and know how to behave as the public face of the boycott.

Parks was arrested on 1 December. The WPC called for a one-day boycott of the buses, on 5 December, in protest against her arrest. The boycott was a huge success – 90% of black people who usually rode on the buses boycotted them. Civil rights activists realised that they could use the situation to get publicity for their cause and make real changes in Montgomery.

Activities ?

1. In groups, list three reasons for Parks' place as the figurehead of the boycott.

2. Choose the reason that you consider the most important and write a sentence to justify your choice.

3. Which reason would you choose if:
   a. you were writing a biography of Rosa Parks?
   b. you were writing a history of the NAACP?
   c. you were writing a book on significant civil rights campaigners?

Figure 1.9 Changes the Women's Political Council (WPC) wanted.

The Montgomery Improvement Association (MIA)

The Montgomery Improvement Association was set up at a meeting at the Holt Street Baptist Church on the evening of 5 December. Its aims were to improve the lives of black people in Montgomery generally and to continue the bus boycott, pressing for the improvements demanded by the WPA (black drivers, fair seating and courtesy from white drivers).

The leadership of Martin Luther King

Martin Luther King was chosen as the leader of the MIA for several reasons.

- He was new in Montgomery, so had no friends or enemies among Montgomery's white officials.
- He was a clergyman so while he was new Montgomery, the black community respected him. Also, he was paid by the church, not a white business that could threaten to sack him.
- He was well educated and believed in black and white Americans working together for civil rights.
- He supported fighting for civil rights – but through non-violent direct action.

Joe Azbell, a white reporter for the *Montgomery Advertiser*, went to the meeting at the Holt Street Baptist Church. A huge crowd had spilled out of the church and into the street, but the crowd let Azbell in because he was a white reporter. He was overwhelmed by King's speech, and the response to it. He wrote an article saying the speech would start a flame that would sweep across America. King was an inspired choice. He understood the importance of publicity and toured the USA making speeches and raising money for the boycott. King became the face, and voice, of the campaign.

Source B

A photograph showing Martin Luther King speaking to the MIA in 1955.

Source C

From a 1973 interview with John Lewis, who went on to become a civil rights activist.

And in spite of his education[,] black people in the South, the masses of black people[,] whether it was in the large urban centers or small towns or rural communities, saw Martin Luther King as one of them. He was a black Baptist preacher and they identified with him. The fact that he was a minister was a real asset. I doubt, if Martin Luther King had been a lawyer, a doctor, whether he would have had the same impact but the fact that he could go into a Baptist church in Montgomery and put the struggle of what he would call freedom and liberation in religious terms, when he could say things like I'm not concerned about the streets that are paved with gold and Pearly Gates, I'm concerned about the streets of Montgomery and the gates of City Hall, or something like that – the people could identify with that. He had a way of sort of capturing the imagination of the masses of black people.

The events of the boycott

On 8 December, members of the MIA met bus company officials who refused to consider any policy changes. That evening the MIA decided to continue the boycott until their demands were met. They knew some people would not be able to walk to work (because of the distance, or because of physical problems). The MIA met with church groups and other organisations to set up a car pool system of lifts. The first car pools began on 12 December and eventually had well over 300 cars.

The boycott made the boycotters' daily lives less comfortable. They faced violence and other harassment. Some lost their jobs. They faced long walks in all weathers, but most did not give in. This persistence brought growing publicity and fundraising for the MIA, which encouraged the boycotters to keep going.

As the boycott went on, the reaction of some white people became more extreme. On 30 January 1956, King's home was bombed, with his wife and young baby inside. Several other homes and churches were bombed. This increased the publicity, which was largely sympathetic to the boycotters. A key policy of non-violent direct action was emerging: the strategy was to make it clear that you are the oppressed group and make your opponent look as oppressive as you could.

Opposition to the boycott

Many white people in Montgomery (from Mayor Gayle, to the bus company owners, to the KKK and WCC) reacted badly to the boycott and tried to oppose it in any way they could. WCC membership rose sharply. In January, Mayor Gayle and several of his officials (including the police commissioner) joined. Source E shows the kind of hostility the boycotters were up against.

Source E

From a racist leaflet distributed by the WCC at a meeting in Montgomery on 10 February 1956. By this point Mayor Gayle and several of his officials had joined the WCC.

When in the course of human events it becomes necessary to abolish the Negro race, proper methods should be used. Among these are guns, bows and arrows, sling shots and knives. We hold these truths to be self evident that all whites are created equal with certain rights; among these are life, liberty and the pursuit of dead niggers.

My friends it is time we wised up to these black devils. I tell you they are a group of two legged agitators who persist in walking up and down our streets protruding their black lips. If we don't stop helping these African flesh eaters, we will soon wake up and find Rev. King in the White House.

MIA arrests

One of the ways that Montgomery officials harassed MIA officials and the boycotters was to arrest them on minor charges, such as speeding. From January 1956, this increased, as did other types of harassment. City officials also looked for ways to bring the leaders of the boycott to trial on more serious charges. On 22 February, 89 MIA members, including King, were arrested for disrupting lawful business due to the boycott. They went to jail and appeared on trial on 19 March. During the trial they brought evidence of the abuses, including murder, inflicted by white drivers. Publicity increased. People began fundraising for the MIA. King was found guilty and ended up paying a $500 fine.

Source D

A photograph showing a car pool pick up in Montgomery, Alabama, in February 1956. Behind the car is an empty Montgomery city bus.

The *Browder v. Gayle* court case begins

The NAACP saw the growing publicity and decided to bring a case to desegregate Montgomery buses (something the MIA had not yet requested). On 1 February 1956, NAACP lawyers filed *Browder v. Gayle* against bus segregations as a violation of the 14th Amendment (the winning argument in *Brown*). The lawyers did not include Rosa Parks, as issues about her arrest could complicate the desegregation case. Instead, the case was in the names of Aurelia Browder and four other women who were arrested in 1955. Once the case was filed, the MIA held a meeting and agreed to demand for desegregation as well.

The Supreme Court decision

Browder v. Gayle came to trial on 11 May. On 5 June, the court stated that buses should be desegregated, giving *Brown* as their reason. The bus company appealed to the Supreme Court but, on 13 November, the Supreme Court upheld the earlier decision and a second appeal was rejected on 17 December. On 20 December, the MIA stopped the boycott. Integrated bus services began the next day.

Reasons for the success of the boycott

A combination of organisation, commitment and publicity were responsible for the success of the boycott and all three were needed for success (see Figure 1.10). Also, the leadership of King and others (see page 37) was crucial in maintaining the commitment of the boycotters and in gaining publicity.

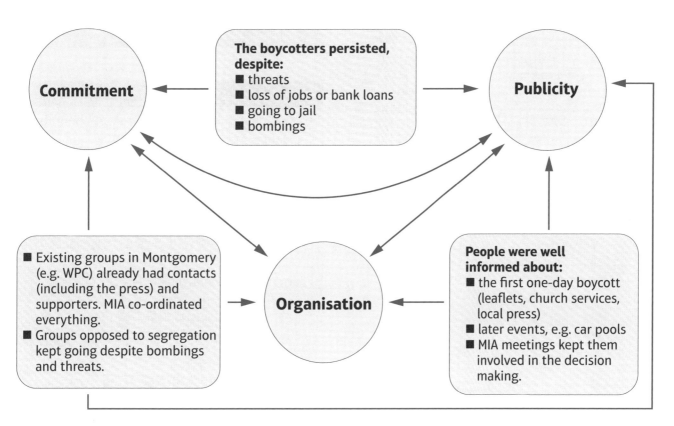

Figure 1.10 Reasons for the success of the Montgomery Bus Boycott. Think about specific examples of these and how they interact.

Interpretation 1

From 'To Walk in Dignity: the Montgomery Bus Boycott' in the *Organisation of American Historians Magazine of History* (2005) by Clayborne Carson.

The ultimate success of the boycott resulted not only from the perseverance of MIA members but also from the determination of the lawyers who challenged segregated bus seating in the courts. Clifford Durr worked closely with black attorney Fred Gray to provide legal defence for Parks and later advised NAACP attorneys involved in the *Browder v. Gayle* (1956) case that struck down the legal basis for segregation on Montgomery's buses, achieving the boycott's objective.

Source F

From a leaflet made by Jo Ann Robinson of the WPC on 1 December 1955. It asks black Americans in Montgomery, Alabama, to participate in a bus boycott on 5 December.

Another Negro woman has been arrested and thrown into jail because she refused to get up out of her seat on the bus for a white person to sit down. It is the second time since the Claudette Colvin case that a Negro woman has been arrested for the same thing. This has to be stopped.

Negroes have rights, too, for if Negroes did not ride the buses, they could not operate. Three-fourths of the riders are Negroes, yet we are arrested, or have to stand over empty seats. If we do not do something to stop these arrests, they will continue. The next time it may be you, or your daughter, or mother.

This woman's case will come up on Monday. We are, therefore, asking every Negro to stay off the buses Monday in protest of the arrest and trial. Don't ride the bus to work, to town, to school, or anywhere else on Monday.

You can afford to stay out of school for one day if you have no other way to go except by bus. You can also afford to stay out of town for one day. If you work, take a cab, or walk. But please, children and grown-ups, don't ride the bus at all on Monday. Please stay off the buses.

Source G

A photograph showing Rosa Parks (at the front, in a dark hat and coat) about to board an integrated bus on 26 November 1956.

Activities ?

1 Complete the following sentences about the Montgomery Bus Boycott:

   a The call for a boycott would have failed without…

   b The threats against the boycotters would have worked without…

   c The car pool system would have failed without…

2 Design a poster that shows the reasons for the success of the Montgomery Bus Boycott. Remember that posters do not use many words – make the reasons you think are more important the biggest.

3 In groups, discuss which you think was the most significant reason for the success of the boycott and explain why.

4 Give a detailed example of an action during the boycott that showed organisation, commitment and publicity and explain how it shows those things.

The significance of Martin Luther King

King became important in the civil rights movement because of his education, non-violent approach, passionate speeches, devotion to civil rights and emphasis on Christian values. He had widespread appeal among black and white people. The Montgomery Bus Boycott was his first significant civil rights protest and he played an important part in keeping the boycotters going, raising funds for the MIA and getting publicity for the boycott.

King's leadership was significant to the boycott because of these factors. However, other people (many of them local) played a significant part in the success of the boycott, and many of these continued to work for desegregation in Montgomery after King had left. The three people below were all involved in setting up the initial bus boycott, they all helped run the MIA and all were arrested with King in January 1956.

- **Jo Ann Robinson**, president of the WPC, taught English at Alabama State College in Montgomery. Since 1954, she had been writing to Mayor Gayle and the bus company about the problems black people faced on the buses. She was one of those who suggested the one-day boycott. She wrote the flyers (see Source F), then she and several of her students printed and dropped them off at various churches and other places to be given out.

- **E. D. Nixon**, an NAACP member, had been campaigning for civil rights in Montgomery for many years before the boycott. It was Nixon that Parks called when she was arrested. Nixon helped set up the boycott and, like King, went on fundraising tours for the MIA. He was well-respected, especially in the black community, but did not have King's education or his ability to make speeches that swayed both black and white people.

- **Ralph David Abernathy** was a clergyman and a Montgomery NAACP member. He worked closely with King during the boycott, often providing the organisation to back up King's calls for action. When King left Montgomery in 1959, Abernathy took over as leader of the MIA.

Extend your knowledge

Martin Luther King's leadership

King was always aware of the impact he was making. His home was bombed during the boycott, while his wife and two-month-old baby daughter were inside. The mayor, the chief of police and a number of policemen arrived. A crowd of over 300 black people were already there. They were clearly very angry and a riot seemed possible. Then King arrived. He checked on his family and then told the crowd that no one was hurt. He stood on his bombed porch with the white officials and did not shout at them or get angry. He asked the crowd not to react violently, but to go home peacefully and remember they were believers in non-violence. They went.

What does this tell you about King? How do you think the white officials felt about what happened after their arrival on King's porch?

Interpretation 2

From *The American Civil Rights Movement* (2001) by Raymond D'Angelo.

E.D. Nixon has always claimed that he was a 'founding father' of the MIA, and a major contributor to the Montgomery bus boycott. In certain crucial respects this was true: Nixon was the one who (with Martin Luther King) brought a grassroots protest to national attention. ... That he was not impressed by and did not appeal to the college-educated, middle-class and largely clerical leadership of the MIA is revealed in Mrs Johnny Carr's comment: 'Mr Nixon was a hardworking man, a fine leader and everything but he [didn't] have that thing that could weld people together in a movement like ours... I have heard Mr Nixon say that "When I walk into an MIA meeting, don't nobody clap or say anything, but when Dr King walks in, everybody stands up and claps."

Importance of the boycott

The boycott was important for several reasons.

- It showed that black people could organise mass resistance and that civil rights campaigns could attract widespread support if they were well organised and well publicised.
- It brought Martin Luther King into the spotlight.
- It showed the importance of publicity in the fight for civil rights, something that was later underlined by the case of the Little Rock Nine (see page 26). Publicity not only brought injustices to light, but also sparked off other boycotts, for example in Tallahassee, Florida.
- It was where the rules of non-violent direct action were first clearly laid out (see Source H).

- It showed how black action set off a negative white response. This helped the civil rights cause because it showed the problems black Americans faced, especially in the South. Civil rights activists later exploited this, holding mass protests where an extreme reaction from white people was likely.

Activity ?

In groups, debate the statement: 'Without Martin Luther King there would have been no bus boycott.' Remember that you have to answer your opponents' points in a debate, as well as make your own. So list not only the points you want to make, but also the points you think the other side will make and how you will argue against them.

Source H

From a leaflet given out in Montgomery on 19 December 1956 (shortened and simplified). The leaflet gave rules for how black Americans should behave on the newly integrated buses.

```
The bus driver has been told to obey the
law. Assume he will help you occupy any
vacant seat.

Do not deliberately sit by a white person,
unless there is no other seat.

If cursed, do not curse back. If pushed, do
not push back. If struck, do not strike back,
but show love and goodwill at all times.

For the first few days try to ride with
a friend in whose non-violence you have
confidence. You can uphold one another by
glance or prayer.

If another person is being molested, do not
arise to go to his defense, but pray for the
oppressor and use moral and spiritual forces
to carry on the struggle for justice.

If you feel you cannot take it, walk for
another week or two. We have confidence in
our people.

GOD BLESS YOU ALL.
```

Source I

A photograph showing one of the first integrated bus rides in Montgomery, Alabama, on 21 December 1956. The man at the front left is the Reverend Ralph Abernathy. The man behind Abernathy is Martin Luther King.

After the boycott

The boycott achieved its aims. Buses were desegregated in Montgomery. However, the white backlash continued. The homes of King and other MIA leaders were firebombed, as were several black churches. Seven WCC members were arrested for the bombings but they were cleared by an all-white jury. Shots were fired at black people riding the buses. Bus services had to be suspended for several weeks, until things calmed down. Though the buses were desegregated, there was no further desegregation in Montgomery for many years – even the bus stops remained segregated.

Interpretation 3

From *Grand Expectations: The United States, 1945–1974* (1996) by James T. Patterson.

The Montgomery Improvement Association, although very well organised and unswerving, did not change formal practices [of segregation] much in Montgomery. Schools, public buildings, hotels, lunch counters, theatres, and churches remained segregated. "White" and "Colored" signs confronted people entering public places. There were still no black bus drivers or black policemen. And would future boycotts be a viable strategy? It would do no good, for instance, to boycott a restaurant or a park from which one was already excluded.

Interpretation 4

From *From Jim Crow to Civil Rights* (2004) by Michael J. Klarman.

The Montgomery bus boycott demonstrated black agency [taking action], resolve, courage, resourcefulness, and leadership. The boycott revealed the power of nonviolent protest, deprived southern whites of their illusions that blacks were satisfied with the racial status quo [segregation], challenged other southern blacks to match the efforts of those in Montgomery, and enlightened millions of whites around the nation and the world about Jim Crow.

The 1957 Civil Rights Act

President Eisenhower had been reluctant to act on civil rights, arguing that real change came from changing the way people think, not forcing them to do something. He knew that many people felt that federal intervention in state government was unconstitutional. However, *Brown*, the Montgomery Bus Boycott and the white backlash they caused led to increasing sympathy for civil rights in the USA (including in Congress) and abroad. The first draft of the civil rights bill called for federal intervention over civil rights violations by states. It faced widespread opposition. Even Eisenhower spoke against it, saying that it was forcing change on people.

The Dixiecrats and the 1957 Civil Rights Act

Although some white politicians in the South supported black voting rights, the Dixiecrats did not. Political opposition to civil rights came from both the Senate and the House of Representatives. Dixiecrats in Congress fiercely opposed any bill supporting the civil rights of black Americans. Strom Thurmond, a leading Dixiecrat, spoke for 24 hours and 18 minutes in a filibuster* that prevented the first vote on the bill. This meant that the bill had to be revised and considered by both houses in Congress all over again.

Key term

Filibuster*

A tactic used by politicians in debates to stop a bill being voted on. There is a time limit on how long most bills can be debated, so the most usual filibuster tactic is to keep talking until the deadline for the bill to be passed is reached.

The 1957 Civil Rights Act, signed on 9 September, allowed federal courts to prosecute state violations of voting rights. However, these prosecutions would be tried in the state by a jury. An all-white jury in the South was unlikely to do anything but dismiss such a prosecution. As a result, the 1957 Civil Rights Act was a positive step forward in showing that the federal government supported civil rights. However, it also showed the power of Southern opposition to civil rights legislation, in its ability to slow it down and block its enforcement.

The Southern Christian Leadership Council (SCLC)

The SCLC was set up in January 1957, to coordinate church-based protest across the South. Among its leaders were Martin Luther King and Ralph Abernathy. Key features of its policies were:

- all segregation to be rejected and protested against
- non-violent direct action tactics
- mass action
- broad-based black and white membership.

The SCLC's first big campaign was centred around voter registration. It wanted enough black voters in the South to have an impact on the 1958 and 1960 elections.

The SCLC worked with black communities to train people for the voter registration tests that they had to pass before they could vote.

Activities ?

1 Draw a timeline for the events of the Montgomery Bus Boycott, starting with the arrest of Rosa Parks and ending with the desegregation of the Montgomery buses.

2 Design a poster urging black people to ride the desegregated buses.

3 List three ways in which the timeline and poster do not tell the whole of the Montgomery Bus Boycott story.

Summary

- On 1 December 1955, Rosa Parks was arrested for refusing to give up her seat for a white man. Bus seating and the behaviour of the white drivers was a long-standing problem in Montgomery.
- A one-day bus boycott on 5 December, to protest against Parks' arrest, was a huge success. That night the MIA was set up with Martin Luther King as its president.
- While the boycott was going on, the NAACP brought *Browder v. Gayle* to the state courts to desegregate Montgomery buses.
- There was a lot of violence against black Americans, including the bombing of the homes and churches of MIA leaders.
- The boycott lasted for 381 days, earned a lot of publicity and made Martin Luther King famous. He went on to help set up the SCLC.
- The 1957 Civil Rights Act was seen by many to be a result of *Brown* and the bus boycott. It proposed federal intervention to make sure black people could register to vote in the South.

Checkpoint

Strengthen

S1 List the causes of the Montgomery Bus Boycott.

S2 Give three reasons for the success of the boycott and give an example of each.

S3 Write a short paragraph to explain how the 1957 Civil Rights Act could be seen as both progress and a setback for civil rights.

Challenge

C1 Write a short paragraph to explain the link between the Supreme Court decisions in *Brown v. Topeka* and *Browder v. Gayle*.

C2 Who were the Dixiecrats and how did they affect the federal government's position on civil rights?

How confident do you feel about your answers to these questions? If you are not sure that you answered them well, compare your answers with a partner and see if you may have missed anything.

Recap: The development of the civil rights movement, 1954–60

Recall quiz

1 What is segregation?
2 What were 'Jim Crow' laws?
3 What was the ruling in *Brown v. Topeka*?
4 What was 'white flight'?
5 How many black students were trying to enrol in Central High School, Little Rock, in 1957?
6 Who was Emmett Till?
7 What were White Citizens' Councils?
8 Who was Jo Ann Robinson?
9 What were the initial demands of the Montgomery Bus Boycott?
10 Who were the Dixiecrats?

Activities

1 Write lists summing up the progress of the civil rights movement due to federal intervention (including Supreme Court rulings).
2 Write a paragraph to explain why some black people in the South might have been opposed to school desegregation.
3 Write a paragraph to explain how federal intervention affected the attitudes of many white people in the South to black Americans.

In the exam you will be asked how useful contemporary sources are for an enquiry. Copy and complete the table below. Support what you say with your own knowledge if it helps you to make your point.

Sources	Enquiry	Ways they are useful
C on page 12 and D on page 13	attitudes to segregation in the South	
E and F on page 27	problems faced by black people due to desegregating schools in the South	
D on page 34 and F on page 36	why the Montgomery Bus Boycott worked	
H and I on page 38	the work of the MIA as the bus boycott ended	

In the exam you will be asked about how historians' interpretations can differ. Copy and complete the table below.

Interpretations	Enquiry	How they differ	Why they might differ
2 and 3 on page 20	the importance of the Dixiecrats		
3 and 4 on page 28	the benefits of school desegregation		
3 and 4 on page 39	the achievements of the Montgomery Bus Boycott		

Writing historically: organising ideas

The most successful historical writing is clearly organised, guiding the reader through the writer's ideas.

Learning outcomes

By the end of this lesson, you will understand how to:

- organise your ideas into paragraphs
- link your paragraphs to guide the reader.

Definitions

Paragraph: a unit of text that focuses on a particular point or idea and information related to it.

How can I organise my ideas into paragraphs?

Look at the notes below written in response to this exam-style question:

> Explain why the Montgomery Bus Boycott was a success. **(12 marks)**

Leadership – King

Organisation – taxis

Support – determination

Media publicity

NAACP court case

Black community and churches

Dealing with the bus company and mayor

Now look at the response below.

Strong leadership was important. The boycott went on for a long time, and it was important to keep people going. The leaders also had to be able to negotiate with the bus company and the mayor: Martin Luther King was important here because he was a newcomer who was also good at making speeches and negotiating. His leadership was a key factor in the boycott's success.

Good organisation was vital for success. It was important to keep people informed of meetings. It was also important to organise alternative transport for those who lived too far away from their work to walk, or who could not walk for other reasons. At first this was done by taxis, but as the boycott went on there were car pools run by various churches and other groups. So these needed someone to organise drivers and times when they were running. People might have dropped out of the boycott if they found it too hard to get to work.

Publicity was also very important. People were well informed about the boycott, with leaflets and church meetings being used to circulate information about the boycott and car pooling. Because of this, it was much easier to organise the boycott. If people had not known specific information like this, the boycott would not have been as successful.

Support of the bus boycott did not ease up even after opposition to it from groups such as the KKK turned violent. The threat of arrest from the police was great, but people were committed to the cause. The Montgomery Improvement Association (MIA), led by Martin Luther King, was set up in December 1955. When it was established, one of its aims was to support the boycott. King was a very good public speaker. He toured the USA to promote the bus boycott. Because of this, more people began to support the boycott.

1. a. What is the key focus of each of these paragraphs?

   b. Why do you think this response chose to focus on these four key areas?

   c. Why do you think this response chose to sequence these four paragraphs in this order?

   d. Which points in the notes have not been included in the final response? Why do you think the writer decided not to include them?

2. Look closely at the structure of the first paragraph. Which sentences:

   a. clearly indicate the central topic of the paragraph

   b. show knowledge and understanding of that topic

   c. explain its significance to the question?

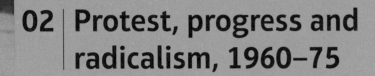

02 | Protest, progress and radicalism, 1960–75

From 1960, support for the civil rights movement grew. The different civil rights groups worked together to plan and carry out larger and larger non-violent direct action protests in the South. However, while methods of protest changed, the reaction of white people in the South did not. The resulting violence from white people inspired disgust around the country and the world. Images such as police setting dogs on black children showed America in a shocking light. The USSR was able to score points in the Cold War by pointing out that while the US claimed it supported democracy and freedom, it could not even protect its black citizens from violence.

This criticism, from both inside and outside the US, forced the federal government to act decisively. By 1966 there was both a Civil Rights Act and a Voting Rights Act in place to protect the rights of black Americans. However, at this point, many white supporters of civil rights felt that their work was done; that the struggle was over. In reality, equality was still a long way off.

In the late 1960s there were very different images of black Americans on television screens. Black Americans were rioting in the streets of cities across the country, especially in the North. In the minds of many Americans in 1975, the image of the civil rights movement was not of a defenceless black person being attacked by a white policeman, but of a young black man throwing a brick or even a petrol bomb in one of the nation's many ghettos.

Why did black protest change so radically in this period?

Learning outcomes

In this chapter, you will study:

- progress and conflict in the civil rights movement, 1960–62
- peaceful protests and their impact, 1963–65
- Malcolm X, his beliefs, methods and assassination
- Black Power and the Black Panthers
- the civil rights movement, 1965–75, including urban riots and the assassination of Martin Luther King.

The Greensboro sit-in

On 1 February 1960, four black students from the North Carolina Agriculture and Technology College in Greensboro, North Carolina, changed the face of civil rights protest. Izell Blair, Franklin McCain, Joseph McNeil and David Richmond shopped at the Greensboro Woolworth's department store, then sat at the lunch counter and waited to be served. The lunch counter was segregated. Staff refused to serve the students and asked them to leave. The students refused. They sat at the lunch counter until closing time.

The next day, about 25 students arrived and sat at the lunch counter in shifts. The local papers reported the story and word spread rapidly. More students joined the sit-in. By 4 February there were over 300 students working in shifts – black and white, male and female. The sit-in spread to other Greensboro segregated lunch counters. Young people in North Carolina read the local news and began to hold their own sit-ins. Within weeks, the sit-ins were spreading and were national news. Hundreds, then thousands, of young black and white people took part.

Organising the protests

Both CORE and the SCLC were asked to send people to train students in non-violent protest tactics. On 15 April 1960, Ella Baker, a civil rights activist and SCLC member, invited student groups to a meeting in Raleigh, North Carolina, to plan student protests across the South. At this meeting, the Student Nonviolent Coordinating Committee (SNCC, pronounced 'snick') was set up, with the aim of using non-violent protest to campaign for civil rights. It built on the non-violent principles developed by CORE and Martin Luther King:

- demonstrate peacefully and visibly
- do not rise to provocation
- show your opponent up as a violent oppressor.

SNCC also provided support to groups. They trained students to cope with the hostility and harassment they faced during sit-ins and other demonstrations. This ranged from swearing, racial abuse, blowing cigarette smoke into their faces, pouring food and drink over them and physical violence.

Source A

A photograph showing the Woolworth's lunch counter in Greensboro, North Carolina, on 2 February 1960 (the second day of the sit-in). Joseph McNeil is on the left and Franklin McCain is beside him. This image was used in a newspaper article in the *Greensboro Record*.

Exam-style question, Section A

Give **two** things you can infer from Source A about the significance of the Greensboro sit-in. Give the detail in the source that tells you this.

4 marks

Exam tip

You infer something from a source by working out something the source does not actually tell you from the detail in the source.

The significance of Greensboro

The Greensboro sit-in was significant for a number reasons.

- Existing civil rights groups helped the sit-ins to spread rapidly, but it was mainly a reaction to the first protest. Young people thought that segregated lunch counters were wrong and were inspired to protest against them.

- Some white southerners joined CORE and SNCC, even when segregationists (those who supported segregation) threatened them.

- The sit-ins and other protests attracted significant numbers of protesters (about 50,000 by mid-April 1960). It was a very visible form of protest that was hard to ignore.

- Everything about a sit-in was open to the media. Unlike boycotting, sit-ins were in public spaces that black people were not supposed to use. With school desegregation, the riots outside schools were visible, but the humiliation of black students inside was not.

- At first, the sit-ins were a largely student, largely black, protest. Then, other people, such as college professors, also took part. By the end of the year, the number of

Extend your knowledge

Earlier sit-ins

In August 1958, in Oklahoma City, a 15-year-old black girl, Barbara Posey, organised a sit-in at a lunch counter. She was a member of the local NAACP. About 85 black children took part in the sit-in. Barbara organised more demonstrations in Oklahoma, the largest of which involved about 500 students. Most stores desegregated after one or two days of protest.

white people joining the protests meant the organisers could use mixed race groups in their protests.

- The sit-ins showed the importance of publicity. Publicity for the Greensboro sit-in grew because the numbers of people involved rose rapidly. When the sit-ins spread, the media saw it as a newsworthy mass movement, and the coverage was mainly supportive.

- Favourable news coverage produced support from black and white people in both the North and South. There were demonstrations across the USA, at local branches of nationwide department stores that segregated their facilities.

Source B

A photograph showing part of the original Greensboro lunch counter in the International Civil Rights Museum in Greensboro, North Carolina. Other sections of the counter are in museums in Washington DC.

Source C

From an interview given in 2015 by Samuel Jones, a student who joined the Greensboro sit-in on the second day. He explained what happened after the store closed on the day of the first sit-in.

```
When they [the four protesters] returned to
the college, a big discussion was held among
the rest of the students. We decided to all go
back to the lunch counter the next day. When
we got there, some of us took a seat at the
lunch counter, in an orderly fashion. After
a while the ones at the counter were asked to
leave. When they left their seats, the rest of
us sat down. This scenario was repeated daily,
until July 26, 1960. When we first started,
none of us realised what we were getting into
or the impact we would make on history.
```

Source D

From an account by Julian Bond, who was one of the first SNCC members. On 15 March 1960, he led a sit-in to desegregate the lunch counter in Atlanta's government offices at City Hall, Georgia.

```
You could say that I was inspired by the
Greensboro sit-in. The Atlanta sit-in was a
logical follow-on from Greensboro, though
we didn't know how big the sit-in movement
would get.

We went into the cafeteria and I collected a
tray of food. When I approached the cashier,
carrying my food, she told me, "This is for
City Hall employees only". I said, "You have
a big sign outside that says, 'City Hall
cafeteria — the public is welcome.'"

She said, "We don't mean it."

She called the police and we were arrested
and taken to jail.
```

Activities ?

1 In groups, decide how useful Sources B, C and D are for an enquiry into the significance of the Greensboro sit-in. List the sources in order of most useful to least useful.

2 Compare the list your group has made with another group. Are they different? Write a short paragraph to explain why your group chose that particular order.

3 Which source would you use to show how people felt about the sit-in at the time? Explain your answer.

Interpretation 1

From *We Ain't What We Ought To Be: The Black Freedom Struggle from Emancipation to Obama* (2010) by Stephen Tuck.

Soon there were wade-ins on the beaches, pray-ins in churches, read-ins in libraries… Whereas African Americans in Montgomery had protested segregation by staying away, this was protest by confrontation. By August 1961, over seventy thousand people had participated in some kind of direct-action protest. Hundreds of thousands more joined economic boycotts supporting the sit ins. Within a year, over one hundred communities had desegregated their lunch counters some – starting with San Antonio, Texas, in March – to pre-empt [prevent] sit-ins from even starting. On July 25, 1960, after renewed demonstrations, the lunch counter in Greensboro's Woolworth's served its first black customer.

THINKING HISTORICALLY ▶ Evidence (2b&c)

Evidence and overall judgements

How successful was the Greensboro sit-in? Study Sources C and D and Interpretation 1.

1 Which of the texts were written on the basis of personal experience of the events?

2 Which of the authors must have based their account(s) on studying evidence rather than on personal experience?

3 Out of Sources C and D, which is most useful in helping assess the overall success of the Greensboro sit-in?

4 When thinking about the question of overall success, does the historian have an advantage over an eyewitness? Explain your answer.

5 If Samuel Jones and the other students had no idea of how successful the sit-in would be, why did they go?

6 Is there information in Interpretation 1 that people in the spring of 1960 probably wouldn't have known? Explain your answer.

7 How do you think the author of Interpretation 1 got their information?

The Freedom Riders

The Supreme Court desegregated state transport in 1956, after the Montgomery Bus Boycott. However, bus station facilities (e.g. toilets and waiting rooms) remained segregated until December 1960, when the Supreme Court ordered their desegregation. In 1961, CORE activists decided to ride buses from the North to the Deep South on 'Freedom Rides' to test if desegregation was happening. They knew it was not. They aimed to spark a crisis and worldwide publicity so that federal government would force states to desegregate.

On 4 May 1961, seven black and six white 'Freedom Riders' left Washington DC on two different buses. The Governor of Georgia urged calm, so the Riders got as far as the border with Alabama with only two of them being arrested and very little violence. However, politicians in Alabama and Mississippi, including John Patterson (Alabama's governor), spoke out against the Riders. The Southern press was united against them. Some northern media accused the Riders of deliberately looking for trouble. Klan and WCC members swore to stop them.

Anniston, 15 May 1961

On 15 May, the first bus reached Anniston, Alabama. Over 100 KKK members surrounded it, slashing the tyres and smashing the windows. The bus left, chased by the mob. The slashed tyres burst when the bus was outside the city. Someone tossed a firebomb into the bus through a broken window and held the doors shut. A white policeman travelling on the bus forced the doors open. The passengers escaped just before the petrol tank exploded. Some were beaten up as soon as they were off the bus. Fred Shuttlesworth, leader of the Alabama Christian Movement for Human Rights (ACMHR) in Birmingham, Alabama, organised cars to take the Riders to Birmingham airport.

Riders on the second bus, not knowing what had happened to the first, arrived in Anniston. They were pulled off the bus and beaten up. They got back on the bus, which drove on to Birmingham. Here, they were beaten up again by KKK members. The Birmingham chief of police, 'Bull' Connor, told the police not to stop KKK members. Eventually the ACMHR got the Riders to the airport. Press coverage of the attacks was a huge embarrassment to the government.

Source E

A photograph showing the burned-out bus used by the Freedom Riders on 15 May 1961. It was taken just outside Anniston, Alabama. All the people in the photo are Freedom Riders.

The rides, and the violence, continue

SNCC were determined not to let the KKK and WCCs win, so they recruited their own Freedom Riders. On 17 May, ten Riders took the bus from Nashville, Tennessee, to Birmingham. No driver would take them further, so they waited in the Birmingham bus station, with an angry mob outside. The publicity forced the federal government to force Governor John Patterson to get them safely to Montgomery. On 20 May, the police escorted the bus to just outside Montgomery, then left.

Hundreds of KKK and WCC members were at the bus station. They beat up the Riders and members of the press. A policeman fired his gun into the air to stop the violence. The mob (over 1,000) roamed Montgomery, attacking black people and setting one boy on fire. The police arrested the Riders for starting a riot.

Despite the violence, more people volunteered for Freedom Rides. In response, the Southern states developed a new tactic. On 24 May, a large police escort accompanied a bus containing Freedom Riders going from Montgomery to Jackson, Mississippi. However, when they arrived in Jackson and tried to use the facilities the Riders were arrested. The federal government did not stop the arrests.

Over the summer, there were over 60 Freedom Rides. Over 300 Riders went to Jackson's segregated jail. Many were beaten and tortured. On 1 November, the federal government said federal officers would enforce desegregation if states did not obey. The Southern States began to desegregate bus facilities and the Freedom Rides ended.

The James Meredith case, 1962

Between 1956 and 1962, some Southern universities desegregated without much trouble. In Georgia, in 1961, the Governor and university officials called on students to accept the situation. In 1962, East Carolina University took its first black student with little violence. Also in 1962, James Meredith re-applied to the University of Mississippi (often called 'Ole Miss') which had rejected him in May 1961. The NAACP had challenged his rejection, arguing that it was because he was black. The Supreme Court ordered the university to admit him. University officials and Ross Barnett (the state's governor) disobeyed the Supreme Court ruling by physically stopping Meredith from registering. Barnett, and several of the officials, were WCC members.

On 30 September, Meredith returned to register, accompanied by about 500 federal officials. A mob of over 3,000, many armed, attacked the federal officials. President Kennedy spoke on television and radio, calling for calm. He was ignored. The mob chanted in favour of Barnett and against the federal government. State police did little to stop cars full of armed men from racing into the town. Fires were started and streetlights were shot out. Bricks, firebombs and other missiles were thrown and guns were fired. The marshals could only use tear gas. Two civilians died. Somewhere between 245 and 375 civilians were injured. Over 160 federal marshals were badly injured, 28 of them were shot. Kennedy sent in federal troops, who eventually stopped the rioting.

Meredith registered on 1 October. Troops guarded him for the whole year it took for him to graduate.

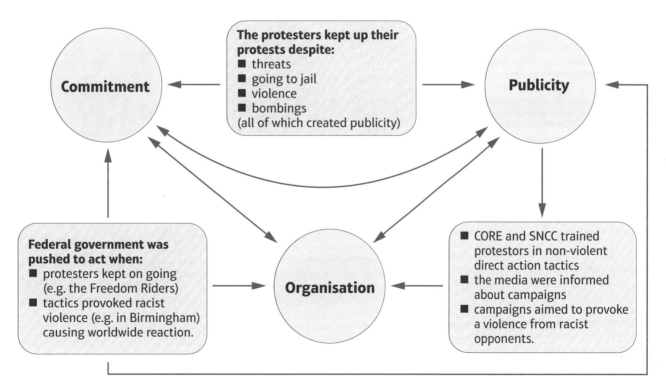

Figure 2.1 Reasons for progress in civil rights 1960–62.

Source F

From a speech made by the Governor of Mississippi, Ross Barnett, which was broadcast on television and radio on 13 September 1962.

We must either submit to the unlawful dictates of the federal government or stand up like men and tell them no... I have made my position in this matter crystal clear. I have said in every county in Mississippi that no school in our state will be integrated while I am your Governor. I shall do everything in my power to prevent integration in our schools. I assure you that the schools will not be closed if this can possibly be avoided, but they will not be integrated if I can prevent it. As your Governor and Chief Executive of the sovereign State of Mississippi, I now call on every public official and every private citizen of our great state to join me.

Source G

From a telegram sent by President Kennedy to Ross Barnett on 30 September 1962.

To preserve our constitutional system the Federal Government has an overriding responsibility to enforce the orders of the Federal Courts. Those courts have ordered that James Meredith be admitted now as a student of the University of Mississippi. Three efforts by Federal law enforcement officials to give effect to the order have been unavailing [unsuccessful] because of your personal physical intervention... supported by state enforcement officers. A fourth was called off at the last minute by the Attorney General on advice from you that extreme violence and bloodshed would otherwise result.

Exam-style question, Section B

Study Sources F and H. How useful are Sources F and H for an enquiry into opposition to desegregation? Explain your answer, using Sources F and H and your knowledge of the historical context. **8 marks**

Exam tip

When considering how useful sources are, be sure to focus on the subject of the enquiry. Consider the information the sources provide. Do not forget to consider the historical context. How might the purpose of the source affect its usefulness?

Source H

A photograph showing federal troops driving into Oxford, Mississippi, on 30 September 1962. Their arrival stopped the rioting that prevented James Meredith from enrolling at the University of Mississippi.

Extend your knowledge

An early university desegregation attempt

In February 1956, the Supreme Court ordered the University of Alabama, in Tuscaloosa, to take its first black student, 26-year-old Autherine Lucy. Before term started, she had received threatening phone calls and hate mail. When term started, KKK crosses were burned on campus. Mobs followed Lucy and there were riots in the city. This was one of the earliest examples of 'white backlash' and was a huge shock to many people. Lucy was banned from the university for causing riots.

The University of Alabama did not desegregate until 1963, and it had to be enforced by federal troops. Governor George Wallace stood in the doorway to stop two black students enrolling.

Why do you think governors in some Southern states made gestures like this?

Activities ?

In groups, discuss Sources F, G and H.

1   How do the Sources F and G show the conflict between federal and state government over the issue of desegregation in education? Write down your findings.

2   What would Source H be most useful to show?

3   Which source would you use to show the issues surrounding desegregating education, if you could only use one? Write a paragraph to explain your choice.

Summary

- On 1 February 1960, four students staged a sit-in at a lunch counter in a department store in Greensboro, North Carolina. It started a mainly local, student-driven mass movement.
- The Student Nonviolent Coordinating Committee (SNCC) was set up as a result of what happened in Greensboro.
- CORE organised a Freedom Ride to test whether bus facilities had been desegregated. The Riders wanted to provoke white violence and create publicity to force federal action. This resulted in the Anniston bus bomb.
- SNCC organised more rides. The publicity forced the government to desegregate bus facilities.
- In 1962, the federal government was forced to intervene to stop riots and enable James Meredith to go to the University of Mississippi as the Supreme Court had ruled he should.
- CORE and SNCC trained protesters in not reacting to white provocation and violence.

Checkpoint

Strengthen

S1 Give at least three reasons why the Greensboro sit-in was significant.

S2 Explain how the Freedom Rides were different from Greensboro and the sit-in movement that followed it.

Challenge

C1 What political factor, produced by the way the USA was governed, was a constant issue in civil rights from 1954 to 1962?

C2 By 1962, it was clear that publicity was going to be a key factor in the fight for civil rights. Why?

How confident do you feel about your answers to these questions? If you are not sure that you answered them well, look back at Chapter 1 for the extra information that you need.

Events in Birmingham

Developments on 11 and 12 May
- desegregation timetable agreed for Birmingham
- black homes and businesses bombed
- first significant riots against white violence
- Kennedy ordered federal troops into Alabama
- over 1,000 black students expelled for missing school through protesting or imprisonment.

Longer term effects
- federal government fear of widespread rioting
- protests in other cities all over USA
- a month later, 143 cities had some desegregation
- many black people felt that progress was too slow and forced desegregation didn't work if local white people didn't accept it
- some black Americans questioned the tactics used by civil rights campaigners, e.g. they felt it was wrong to put children in danger in protests
- many more Americans saw civil rights as most urgent issue for the USA
- government produced a tougher civil rights bill.

Figure 2.2 The significance of Birmingham.

In October 1961, civil rights groups including SNCC and the NAACP organised a campaign of marches, boycotts and other protests against segregation in Albany, Georgia. The state police arrested protesters but did not publicly use violence. There was little publicity. In December 1961, Martin Luther King and other SCLC members joined the campaign. This produced some publicity but, even so, little was achieved without the publicity that violence from white people produced. A new strategy was needed if the civil rights movement was going to attract the publicity it needed to force change.

The campaign in Birmingham, Alabama

On 2 April 1963 SNCC, SCLC and ACMHR (see page 48) began Campaign 'C' (for 'confrontation'), to end segregation in Birmingham. They targeted Birmingham because it was completely segregated and because black Americans had often been attacked there (the city was nicknamed 'Bombingham' due to the regular bombing of black churches, homes and businesses there). It was also where 'Bull' Connor (see page 48) was the chief of police and it was believed that he could be easily provoked into using violence against peaceful protesters.

- Campaign 'C' included sit-ins, mass meetings, peaceful protest marches and a boycott of shops. Hundreds of people took part, inspired by Fred Shuttlesworth of the ACMHR and Martin Luther King, who were among the hundreds of protesters arrested in the first few weeks.

- Most of the adults who had protested were now in jail. So, James Bevel of SNCC trained young black people to demonstrate. On 2 May, about 6,000 of them marched. Most were students, but some were as young as six years old. Over 900 people of all ages were arrested.

- The next day, 3 May, more young people marched. The jails were full, so 'Bull' Connor ordered the police to use dogs and fire hoses on the protesters. The news reports and photos of this event spread worldwide, causing horror. President Kennedy said that the photos (such as Source A) made him feel sick and ashamed. It also gave the USSR Cold War propaganda* ammunition.

Source A

A photograph showing a young man being attacked by a police dog in Birmingham, Alabama, on 4 May 1963.

Key term

Propaganda*

A way of controlling public attitudes. Propaganda uses things like newspapers, posters, radio and film, to put ideas into people's minds and therefore shape attitudes.

Extend your knowledge

Walter Gadsden

The young black man under attack in the photo (Source A) is Walter Gadsden, a student. He was not even taking part in the Birmingham protest, he was watching the protest from the side of the road. One of photographer Bill Hudson's photos of the attack became famous worldwide as an example of Birmingham police brutality.

Activities ?

1 Imagine you are a journalist working for a northern newspaper in the USA, present at the events in Birmingham on 3 May 1963. Write a headline for an article about what you saw. Remember that headlines need to be short and grab attention.

2 Write the first paragraph of the article that follows. The first paragraph should sum up the article for the reader – try to tell the whole story in about 50–100 words.

3 How might a southern newspaper, with an owner who is a WCC member, tell the story differently? Write a new headline and first paragraph for that newspaper.

Interpretation 1

From an article written for the Organisation of American Historians *Magazine of History* in 2005 by Erin Cook and Leanna Racine. Here, they are writing about the events that followed 3 May.

The next day [4 May 1963] newspapers around the country carried shocking images of the violence taking place in Birmingham. Pictures of children being attacked by dogs, of fire hoses knocking bodies into the street and up against buildings, and of women being beaten by policemen helped awaken the "moral conscience of the nation." On May 10, an agreement was announced resulting in the desegregation of many of Birmingham's public facilities.

Figure 2.3 The lessons of Birmingham.

Interpretations (4b)

Method is everything

A spectrum of historical methodology

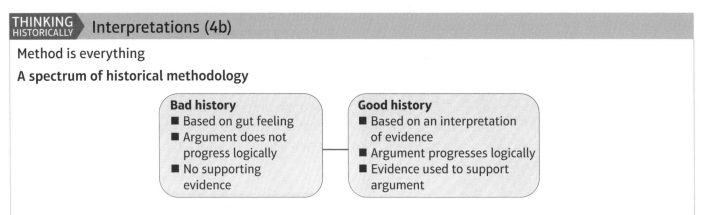

Conclusion 1

What happened in Birmingham was terrible. The police should never have set dogs on people like that, or locked up young children in jail.

Conclusion 2

Birmingham was known as 'Bombingham' for the regular bombing of black churches and homes. The protest campaign began on 3 April. So many adults were jailed that most of the marchers on 2 May were young people. They were fire hosed and attacked by police dogs. This caused outrage around the world and pushed the government to consider a much stronger bill on civil rights.

Conclusion 3

The campaign in Birmingham was a huge success for the civil rights movement. It gained widespread publicity. When people saw the photos and the TV images of young people being knocked over by fire hoses or attacked by dogs, support increased for the movement and for the passing of the Civil Rights Act. The reports about children as young as nine being locked up were also shocking.

Work in pairs. Read the above conclusions and answer the questions.

1 In what ways do the conclusions differ from one another?

2 Look carefully at the spectrum of methodology.

   a Where would you place each student's conclusion on the spectrum?

   b What evidence would you use to support your choice?

   c Suggest one improvement to each conclusion that would move it towards 'good' historical writing.

How important is it that we know what to look for when we are reading and evaluating historical writing?

The March on Washington, 28 August 1963

Almost immediately after Birmingham, civil rights leaders planned a protest march involving people from all over the USA: the March on Washington for Jobs and Freedom. Washington DC was chosen as the location because the White House and Congress were there. Over 250,000 people, about 40,000 of them white, took part.

It was, at the time, the largest political gathering in US history. Despite fears the protest would turn violent, it was peaceful and good-humoured. It was broadcast live on television around the world. It began with the National Anthem and a prayer. Then civil rights activists made speeches. King spoke last. His speech (Source B) confirmed him, for many people, as the spokesman for the civil rights movement.

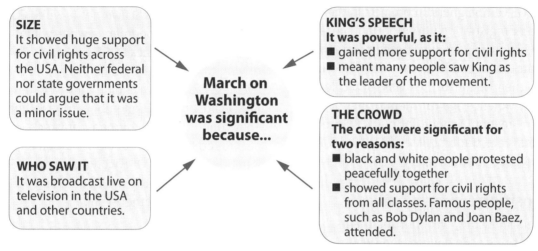

SIZE
It showed huge support for civil rights across the USA. Neither federal nor state governments could argue that it was a minor issue.

WHO SAW IT
It was broadcast live on television in the USA and other countries.

March on Washington was significant because...

KING'S SPEECH
It was powerful, as it:
- gained more support for civil rights
- meant many people saw King as the leader of the movement.

THE CROWD
The crowd were significant for two reasons:
- black and white people protested peacefully together
- showed support for civil rights from all classes. Famous people, such as Bob Dylan and Joan Baez, attended.

Figure 2.4 The significance of the March on Washington.

Source B

From Martin Luther King's speech at the Lincoln Memorial on 28 August 1963.

I have a dream that one day this nation will rise up and live out the true meaning of its creed, "We hold these truths to be self-evident, that all men are created equal." I have a dream that one day on the red hills of Georgia, sons of former slaves and the sons of former slave owners will be able to sit down together at the table of brotherhood. I have a dream that one day even in the state of Mississippi, a state sweltering with the heat of injustice, sweltering with the heat of oppression, will be transformed into an oasis of freedom and justice. I have a dream that my four little children will one day live in a nation where they will not be judged by the colour of their skin, but by the content of their character.

Activity ?

In groups, discuss why Source B was seen as such an inspiring speech. Think of at least one example of King's use of language and his use of images of the past and the future that produce an emotional effect.

Exam-style question, Section A

Explain why tactics used by the civil rights movement changed in the years 1960–63. You may use the following in your answer:

- the Greensboro sit-in
- federal government reaction

You **must** also use information of your own. **12 marks**

Exam tip

When answering a question like this, it is a good idea to refer to the bulleted points in your answer. However, to get the top marks you must also give information of your own to support your answer.

Freedom Summer, 1964

The right to vote only helped black Americans if they were registered to vote and not prevented from voting. Between 1962 and 1964, about 700,000 black Americans in the South registered to vote. However, in the countryside and the Deep South the number of black people registered to vote hardly rose at all.

In 1964, SNCC and CORE set up 'Freedom Summer' in Mississippi. About 1,000 volunteers went to Mississippi to work with local campaigners on projects in the black community. Voter registration was important, because 1964 was an election year. Most volunteers were white college students from good families, chosen because they could pay their way. Also, their class and colour would make any violence against them bigger news. Some taught in Freedom Schools for black children, others held voter registration classes to teach locals how to pass the voter registration tests.

White opposition

SNCC volunteers knew they were putting themselves and black Mississippians in danger. Many white Mississippians called the project an invasion and argued that the northern students did not understand the South. There were over 10,000 KKK members in Mississippi. Before the 'invasion' they burned 61 crosses, at the same time, across the state to show their power and anger. During the summer they burned 37 black churches and 30 homes. They beat up countless volunteers and local black people. Many black people lost their jobs for going to civil rights meetings, trying to register to vote or allowing their children to go a Freedom School. About 17,000 black people tried to register to vote that summer; only 1,600 succeeded.

The Mississippi murders

On 21 June, Michael Schwerner (a white CORE field worker), Andrew Goodman (a white volunteer) and James Chaney (a black CORE worker) were arrested while driving to Schwerner's home. They were released that evening. On their way home they were murdered by the KKK. CORE and SNCC members tried to find their bodies. They found the car, a burned-out wreck, on 23 June. They also found the bodies of eight black men; three were later identified as CORE workers. Chaney, Goodman and Schwerner were not found until 4 August. They had been shot. It became another scandal.

When the summer ended, most of the volunteers had to go back to college, but SNCC continued to work for voter registration rights across the South. Freedom Summer had a variety of consequences that can be seen as good for the civil rights movement, or not (see Figure 2.5).

Figure 2.5 Consequences of the Freedom Summer.

Selma

Alabama was another southern state needing federal action on desegregation. In the spring of 1965, SNCC was still working for voter registration, but white officials had many methods of stopping black people from registering (see page 13). Selma was in Dallas County, where more black people were entitled to vote than white people, yet only 1% of them were registered to vote. Few black people were applying, despite SNCC's work. Fear of violence stopped many – Selma had the largest WCC in Alabama.

King comes to Selma

- Local groups invited the SCLC and King to campaign in Selma. They arrived in January 1965, at the same time as President Johnson was stressing the need for a Voting Rights Act (see page 58) to make voting tests fair and help black Americans qualify to vote.

- In Selma, people protested against the voter registration tests. Others tried to register to vote. There were confrontations with the police and violent arrests. Johnson again spoke in favour of voter registration and the number of protesters rose, as did the violence. One protester died.

- On Sunday 7 March, about 600 protesters set out to march from Selma to Montgomery. State troopers stopped them at the Edmund Pettus Bridge, just outside Selma, firing tear gas and attacking protesters with clubs and electric cattle prods. The protesters fled, chased by troopers. Once more, the USA made world headlines for its abuse of black people.

- In both parts of Congress, many spoke against the violence and in favour of voter registration. All over the country people marched in support of those attacked on 7 March on what came to be called 'Bloody Sunday'. Hundreds of people, black and white, set off to join the marchers.

- Johnson used an executive order to federalise the state national guard. They then escorted the marchers from Selma to Montgomery on 21–24 March. King led the march and gave a speech to a crowd of 25,000 in Montgomery on 25 March.

Source C

From an interview with John Lewis, a civil rights activist and chairman of SNCC, in 1973.

If there is any single event that gave birth to the Voter Rights Act, it was the Selma effort. March 7th was just sort of a combination of things. We had had a series of protests, organizing efforts in Selma in late '63 and some in '64 and '65. ... Some of the people in SNCC felt that Martin King shouldn't come into Selma and some of us felt that he should. I was one of the ones that felt that he should, that he would bring some attention to the problem and help dramatize the problem.

Source D

A photograph showing a protest march in New York on 15 March 1965, held as a result of the events in Selma, Alabama, on 7 March.

Pressure on Congress

The assassination of President Kennedy (who had introduced a strong Civil Rights bill) and the growing protests led to a greater awareness of the issue of civil rights in the USA. The strong support for the protesters put increasing pressure on Congress to pass laws to protect the civil rights of black Americans.

Key Civil Rights Laws

The Civil Rights Act of 1964

The 1964 Civil Rights Act, signed on 2 July 1964:

- banned discrimination in voter registration tests

- banned discrimination in public spaces and businesses with branches in more than one state

- banned job discrimination; set up an Equal Opportunities Commission to enforce it

- gave the government the power to force school desegregation

- gave the government the right to remove federal funding from state projects that discriminated.

The act made significant changes in theory, but did not abolish discrimination. The problems of enforcing federal laws in Southern states remained. There was nothing to impose fair voter registration. The Equal Opportunities Commission could only investigate complaints: many southern black people feared to complain. Also, the Commission staff was small; uninvestigated cases soon piled up. Businesses and schools in the Deep South continued to find ways around desegregation.

The Voting Rights Act of 1965

On 6 August 1965, President Johnson signed the Voting Rights Act. It set up:

- one voting registration requirement, enforced by federal government; states could set qualification rules with federal government approval

- federal officials to run voter registration in any state and in all states where under 50% of those qualified to vote were registered.

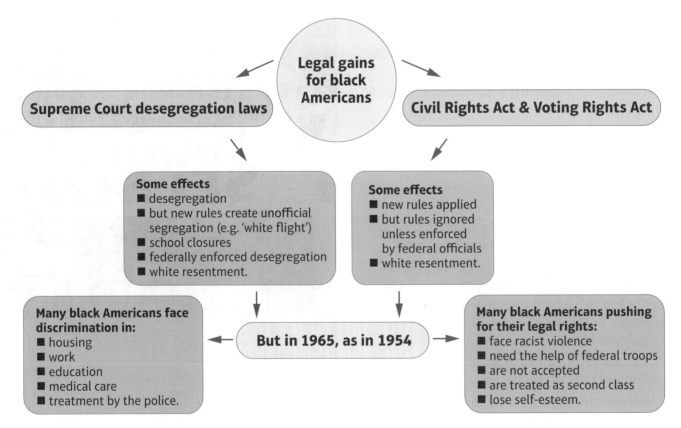

Figure 2.6 Reasons for growing anger among black people.

By the end of 1965, federal registrars had enrolled 79,593 voters. They would probably not have been registered without federal intervention. However, registration was a slow process, because the federal officials were trying to impose black voter registration in areas that did not want black people to vote. By the end of 1965, there was a growing level of frustration among black people about how far the campaign for civil rights had actually improved their lives.

The civil rights movement had fought hard to gain all kinds of rights for black Americans. The laws that had been passed to grant them those rights should not have been necessary – they were rights that the Constitution gave to all US citizens. Figure 2.6 on page 58 shows the reasons for frustration among black people.

The roles of Kennedy and Johnson

The Justice Department dealt with civil rights: either enforcing laws supporting it, or stopping state-authorised violence against black Americans. The Attorney General ran the Justice Department. However, presidents could intervene; mainly by using executive orders to federalise state troops or to send in federal troops to stop violence. Presidents could also speak in favour of civil rights and against state discrimination. They could show they favoured civil rights by appointing black people to high-level positions in their administration. Figure 2.7 shows what Kennedy and Johnson did.

KENNEDY

- Appointed black people to high-level jobs, Thurgood Marshall in the courts; Robert Weaver in his administration
- Pressed for laws – but assassinated before civil rights bill was passed
- Intervened using executive orders – sent federal troops to 'Ole Miss'
- Personal pressure – pressed for escorts for the Freedom Riders

Support civil rights

JOHNSON

- Appointed black people to high-level jobs – Thurgood Marshall into the Supreme Court; Patricia Harris as a US ambassador
- Pressed for laws – secured the Civil Rights Act and Voting Rights Act
- Intervened with executive orders – federalised the Alabama state national guard to escort marchers from Selma to Montgomery
- Personal pressure – pressed Southern politicians to support civil rights bill

Support civil rights

Figure 2.7 How Kennedy and Johnson supported civil rights.

Kennedy and Johnson both supported civil rights, but they had to balance this against political considerations. They needed the support of ordinary American voters and the members of Congress (including the southern Dixiecrats) who opposed civil rights. Also, they wanted to minimise federal intervention in state affairs. What this meant in practice was that they intervened when situations got out of hand. Kennedy had pushed for a strong civil rights bill after Birmingham, but did not live to see the bill become law – he was assassinated on 22 November 1963. Johnson, the Vice President, became President. He was from the South and, while not a Dixiecrat himself, had good relations with the Dixiecrats. He used this to press Southern representatives to agree to pass the Civil Rights Act. He spoke of the bill in Congress as the best way to honour Kennedy's memory. He invited King to the signing of the Act and also pushed through the Voting Rights Act in 1965.

Source E

From a speech made by President Kennedy on 11 June 1963 that was broadcast on radio and television.

The heart of the question is whether all Americans are to be afforded [given] equal rights and equal opportunities, whether we are going to treat our fellow Americans as we want to be treated. If an American, because his skin is dark, cannot eat lunch in a restaurant open to the public, if he cannot send his children to the best public school available, if he cannot vote for the public officials who represent him, if, in short, he cannot enjoy the full and free life which all of us want, then who among us would be content to have the color of his skin changed and stand in his place? Who among us would then be content with the counsels [advice] of patience and delay?

Source F

A photograph showing President Johnson shaking hands with Martin Luther King after signing the Civil Rights Act on 2 July 1964, in a televised broadcast. He is giving King one of the pens he used to sign.

Source G

From the speech made by President Johnson on the signing of the Voting Rights Act of 1965.

And then last March, with the outrage of Selma still fresh, I came down to this Capitol [where Congress meets] one evening and asked the Congress and the people for swift and for sweeping action to guarantee to every man and woman the right to vote. In less than 48 hours I sent the Voting Rights Act of 1965 to the Congress. In little more than 4 months the Congress, with overwhelming majorities, enacted one of the most monumental laws in the entire history of American freedom.

Activities ?

1 Look back at Chapter 1 and note down the key features of the different civil rights protests between 1954 and 1960.

2 Draw a flow diagram showing how civil rights protests changed between 1954 and 1965. Think about the types of protest used and the scale of the protests.

3 In two groups, prepare a debate on the statement: 'The role of protest was more important than the role of presidents in improving civil rights.' One group will support the statement, the other will reject it.

Summary

- The SCLC, especially Martin Luther King, drew publicity to the civil rights protests that they joined.
- The civil rights movement provoked a violent reaction from some white people in Birmingham, Alabama. The publicity helped to influence President Kennedy to call for a civil rights bill.
- The size of the crowds in the March on Washington underlined the importance of civil rights issues in the USA. Martin Luther King's speech showed his significance to the movement.
- President Johnson made sure the Civil Rights Act was passed after the assassination of President Kennedy.
- The events of Freedom Summer (1964) and Selma (1965) led President Johnson to press for the Voting Rights Act.

Checkpoint

Strengthen

S1 Can you explain why the Freedom Summer campaign made some white Southerners so angry?

S2 Write a short paragraph to explain why the Voting Rights Act was so important.

S3 List at least three ways in which President Kennedy and President Johnson played a significant role in helping civil rights.

Challenge

C1 Give one social, one cultural and one political reason to explain why civil rights protest escalated between 1960 and 1965.

C2 Explain what was significant about the violence in Birmingham and at Selma.

How confident do you feel about your answers to these questions? If you are not sure that you answered them well, discuss the questions with a partner and then rewrite the answers together.

Learning outcomes

- Understand Malcolm X's beliefs and methods, and his change in attitude.
- Understand the reasons for the emergence of Black Power.
- Understand the methods and achievements of the Black Panthers.

Key term

Black nationalism*

American black nationalists believed black people would never be equal in integrated communities. Their aim was to create a separate black nation, with black people living and working in their own communities, not integrating, as a first step.

Extend your knowledge

Why Malcolm X left the NOI

Followers of the NOI read the Quran, worshipped Allah and said Muhammad was their prophet, just as Muslims did. They also saw their own leaders as prophets. The NOI leader when Malcolm X joined was Elijah Mohammad. He was supposed to live a good, honest life. However, in 1964 Elijah told Malcolm he had had affairs (and several children) with many women. He asked Malcolm X to help cover this up; this was the main reason Malcolm left the NOI. Elijah Mohammad did not want him to leave, but was also jealous of his increasing importance within the organisation.

Why do you think the NOI reacted so badly to Malcolm X starting his own religious organisation?

Malcolm X

Malcolm X was born Malcolm Little on 19 May 1925. His father, a Baptist minister, was murdered when Malcolm was six. His mother had a breakdown and the children were put in foster homes. In 1946, Malcolm went to prison for burglary. While there, he joined the Nation of Islam (NOI), which shared many Muslim beliefs but also believed in black nationalism*. The NOI said white Americans deliberately held black people back, and that black people needed their own state. Until then, black Americans should live and work in black communities, pressing for equal facilities, but not trying to integrate.

Malcolm changed his name to Malcolm X, replacing a 'slave' surname with 'X' for the unknown tribal name of his African ancestors. Once out of prison, Malcolm X became an NOI minister, then its spokesman. He was clever, articulate and passionate. In 1952, the NOI had 500 members, but by 1963, it had 30,000. Many people gave much of the credit for this to Malcolm X's campaigning.

Malcolm X's beliefs

Malcolm X rejected non-violent direct action, especially its stress on not retaliating to white violence. He said what many more black people were starting to think – that non-violent direct action was not working. Legal pressure, federal intervention, even the Civil Rights Act (1964) and the Voting Rights Act (1965) had not brought black people the equality guaranteed by the Constitution. He criticised civil rights leaders such as King, for trying to work with white people to gain equality. He believed white Americans, no matter how well-intentioned, would always see black people as second-class citizens. Inequality was clear to see, across the USA and especially in the cities. Malcolm X showed that he understood the increasing frustration of black people, especially young men in the ghettos.

In 1964, Malcolm X left the NOI and started his own religious organisation, Muslim Mosque Inc. The NOI made speeches against him and sent death threats. Malcolm went on a pilgrimage to Mecca, the holiest site in Islam, and returned with changed views. He was more willing to consider integration and accept white help. He set up the Organisation of African American Unity civil rights group and said it would work with other civil rights groups. He held meetings with members of SNCC and spoke to civil rights groups with a significant white membership, such as CORE.

Source A

A photograph showing Malcolm X and Martin Luther King meeting for the first and only time, on 26 March 1964. They met by accident in Washington while protesting about the attempt of a few senators to stop the civil rights bill being passed.

Extend your knowledge

Changing beliefs

Malcolm X's early speeches are full of violent language, although he always said that he was only saying that black people should fight back if attacked, not start any violence. He was also very clear in these speeches that, no matter how well-meaning white people were, whites would never want black equality, because it would come at the expense of white people. He rejected offers of help from white people and would not hold discussions with white politicians or officials. After 1964, he was more open to accepting white help.

Assassination

The shift in Malcolm X's beliefs made the Nation of Islam determined to kill him. They firebombed his home several times. He had to travel everywhere with bodyguards. On 21 February 1965, he was making a speech in New York when three members of the Nation of Islam rushed the stage and shot him 15 times. Over 15,000 people went to his funeral on 27 February. After Malcolm X's death, many people focused more on his early beliefs and criticism of non-violent direct action than they did on his later shift in attitude. Since 1965, a rising number of black people rejected non-violent direct action and saw black nationalism and black self-defence against white violence as the next step in the fight for civil rights.

THINKING HISTORICALLY ▶ Interpretations (2a)

The importance of selection

Historians do not aim to tell us about the whole past – there is just too much of it. They need to choose which aspects of the past to investigate and which details are most important to examine. For example, an overview history of military strategy during the First World War would be unlikely to examine witness statements about conditions in the trenches in detail, whereas a work about the experience of the ordinary soldier might examine such witness statements in great depth.

> **The life of Malcolm X – key information**
>
> A) he joined the Nation of Islam while in prison: they believed in separatism
>
> B) he became spokesman for the Nation of Islam
>
> C) he was a powerful and convincing speaker
>
> D) he thought non-violent direct action didn't work
>
> E) he felt black people should defend themselves against action
>
> F) he was a Muslim
>
> G) he rejected the idea of negotiating with white politicians
>
> H) he spoke the language of angry young people in the cities
>
> I) he left the Nation of Islam
>
> J) he came to believe integration might work
>
> K) he came to feel that it was possible to work with non-violent civil rights groups
>
> L) he came to feel that it was possible to work with white people

Often historians have to focus on a particular question to investigate. What information from points A–L would you use to write about the topics below (you can choose up to four pieces of information)?

1. What Malcolm X's early beliefs were.

2. How Malcolm X's beliefs were different from those of Martin Luther King.

3. How Malcolm X's views changed.

4. Malcolm X's popularity.

With a partner, discuss the following questions and write down your conclusions:

5. Why is it important to be selective about the information that you put in your historical writing?

6. How important are the questions historians ask, in deciding what information is included in their writing?

Black Power

From 1963, a growing number of black Americans disagreed with non-violent direct action (see Figure 2.6 on page 58). A new way to protest emerged alongside non-violent direct action: the Black Power movement. 'Black Power' was a slogan used by black radical groups. These groups had different beliefs and ideas, but most of them:

- encouraged black people to be proud of their heritage and culture
- rejected help from white people and argued that black people should rely on themselves
- argued against forced integration, saying it would not produce real equality

- were influenced by Malcolm X
- used militant* language and spoke about revolution.

Black Power had the most support among the poor, because many groups talked not just about power but also about a social revolution to improve the lives of poor black people, especially in ghettos. Black Power campaigns were focused on local issues and they often achieved results. Figure 2.8 on page 65 shows reasons for the growth of the Black Power movement.

> **Key term**
>
> **Militant***
>
> In favour of confrontation or violence in support of a cause.

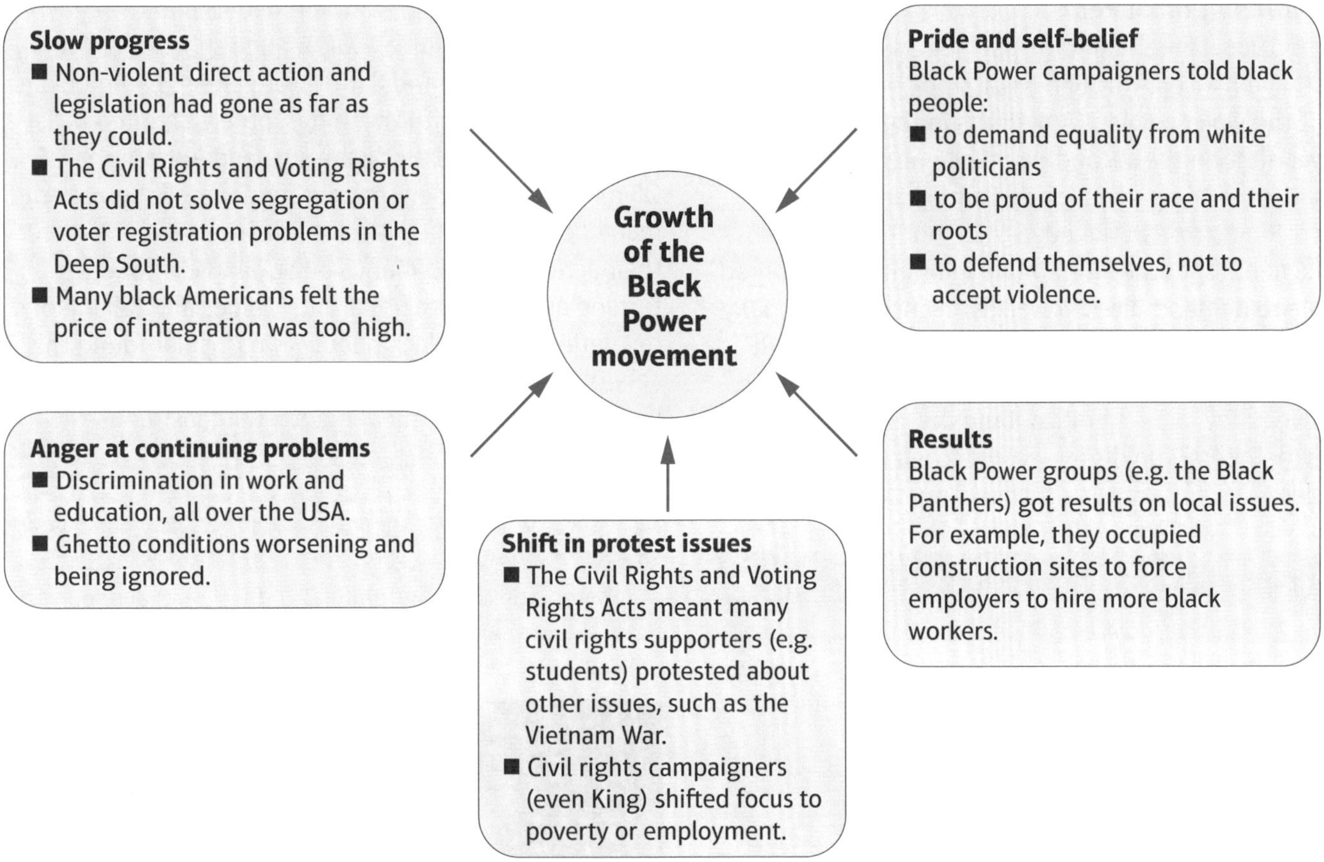

Slow progress
- Non-violent direct action and legislation had gone as far as they could.
- The Civil Rights and Voting Rights Acts did not solve segregation or voter registration problems in the Deep South.
- Many black Americans felt the price of integration was too high.

Growth of the Black Power movement

Pride and self-belief
Black Power campaigners told black people:
- to demand equality from white politicians
- to be proud of their race and their roots
- to defend themselves, not to accept violence.

Anger at continuing problems
- Discrimination in work and education, all over the USA.
- Ghetto conditions worsening and being ignored.

Shift in protest issues
- The Civil Rights and Voting Rights Acts meant many civil rights supporters (e.g. students) protested about other issues, such as the Vietnam War.
- Civil rights campaigners (even King) shifted focus to poverty or employment.

Results
Black Power groups (e.g. the Black Panthers) got results on local issues. For example, they occupied construction sites to force employers to hire more black workers.

Figure 2.8 Reasons for increased support for the Black Power movement.

Stokely Carmichael

After the Voting Rights Act, SNCC continued helping black people to register to vote. Many people said there was no one to vote for who cared about black rights. Stokely Carmichael of SNCC, along with others, set up the Lowndes County Freedom Organisation as a party to represent black Americans. The party symbol was a panther and its slogan was 'Vote for the panther, then go home'. Many did just that. The panther became, for the first time, a symbol of black rights. In May 1966, Carmichael was elected chairman of SNCC. He had believed in non-violent direct action but now felt the fight for civil rights needed to change. He brought more people who believed in Black Power into SNCC and started more SNCC campaigns in the North, especially in city ghettos.

Activities   **?**

1   Design a poster for a Black Power group. Show what makes your group worth joining.

2   In groups, choose one word to summarise each reason in Figure 2.8 and decide if it is a social, political, economic or cultural reason.

3   How might the passing of the Civil Rights Act and the Voter Registration Act be a problem for the civil rights movement in:
    a   keeping white support
    b   keeping activism going in the Deep South?

The March Against Fear

In June 1966, James Meredith (see page 49) led the March Against Fear through Mississippi, protesting about the violence black Americans in the South faced. He was shot on the second day. While he was in hospital, Martin Luther King and Stokely Carmichael led the march. King stressed the need to be non-violent, but Carmichael's speeches were more militant and he urged people to demand Black Power. Carmichael swept many people along with his more radical beliefs. Both CORE and SNCC became less welcoming to white supporters. However, they lost a significant number of their original black members who disagreed with their new, radical, policies.

Source B

From *Voices of Freedom*, a book on civil rights that contains recollections of those who took part. David Dawley, a white student who joined the March Against Fear, remembers how attitudes changed.

```
One afternoon in Greenwood [in Mississippi],
I was in a crowd that was listening to
speakers from a porch. Willie Ricks from
SNCC was introduced and Willie Ricks was
angry and he was lashing out at Whites like
a cracking whip. And as he talked, there
was a chill, there was a feeling of a rising
storm... As Willie Ricks asked people what
they wanted and they answered, "Freedom
now," Willie Ricks exhorted [encouraged] the
crowd to demand not freedom now, but Black
Power. He kept talking at the crowd and when
he asked what they wanted, they answered,
"Freedom now," but more answered "Black
Power," until eventually Black Power began
to dominate, until finally everyone together
was thundering, "Black Power! Black Power!"
And that was chilling, that was frightening.
```

The Mexico Olympics, 1968

Black Power rejected white people. It also scared them, because it talked of violent revolution. Many Black Power groups used the symbol of a raised, clenched fist. At the 1968 Mexico Olympics, black Americans Tommie Smith and John Carlos won the gold and bronze medals in the 200 m race. The US national anthem was played as they were given their medals and they gave the Black Power salute. It was a huge shock and a very political act. Smith and Carlos were booed by Americans in the crowd; some threw things, others shouted racist abuse. Smith and Carlos were suspended from the US Olympic team. US newspapers condemned them, as did many politicians. They received death threats. However, their action inspired many young people who were turning away from their parents' values and talking of revolution. Young black people in particular found this very public expression of black pride an inspiration to join the Black Power movement, or at least to use its more confrontational tactics.

Source C

A photograph showing Tommie Smith (centre) and John Carlos (right) giving the Black Power salute at the Mexico Olympics in 1968.

The Black Panthers

The Black Panthers were one of the largest Black Power groups, one of the most feared and, in their own view, one of the most misunderstood. They were set up in California in October 1966 by Huey P. Newton and Bobby Seale. They attracted media attention when they went to the State Capitol in Sacramento carrying guns, to protest against a proposed law to stop people openly carrying guns. The sight of armed black men in the State Capitol made the news. The Panther movement took off.

The Panthers believed that white officials and police were not supporting black communities. They said black people needed black officials and police who would work for the community. However, unlike many other Black Power groups, they were willing to work with white people who shared their beliefs. They originally called themselves 'The Black Panther Party for Self-Defense'. Each group had their own version of the 'Ten Point Programme' (see Source D) and each had their own version of the Panther 'uniform': black beret, black trousers and black leather jacket.

Most Black Panther groups saw themselves as the police and social workers that their black communities needed but did not have. They:

- patrolled the streets in black communities to keep them safe
- worked to create 'rainbow coalitions' to encourage cooperation between non-white city gangs that usually fought each other
- controlled the traffic around schools with no pedestrian crossings, where children were regularly hit by cars
- continually pressed local white government officials to provide street lighting, pedestrian crossings and various kinds of aid for ghetto communities
- ran courses on black history and citizens' rights
- carried guns for self-defence and tape recorders so they could tape police harassment
- organised medical clinics and provided free shoes for poor black people
- ran breakfast clubs for poor black children before school.

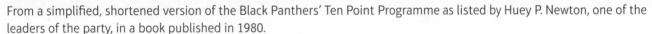

Source D

From a simplified, shortened version of the Black Panthers' Ten Point Programme as listed by Huey P. Newton, one of the leaders of the party, in a book published in 1980.

1 We want freedom. We want the power to run our black community.

2 We want full employment for our people.

3 We want an end to the robbery by the capitalists of our black community.

4 We want decent housing fit for the shelter of human beings.

5 We want education for our people that exposes the true nature of this decadent American society. We want education that teaches us our true history and our role in present-day society.

6 We want all black men to be free from having to serve in the military forces.

7 We want an immediate end to Police brutality and murder of black people.

8 We want freedom for all black men held in prisons, federal or state.

9 We want all black people who are brought to trial to be tried by a jury from their black community.

10 We want land, bread, housing, education, clothing, justice and peace.

Source E

From a 2001 interview with Raney Norwood, from North Carolina, who joined the Panthers in 1967.

What really caught my attention was, a group of Black Panthers came in from High Point. And they weren't really recruiting at the time. What they were trying to do was help. So we decided to just hang out with them, just see what it's all about. When we were just hanging out with them, they taught us a lot. It was not hatred. They were teaching us what was really going on. What I mean by that, they were showing how our black younger kids were being sent to school with no breakfast. They were sitting there with not half of the books they need. So then we started selling newspapers for the Panthers. So we became more and more interested. We decided to join up. And the thing about it back then, when you became a Panther and you came back into the black neighborhood, it was hard for them to accept you because they was afraid. We might have been troublemakers, we might have been the type to kill police officers.

What did the Panthers achieve?

The Panthers did, at a local level, help to improve living conditions in ghetto communities. Their health clinics and breakfast clubs were particularly successful, and improved the lives of many black Americans. However, there was another side to what they did. The money that they raised for their welfare projects came mostly from black businesses, but not all of these businesses contributed willingly. Some Panthers were arrested for robbing banks to fund their projects. Also, their policing of the streets was, for many groups, as much about provoking the police (who they called 'pigs') and engaging in shoot-outs as it was about policing the community.

In July 1967, California passed a law that made it illegal to carry guns in public places. Huey Newton was then badly wounded in a shoot-out with the police in October and charged with murder. The Panthers concentrated on a campaign to 'Free Huey' and the publicity led to many more people joining the Panthers. By late 1968 there were 25 cities with Panther groups and many more Panther members across the country. Even so, there were never more than about 2,000 Panthers.

Source F

A photograph of a Black Panther Party march in New York, in 1968.

Activities

1 Look at Source E. What impression does it give of the Black Panthers? List the detail in the source that gives this impression.

2 In groups, discuss the impression of the Black Panthers given by Sources E and F. List the aspects of the Black Power movement you would use each source to illustrate.

3 Choose **one** of the following statements to best sum up each source: made white people fearful; encouraged young black people; helped the community; rejected help from white people; improved ghetto conditions and opposed police brutality. Write a sentence to justify each choice.

Exam-style question, Section B

Study Sources D and E. How useful are Sources D and E for an enquiry into the aims of the Black Panthers? Explain your answer, using Sources D and E and your knowledge of the historical context. **8 marks**

Exam tip

When considering how useful sources are, think about how the type of source (e.g. interview, pamphlet, photograph) might affect its usefulness.

Interpretation 1

From *The Civil Rights Movement* (2004) by historian Mark Newman. He is considering the effects of the Black Power movement.

In some ways a continuation of the civil rights movement's concerns and in others a departure from them, Black Power divided the national civil rights coalition, alienated white supporters, destroyed SNCC, decimated [ruined] CORE, produced a range of competing visions, and fanned an already advanced white reaction against black demands for the substance [actual] equality. Black Power was part of a new wave of black nationalism which boosted black pride, consciousness and identity, but enjoyed little success politically.

Interpretation 2

From *We Ain't What We Ought To Be: The Black Freedom Struggle from Emancipation to Obama* (2010) by historian Stephen Tuck. He is considering the effects of the Black Power movement.

Most [Black Power] groups combined racial pride and political goals. Many focussed on the poor, condemned middle-class black leaders, called for reparations [compensation payments] to be paid for slavery, and identified with nonwhite protest abroad. … These Black Power groups had plenty of slogans, but they went far beyond posturing [doing things for effect]. Black Power was often entirely practical when applied to a particular place at a particular moment. Revolutionary trade union movement demanded more black jobs and black representatives in decision making. Black Power student groups demanded more black faculty members [teaching staff], better treatment of black staff, and courses on black history.

Summary

- Malcolm X had a more confrontational approach to civil rights. However, he began to work with other civil rights groups, such as SNCC and CORE, before his assassination in 1965.
- The Black Power movement emerged due to growing dissatisfaction with the lack of progress that non-violent direct action had made in achieving real change for black people.
- SNCC, under the leadership of Stokely Carmichael, and CORE became more radical.
- There was negative publicity for black athletes who gave the Black Power salute at the Mexico Olympics in 1968.
- The Black Panthers, set up in California in 1966, said they provided ghetto communities with the care that white officials did not provide.

Checkpoint

Strengthen

S1 Choose what you think is the most important reason for the emergence of Black Power. Explain your choice in a sentence.

S2 Explain the significance of the Black Power salute at the 1968 Olympics.

S3 Think of four different ways in which the Black Panthers helped ghetto communities. For each of them, write down the way followed by 'but' and a downside of this.

Challenge

C1 Give one social, one cultural, one economic and one political reason to explain why Black Power became significant in the mid-1960s.

C2 Why do you think the Black Panthers were a city-based movement?

How confident do you feel about your answers to these questions? If you are unsure, try planning them with diagrams that show the key points and make links between them.

2.4 The civil rights movement, 1965–75

Learning outcomes

- Understand the riots of 1965–67 and the Kerner Report.
- Understand King's campaigns in the North and the impact of his assassination.
- Understand the extent of progress in civil rights by 1975.

Between 1964 and 1968 there were 329 major riots in 257 US cities. They resulted in 220 deaths, 8,371 severe injuries and 52,629 arrests. The first large-scale riot was in New York City in July 1964, two weeks after the Civil Rights Act was signed. It began when a policeman shot a young black man, but it was also a reaction to ghetto conditions and violence in Mississippi (see page 56). Riots followed in other Northern cities. The next major riot was in the Watts district of Los Angeles in August 1965. It was set off by police violence while arresting a young black man, but it was also a reaction to ghetto conditions and the violence in Selma (see page 57).

After this, there were summer riots every year in different cities, mainly in the North (the worst being in Chicago and Cleveland in 1966, and Newark and Detroit in 1967). Summer was when ghetto conditions were at their worst, and the heat made tempers short.

Why were there riots?

While specific incidents sparked off the riots, the long-term cause was the problems faced by black Americans in city ghettos.

- **Police discrimination:** the police seemed more concerned with harassing young black men than keeping the ghettos safe. They were quick to shoot 'suspects'. In the 30 months before the Watts riots, the police shot 65 black people (27 were shot in the back and 25 were unarmed).
- **Discrimination by white officials:** city officials did not respond to complaints about issues such as badly-repaired roads or landlord harassment.
- **They were twice as likely to be unemployed:** workers mostly had unskilled, low-paid jobs.
- **They were more than twice as likely to be poor:** landlords, mostly white people, crowded them into cramped, badly repaired over-priced housing.
- **Poor quality education:** schools were run down, under-equipped and lacked funding.

Exam-style question, Section A

Give **two** things you can infer from Source A about the Watts riots in 1965. Give the detail in the source that tells you this.

4 marks

Exam tip

You infer something from a source by working out something the source does not actually tell you directly. In this case, think about who you can see, where they are and the time of day.

Source A

A photograph showing the army patrolling Watts during the riots of 1965. It was taken by the US news photographer for the French newspaper *Paris Match*.

The pattern of the riots

While over 80% of the rioters were young black men, they had support in the community. Many black people saw the riots as a reaction to the actions of white people. Black violence during the riots was mostly aimed at property (such as white-run stores that discriminated against black people) not white people. More black people died in the riots than white, often shot by white police or troops.

The Watts riots led more black people to join Black Power groups, and more white people to react against calls for equality. On the other hand, the publicity drew attention to ghetto problems. Martin Luther King visited Watts during the riots and decided that the SCLC must campaign in the North. President Johnson said the riots convinced him to put more money into improving ghettos. The riots usually followed the pattern shown in Figure 2.9.

Timeline
Major riots 1964–67

1964 New York, Philadelphia, Rochester

1965 Los Angeles

1966 Chicago, Cleveland

1967 Newark, Detroit

Figure 2.9 The pattern of the riots.

The Kerner Report, 1968

In July 1967, President Johnson set up an enquiry into the riots. The 1968 Kerner Report said that:

- the riots were the result of ghetto conditions produced by segregation and discrimination
- the riots came after white officials failed to fix problems that the black community had pointed out
- white officials should listen to the black community and involve black people in solving problems
- the police should change their policing to provide more protection in the ghettos
- the police needed to change their unfair, and sometimes brutal, treatment of black people
- during the riots the police had made the situation worse by using violence
- federal money given after the riots to improve conditions was usually spent on training and equipping the police with even more weapons to deal with riots
- there was no serious attempt to improve the ghettos or to win the trust of the black community
- the media had sensationalised the riots, almost always exaggerating the damage, numbers of dead and the amount of federal aid given afterwards.

Source B

From the introduction to the Kerner Report (1968), which was an enquiry into the cause of urban riots in the 1960s. The enquiry was set up by President Johnson.

This is our basic conclusion: Our nation is moving toward two societies, one black, one white — separate and unequal. Reaction to last summer's disorders has quickened the movement and deepened the division. Discrimination and segregation have long permeated [been a part of] much of American life; they now threaten the future of every American. This deepening racial division is not inevitable. The movement apart can be reversed. Choice is still possible.

Why did rioters damage 'their' property?

Black Americans in the ghettos were caught in a trap of constant racial discrimination. Shops run by white people often charged more than the average price for goods. White landlords, and government housing, often charged black people high rents to crowd into buildings with poor facilities (e.g. plumbing and windows were not repaired, a whole building might only have one toilet). The fire brigades were often slow to answer calls from the ghetto, or never came. Rubbish collection was not regular and rubbish piled on the streets, attracting rats.

The reaction of white people to the riots often included surprise that the rioters damaged 'their' own shops and homes in their community. How does this misunderstand the situation?

Activity   **?**

In groups, discuss the statement: 'The riots damaged the civil rights movement and did no good.' How far do you agree with this judgement? Make a list of evidence to support it and evidence against it. Which list is longest? Do all groups have the same result?

King's campaign in the North

King, shocked by his visit to Watts, wanted to show that non-violent direct action could still produce results. When the Coordinating Council of Community Organisations of Chicago (CCCO) asked the SCLC to join a non-violent campaign for fairer housing in 1966, the SCLC accepted.

- James Bevel from the SCLC helped the (CCCO) to organise tenants' associations to fight the Chicago Real Estate Board's segregated housing and unfairly high rents.

- Jesse Jackson from the SCLC helped to organise Operation Breadbasket: boycotts to pressurise white businesses to employ more black people.

- On 7 January 1966 the SCLC officially announced plans for a Chicago Freedom Movement and King went to Chicago.

- King called meetings and arranged demonstrations. King and the SCLC had support, but it was far from complete. Many of Chicago's black politicians opposed the campaign.

- The SCLC also found it hard to connect with the ghetto gangs. In the South, black churches were the focus of most communities and King's message of peaceful non-violence worked well. It still worked with church groups in Chicago, but it was not enough to be effective across the city.

Source C

A photograph showing a non-violent direct action protest in Chicago on 25 June 1966. Demonstrations organised in the city showed that non-violent direct action could still draw a lot of support.

The campaign

King faced a very different opposition than he had faced in the South. Chicago's Mayor, Richard Daley, used words, not weapons. In negotiations with King he sounded reasonable and supportive of civil rights – but did nothing. The Chicago Freedom Movement planned marches through white neighbourhoods, to start in July. It hoped to provoke a violent response and to gain publicity and sympathy.

Before the marches could begin, a riot broke out. King was there at the time, but his appeals for calm were ignored and he was abused for not achieving any gains in Chicago. State troops were called in to stop the riot and Daley accused the SCLC of encouraging it. Despite this, the Chicago Freedom Movement went ahead with their marches through white neighbourhoods. They produced a violent response and the expected publicity, but the publicity was far less supportive than it had been to the backlash from white people in the South. Even so, Daley agreed to meetings with the Chicago Freedom Movement and Chicago Real Estate Board, which led to an agreement on fairer housing practices. King and many of the SCLC, feeling their job was done, left Chicago.

Source D

From an interview given in 1989 by Albert Raby of the Coordinating Council of Community Organisations of Chicago. This was the group that invited King and the SCLC to Chicago.

Mayor Daley had said that there was no ghettos in the city and that the racial composition of the city was as a result [of] people's desires, that you could live really anywhere you wanted to, but people just chose to live where they were. So that our decision to go [to] real estate agencies in White communities and ask to look at property which is available created an environment in which the White community reacted negatively and threatened us. And the situation, or the attitude of the movement was that we were not going to be frightened out of these neighborhoods... and that the city had to admit that there was in fact segregation and initiate programs to remedy that.

Failure or success?

King spoke of the campaign as a success: there had been peaceful demonstrations and there was an agreement. Operation Breadbasket kept running. It helped black people to find jobs in white-owned businesses. It became a key protest organisation in Chicago. The whole campaign was seen as a failure because:

- There had been violence on both sides during the campaign and King had not been able to stop the riot that broke out before the marches.
- Daley ignored the agreement he had made with the Chicago Freedom Movement, and Chicago Real Estate Board housing policies did not change. The CCCO had warned King that this would happen. When King and the SCLC left, the CCCO found it hard to keep up the pressure on Daley on their own.
- The government did not push Daley to carry out the agreement. Relations between Johnson and King were strained as King opposed the Vietnam War more publicly.

Source E

From an interview given in 1990 by Bob Lucas of CORE. He is talking about the last of the black marches through white neighbourhoods in Chicago, held after King left, during which there was some black retaliation to white violence.

I felt really good about the blacks catching the missiles and throwing them back [on their marches through the white neighbourhoods] because it sorely indicated to the whole world that nonviolence had worked in the South but it wasn't about to really work in the North.

After Dr. King left the city in late August of 1966, having failed really in Chicago, we began to notice a wider split between the blacks and the whites in the civil rights movement. As long as Dr. King was here, that was sort of held at bay, out of respect for him.

Activities ?

1 In groups, choose three significant reasons for calling the Chicago campaign a failure and three significant reasons for calling it a success.

2 Which argument do you agree with? Make a poster to convince others of your choice.

The Assassination of Martin Luther King

At just after 6 pm on 4 April 1968, Martin Luther King was assassinated. He was shot while standing on the balcony of a motel in Memphis, Tennessee. He had arrived the day before, to prepare for a march supporting striking rubbish collectors. At the same time, he was planning a large 'Poor People's Campaign' on behalf of all the poor, not just poor black people.

In the weeks after King's death:

- There were riots in 172 towns and cities all over the USA, both in places that had riots in earlier year and in those that had not. By 9 April, the day of King's funeral, 32 black people were dead, over 3,500 had been seriously injured and 27,000 had been arrested. $45 million of damage had been caused.

- The Poor People's Campaign that King had planned went ahead. A large, integrated group of poor marchers marched on Washington and set up camp there, within view of the Capitol. The campaign, which many of the SCLC leaders had warned King might not succeed, failed. The SCLC leaders and the protesters argued and it poured with rain. The camp broke up after only a few weeks.

- The 1968 Civil Rights Act was quickly passed. It included a section about fair housing, covering rental housing and housing sales made after the passing of the act. The act gave federal protection to civil rights workers, although it also made punishment for rioting more severe.

Later impact

National civil rights groups lost membership, funding and support from white people. This was not simply a result of King's death. From 1965, white public opinion had been less supportive of civil rights. This was partly because, with the Civil Rights Act and the Voter Registration Act, many white people saw the battle as won. The Northern riots caused a drop in white people's support for civil rights and even King himself. However, King was still the person most white people related to; his death likely accelerated white people's opposition to black people's demands for equality.

Many black Americans became more radical after King's death. In 1969, SNCC changed the 'N' in its name from 'non-violent' to 'national' – and lost almost all of its original members. The result of many black people becoming more militant and many white people opposing black equality meant increasing conflict, rather than agreement, on civil rights.

Source F

A photograph showing the moments immediately after Martin Luther King was shot. The people on the balcony with him are pointing to the window where the shot was fired from.

Civil rights and progress, 1969–75

Black protest after 1969 split many ways. Local protest still addressed issues such as desegregation or equal employment, while large-scale protests were likely to be about single issues. The Black Panthers, for instance, held national protests about what they saw as the wrongful imprisonment of some of their members. These large protests drew in other, non-black, protest groups.

The issue that drew in the most people, from many different races and classes, was US involvement in the Vietnam War. As the USA became more involved in the war, public anti-war feeling increased. Black Americans were particularly angry that their demands for civil rights were not being met, yet they were expected to join the army and fight. For example, the famous boxer, Mohammad Ali refused to fight because he had no quarrel with the Vietnamese and said it was wrong to fight for the USA when the government was denying black people their human rights.

A new president: more rights?

Richard Nixon became president in 1969. As vice-president (1953–61), and in his presidential election campaign, he spoke up for civil rights. However, like earlier presidents, he was careful to balance the need for black votes against the need to keep the Southern vote – which was still largely against the enforcement of civil rights. Many of the reforms he introduced were sold to the white community as being likely to stop riots. For instance, he encouraged black businesses and black home ownership, saying people would be less likely to destroy their own property which they owned.

- He set up funding and training for black people setting up businesses in black neighbourhoods.
- He gave tax breaks to white-owned businesses that set up branches in black neighbourhoods.
- He pressed for 'affirmative action' – the deliberate choosing of a black person for a job over a white person. He saw this as a way to get more job equality. It was introduced first in the building industry and then extended to other industries.
- He made sure that there were more black officials in the White House. James Farmer, who had been a CORE official, was given a high-level job in the Department of Health, Welfare and Education.

Source G

A photograph showing the boxer Mohammad Ali with a group of Black Panthers in 1969. Ali had refused to go to fight in Vietnam, saying he had no quarrel with the Vietnamese.

Extend your knowledge

Shirley Chisholm

Shirley Chisholm grew up in New York. She became a teacher in 1946, joined the NAACP and was involved in local politics. In 1968, she was the first black woman to be elected to the House of Representatives in Congress (for the Brooklyn district of New York). She campaigned for black rights and women's rights. In 1971, she ran to be the Democratic candidate for president to oppose the Republican president, Nixon. She had some support, but not enough to win the nomination. She stepped down to support George McGovern: a white, male, candidate.

What does her story suggest about the extent of the progress on civil rights?

Progress by 1975

In 1970, the Voting Rights Act was revised to ban state literacy tests. In 1975, it was revised to include Hispanic, American Indian and other races. It reflected the move in civil rights protest towards campaigning for the rights of other minority groups.

By 1975, the fight for equality for black Americans was far from won. In 1954, the federal government and civil rights campaigners had hoped that enforced changes would change thinking and that the next generation would be more integrated and accepting. Instead, they found that racism ran deeper in the USA, North and South, than many had thought. They also found that desegregation was patchy and not always useful to black people. School integration, enforced or otherwise, was not necessarily benefiting black students as much as they had thought. Figure 2.10 shows how 'progress' could be interpreted differently.

Interpretation 1

From *The American Dream* (1996) by historian Esmond Wright. Here, he is considering whether there had been progress in civil rights by the mid-1970s.

Despite the civil rights gains of the 1960s, however, racial discrimination and repression remained a significant factor in American life. Even after President Johnson declared a war on poverty and King initiated a Poor People's Campaign in 1968, the distribution of the nation's wealth and income moved towards greater inequality in the 1970s. Civil rights advocates acknowledged that desegregation had not brought significant improvement in the lives of poor blacks.

Interpretation 2

From *The Civil Rights Movement* (2004) by historian Mark Newman. He is considering whether there had been progress in civil rights by the mid-1970s.

By the early 1970s, the African-American struggle for equality had made some significant gains. Between 1964 and 1970, the number of southern black elected officials had increased from fewer than 25 to over 700. Racist demagoguery [language] declined in southern elections, and white candidates increasingly sought to attract black voters… By 1972 most southern states had moderate executives [state officials]. Andrew Young, who had resigned from SCLC in 1970 to enter politics, was elected to the US House of Representatives in 1972. A year later, Maynard Jackson became Atlanta's first African-American mayor.

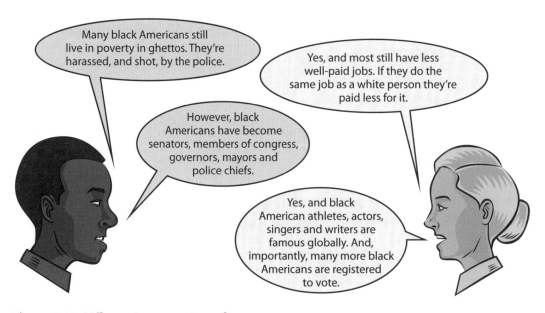

Figure 2.10 Different interpretations of progress.

Exam-style question, Section B

Study Interpretations 1 and 2. They give different views on progress in civil rights by the mid-1970s.

What is the main difference between these views?

Explain your answer, using detail from both interpretations. **4 marks**

Exam tip

When answering a question about how interpretations differ, remember that the question is only worth four marks, so do not spend too long on it.

Activity

In groups, prepare one person in each group to role-play a discussion of progress in civil rights between 1954 and 1975.

Group 1 will prepare to argue that there has been significant progress.

Group 2 will prepare to argue that there has been hardly any progress.

Go back through Chapters 1 and 2 to collect evidence to support your interpretation. Make sure to use both sources and interpretations to support your interpretation, as well as the information in the text.

Summary

- Between 1964 and 1968 there were over 300 major riots in over 250 US cities.
- The riots were set off by an incident in the city, often involving the police, but they were also a reaction to ghetto conditions.
- The Kerner Report said that the US was developing two societies and black people were being discriminated against at every level, including by white officials and the police.
- King and the SCLC went to Chicago in 1966 to help local campaigns for fairer housing. The campaign attracted support, but in July there were riots in the ghetto.
- Mayor Daley of Chicago agreed to talks with King, the SCLC and local civil rights campaigners. He made promises about fairer housing, but he did not carry them out.
- King then began to organise a big demonstration in Washington: the Poor People's Campaign, addressing the issue of poverty for black and white Americans.
- On 4 April 1968, King was assassinated. Widespread riots followed.
- After King's death civil rights groups worked together less, so there were fewer big protests. Also, black protest became more radical. Support for civil rights protest dropped as the Vietnam War became more of an issue.

Checkpoint

Strengthen

S1 List at least four steps in the build-up to a city riot in the late 1960s.

S2 Explain the significance of police attitudes to black Americans in the development of a riot.

S3 Explain why the Chicago campaign might be called a failure.

S4 Explain why civil rights campaigning had less support after 1968.

Challenge

C1 Give one social, one economic and one political reason to explain why there were so many riots between 1964 and 1968.

C2 Explain what was significant about King's campaign in Chicago in 1966.

How confident do you feel about your answers to these questions? If you are not sure you answered them well, ask your teacher for some guidance and then try them again.

Recap: Protest, progress and radicalism, 1960–75

Recall quiz

1 What happened at Greensboro, North Carolina, on 1 February 1960?
2 What did the Freedom Riders do?
3 What was the James Meredith case about?
4 What was the nickname of Birmingham, Alabama?
5 What was the destination of the March for Jobs and Freedom in 1963?
6 Who were the three Freedom Summer campaigners murdered in Mississippi in 1964?
7 What was the Nation of Islam?
8 Who was Stokely Carmichael?
9 What was the Kerner Report?
10 Who was assassinated on 4 April 1968?

Exam-style question, Section B

How far do you agree with Interpretation 1 about the impact of the Black Power movement? Explain your answer using Interpretations 1 and 2 and your knowledge of the historical context.

Exam tip

When considering how far you agree with an interpretation you are expected to weigh up one interpretation against the other. You need to use exact details from the interpretations and your own knowledge.

In the exam, you will be asked how useful contemporary sources are for an enquiry. Copy and complete the table below. Support what you say with your own knowledge if it helps you to make your point.

Sources	Enquiry	Ways they are useful
B on page 46 and D on page 47	The impact of the Greensboro sit-in	
G and H page 50	Federal involvement in the James Meredith case	
C and D on page 57	The significance of the Selma to Montgomery march	
B and C on page 66	The impact of black power on white people	

In the exam, you will be asked about how historians' interpretations can differ. To find out why interpretations give different impressions you need to ask:

- Are they thinking about the same aspect of the topic?
- Might they have given weight to different sources (look carefully at both sources on your paper, as well as the interpretations; the sources will have been carefully chosen to help you)?

Interpretations	Enquiry	How they differ	Why they might differ
1 and 2 on page 69	The impact of the Black Power movement		
1 and 2 page 76	Progress in civil rights by the mid-1970s		

03 | US involvement in the Vietnam War 1954–75

In 1939, at the outbreak of the Second World War, Vietnam was just one of the French colonies in Indochina (an area including modern day Vietnam, Cambodia and Laos). It was a poor country with very little industry or goods worth trading for. Yet this small nation dragged the richest and most powerful nation in the world, the USA, into a war that the USA found impossible to win. How did the USA get involved?

The USA became involved in Vietnam because of the Cold War that developed after the Second World War. The Cold War was a war of ideas between the USA and the USSR. The USA supported ideas of democracy, individual choice and economic freedom. The USSR supported ideas of equality, state control and economic restriction. Both sides were powerful enough that a war between them would be devastating. So, instead of fighting directly, the capitalist USA and the communist USSR jostled to win other countries onto their side. They did this by influencing the outcome of wars in other countries by 'limited war': sending supplies and training troops but not sending troops to fight. This is how the USA became involved in Vietnam. There was a possibility that the whole of Vietnam might become communist and the USA wanted to stop that happening.

Over time, the USA was increasingly sucked into the war, sending hundreds of thousands of troops. But, in the end, it failed to stop all of Vietnam becoming communist, losing thousands of men and spending billions of dollars in the process. Why couldn't the USA win the war in Vietnam, despite its huge army, wealth and technologically advanced weapons?

Learning outcomes

In this chapter, you will study:

- the end of French rule in Vietnam
- reasons for US involvement in Vietnam 1954–63
- the escalation of the conflict under President Johnson
- the nature of the conflict in Vietnam, 1964–68, including Vietcong guerrilla tactics, US methods and the significance of the Tet Offensive
- changes under Nixon, including Vietnamisation, the Nixon Doctrine and attacks on Cambodia, Laos and North Vietnam.

The end of French rule in Vietnam

On 13 March 1954, a battle began between Vietnamese and French troops at Dien Bien Phu. There were two main reasons for the battle.

- Vietnam was a French colony*. France lost control of Vietnam when Japan occupied it during the Second World War. When the war ended, France wanted to regain control of its colony.
- The Vietnamese Vietminh, led by Ho Chi Minh, wanted Vietnamese independence.

When Japan surrendered in August 1945, Ho Chi Minh announced that Vietnam was now the Democratic Republic of Vietnam – an independent country free from French colonial rule. Ho Chi Minh wanted the USA to help him to secure Vietnam's independence from the French, but they were reluctant because they feared Ho would make Vietnam communist.* The USA wanted Vietnamese independence, but not as a communist country.

Support for Ho Chi Minh was weak in the south. Here, French troops marched in and set up the State of Vietnam, ruled by Bao Dai (who they controlled). Bao Dai was anti-communist. Then, in 1949, China became a communist country. Fears of the spread of communism grew when China sent the Vietminh supplies, advisers and troops. In response, the US began to send the French supplies and military advisers. Many advisers were soldiers and wore uniforms; but were told to advise, not fight. By 1954, the USA was paying about 80% of the cost of France's war with the Vietminh.

Key terms

Colony*

A place controlled by another country, politically and economically.

Communist*

A communist government owns all the businesses and land in the country it controls. Everyone works for the government. In return, the government provides everyone in the country with everything they need, such as food, homes, healthcare and education.

Source A

A photograph showing villagers taking supplies to the Vietminh surrounding Dien Bien Phu in 1954. Many of the paths up the mountains were much narrower and steeper than this one.

Dien Bien Phu

The French built an airstrip at Dien Bien Phu to lure the Vietminh into battle, brought in 15,000 troops and waited for an attack. They had no idea that they were surrounded by 50,000 Vietminh with anti-aircraft guns and other artillery, which they had spent months getting up into the mountains. The Vietminh also had 50,000 troops in reserve and about 200,000 civilian workers. The fighting at Dien Bien Phu lasted 55 days. On 7 May 1954, the French surrendered.

Why did the Vietminh win?

Figure 3.1 shows the main reasons for the Vietminh victory. The French had asked the USA for military help. President Eisenhower had considered it, and even considered using atom bombs, but he felt Congress would refuse to send in troops. The USA had just ended a war in Korea, with 34,000 American lives lost and nothing gained. Very few Americans wanted another war.

Local conditions
The Vietminh understood the country:
- they saw the French had built a trap for themselves
- they saw access to the mountains as possible.

Local support
The Vietminh had local support. Villagers:
- helped dig five new roads to move supplies
- helped move supplies
- spied on the French.

Why the Vietminh won at Dien Bien Phu

China's help
China supplied the Vietminh with:
- weapons and ammunition
- 20,000 bikes to move supplies
- help in planning
- some troops.

French problems
- Underestimated support for the Vietminh
- Didn't expect the Vietminh to be so well armed
- Supply planes were shot down by Vietminh anti-aircraft guns
- The troops lacked commitment; many were German, not French troops defending their colony.

Vietminh commitment
The Vietminh army:
- worked day and night to build roads and move supplies
- were fighting for independence from French rule.

Figure 3.1 Why the Vietminh won at Dien Bien Phu.

Key terms

Accord*

A formal agreement.

DMZ (demilitarised zone)*

An area where all military activity is forbidden.

The new government of Vietnam

The day after the French surrender, representatives from nine countries met in Geneva to discuss what was to happen to Vietnam. On 21 July, a partial agreement was reached: the Geneva Accords*.

- Vietnam was to be temporarily divided along the 17th parallel (see Figure 3.2), separated by a demilitarised zone (DMZ)* that no troops could enter.

- Ho Chi Minh would run the northern part (Democratic Republic of Vietnam) from Hanoi. It was a smaller area of Vietnam than the Vietminh held when the war with France ended.

- Bao Dai would run the southern part (the State of Vietnam) from Saigon. Later, he made Ngo Dinh Diem Prime Minister in June 1954. Bao Dai then went to France and Diem (also fiercely anti-communist) ran the country.

- Vietnamese troops, and people, could move north or south for 300 days after the agreement.

- No foreign troops could set up bases in either part of the country.

- In July 1956, elections would be held (supervised by international observers) across both parts of Vietnam to decide on the government of a united Vietnam. No system was suggested for the elections.

The countries at Geneva were: Cambodia, China, France, Laos, the UK, the USA, the USSR and North and South Vietnam. The USA and South Vietnam refused to obey the Accords. North Vietnam had wanted to divide Vietnam further south, at the 13th parallel, and to hold elections in six months. China pushed it to give in. So, both Vietnamese governments were unhappy with the Accords.

Figure 3.2 How Vietnam was divided.

Activities ❓

1   In groups, discuss whether the Geneva Accords were a good basis for peace. Consider:

    a where the division was set up

    b who was in power in South Vietnam

    c the arrangement for elections

    d who actually agreed with the Accords.

2   List two inferences you could make from Source A (page 80) about support for the Vietminh in 1954.

3   Draw a concept diagram to show how the reasons for the Vietminh's success in 1954 are linked.

Greater involvement under Eisenhower

After the Geneva Accords, Eisenhower could have brought all US advisers home, leaving Vietnam to work towards the elections to reunite the country. Instead, he committed more US aid to South Vietnam, even after the French left.

The 'domino theory'

The most significant reason for greater US involvement in Vietnam was fear of communism. Eisenhower feared that if Vietnam became communist, other countries in Southeast Asia would follow. This became known as the 'domino theory' (see Source B). Eisenhower set up the South East Asia Treaty Organisation (SEATO) in September 1954 with the USA, the UK, France, New Zealand, Australia, Pakistan, the Philippines and Thailand as members. They agreed to act together, by force if necessary, to stop communism spreading in Southeast Asia.

Source B

From a press conference given by President Eisenhower on 7 April 1954. He was asked why Indochina (Vietnam, Cambodia and Laos) was important.

Finally, you have broader considerations that might follow what you would call the "falling domino" principle. You have a row of dominoes set up, you knock over the first one, and what will happen to the last one is the certainty that it will go over very quickly....

Asia, after all, has already lost some 450 million of its peoples to the Communist dictatorship [when China became communist], and we simply can't afford greater losses.

But when we come to the possible sequence of events, the loss of Indochina, of Burma, of Thailand, of the Peninsula [British Malaya], and Indonesia following, ... now you are talking really about millions and millions and millions of people.

Source C

From a letter written by Eisenhower to Diem, on 23 October 1954. It was written in response to a request by Diem for military and economic aid.

The purpose of this offer is to assist the Government of Viet-Nam in developing and maintaining a strong... state, capable of resisting attempted subversion or aggression through military means. The Government of the United States expects that this aid will be met by performance on the part of the Government of Viet-Nam in undertaking needed reforms. It hopes that such aid, combined with your own continuing efforts, will contribute effectively toward an independent Viet-Nam... with a strong government.

Why was Diem's government weak?

Diem's government in South Vietnam did not have widespread support. There were doubts that the army would back the government if fighting broke out.

- There were still many communists in South Vietnam. They controlled some northern areas.
- Other religious, political and criminal groups had many supporters and their own armies.
- Diem was Catholic; most Vietnamese were Buddhist. Religious clashes were common and Buddhists assumed Diem favoured the Catholics, which he did.
- Diem mainly gave government jobs to his family members and Catholics, excluding other groups.
- Diem's government was Saigon-based. He had little respect for the peasants in the villages and did not make reforms to gain their support. Many villages were run by corrupt officials or greedy landlords who held most of the land.

Exam-style question, Section A

Give **two** things you can infer from Source C about the reasons for US involvement in Vietnam. Give the detail in the source that tells you this. **4 marks**

Exam tip

You infer something from a source by working out something the source does not actually tell you, using the detail in the source. Remember to make an inference about the enquiry in the exam question.

Keeping Diem in power

Eisenhower supported Diem by sending more advisers to train the South Vietnamese army (ARVN). He wanted the ARVN to win control of South Vietnam and for the US to fight a limited war*, without US troops. He did not want to trigger a war with China and the USSR, which might lead to the use of nuclear weapons.

In October 1955, Bao Dai spoke against Diem's policies. Diem's response was to hold a referendum* with people voting for him or Bao Dai as their leader. US officials helped run the elections, which were widely seen as fixed. Diem won. He said Vietnam was now the Republic of Vietnam and he was its president. He changed the government and (in June 1956) stopped villages electing their own officials. He put widely-resented government officials in charge. As Diem grew more unpopular in South Vietnam, so did the USA.

Key terms

Limited war*

A war where a country supports a side in a conflict by, for example, sending them supplies and training their troops, but not by sending any of their own troops to fight.

Referendum*

A countrywide vote on a single issue.

No elections

On 16 July 1956, Diem refused to hold elections. He said his government had not existed when the Geneva Accords were agreed, so did not have to obey them. The US supported Diem, fearing a communist government would be elected. Vietnam remained divided at the 17th parallel. Eisenhower sent more aid, despite warnings it would make South Vietnam dependent on the US.

Diem became less and less democratic. US advisers said he needed to use force to stay in power, after which he could make reforms and hold elections.

Source D

A photograph showing South Vietnamese men looking at a poster before the 1955 referendum. The poster stresses that Bao Dai was living an extravagant life in France, not working for the people in South Vietnam.

However, Diem continued to oppress many South Vietnamese, and he did not make reforms. He took US money, but not US advice. He assured Eisenhower that the South Vietnamese people supported him. He may or may not have believed this, but he hoped the USA would. He began a campaign against opponents, especially communists.

- He began to arrest political and religious opponents.
- His 'denounce a communist' campaign urged people to report communists to the government.
- In 1957, he sent the ARVN into the countryside to find and arrest communists. The ARVN arrested about 65,000 suspected communists, and killed about 2,000.

The situation worsens

The remaining communists fought back, both against the ARVN and the local officials Diem had forced on them. By March 1958, over 400 officials had been killed. From this point on, various revolutionary groups in South Vietnam fought against Diem's government. Diem, and most Western countries, called them all the 'Vietcong' (or VC) – short for 'Vietnamese Communists'.

The North Vietnamese supported the Vietcong in the hope of starting a revolution in South Vietnam. However, the executions (and oppression) by the South Vietnamese government increased, and there was no revolution. In May 1959, the North Vietnamese, with China's support, decided to act. They sent North Vietnamese troops and weapons into South Vietnam along the Ho Chi Minh Trail*. North Vietnamese troops trained the VC and fought alongside them. Diem's actions had led to a civil war.

Figure 3.3 Why Diem could not win.

> ### Key term
>
> **Ho Chi Minh Trail***
>
> A series of dirt paths and smaller trails, which ran mainly through Laos and Cambodia from North Vietnam into South Vietnam. North Vietnam used it to send troops and supplies to support the Vietcong in South Vietnam. It was later paved.

> ### Extend your knowledge
>
> **The Ho Chi Minh Trail**
>
> The main part of the Trail ran through Laos and Cambodia and it took over a month to get from one end of it to the other.
>
> After 1960, as the North Vietnamese poured troops and supplies into South Vietnam, the main path became wider. By 1974, some of it was paved and there were underground hospitals, weapon stores and fuel storage tanks.
>
> Why do you think as much of the trail as possible ran through Laos and Cambodia?

Figure 3.4 The Ho Chi Minh Trail.

Key terms

Guerrillas*

Fighters who avoid big battles and attack their enemy by blowing up roads and bridges, ambushing them and striking them with sudden 'hit and run' attacks.

Counter-insurgency*

Fighting guerrillas both by military attacks and by winning the support of the local population.

Pacification*

Winning over the 'hearts and minds' of the local population, so they do not support guerrillas.

A more organised opposition

In November 1960, some army leaders tried to overthrow Diem. They failed. Relations between Diem and the USA worsened. He blamed the USA for the plot. The USA urged Diem to be more democratic and to make himself more popular in the villages by making reforms. He ignored the advice. US support of Diem was increasingly unpopular, at home and abroad.

Then, in December, the Vietcong joined with other anti-Diem groups to form the National Liberation Front (NLF). It organised political opposition to Diem. Members went into the villages by night and urged the villagers to disobey the government officials and to support local Vietcong groups. They worked to win the villagers over to communism. Diem's city-based government looked down on the villagers and did little to gain their support. By the end of 1960, less than half of South Vietnam was under government control.

Greater involvement under Kennedy

Kennedy became president in 1961. He agreed with the domino theory and the idea of limited war. He sent more advisers to South Vietnam (about 16,000 more by November 1963). Kennedy said normal fighting tactics were failing. By early 1961, there were 12,000 Vietcong (VC) guerrillas* in the South; over half the country was under some level of communist control. He told advisers to use counter-insurgency* tactics to isolate the VC. He wanted US and South Vietnamese (ARVN) troops to hunt out the VC, not just to try to lure them into battle. He also wanted a policy of pacification*: for troops and the South Vietnamese government to win the support of the villagers.

- It was hard for the ARVN to win over the villagers. Many ARVN officers looked down on the villagers, while many villagers saw the ARVN as part of the corrupt government system.

- US Special Forces ('Green Berets') went to train villagers to protect their villages from the VC. However, they were in villages during the day and returned to their camps at night. The VC then visited the villages at night. The Green Berets worked to win the villagers' trust (including learning the language), but as foreign soldiers it was difficult.

January 1961
$40 million to train ARVN

October 1961
Kennedy orders a report on sending in US troops

December 1961
Kennedy authorises use of defoliant chemical sprays to kill crops and jungle plants

December 1961
US helicopters and pilots sent to transport ARVN

Figure 3.5 Increased involvement in Vietnam under Kennedy.

The Strategic Hamlet Program

US advisers supported Diem's setting up of strategic hamlets: large new villages (surrounded by barbed wire and guarded by the ARVN) with facilities such as schools and clinics. This was to stop the VC from recruiting villagers or getting supplies from them. People were to move to these villages from smaller ones nearby, making them feel safe, cared for and supportive of the government.

In January 1962, work began on the Strategic Hamlet Program. About 800 Green Berets helped set up the hamlets, reporting 5,000 built or being built by September 1962. However, building a strategic hamlet was not enough. Both the US advisers and Diem's government ignored the fact that villagers did not want to leave their homes, the graves of their ancestors and nearby family members. Diem's government also failed to provide the villagers with enough food, so many villagers went hungry and some even starved. This was unlikely to produce support for the government.

Source E

From an interview with Ngo Vinh Long in 2003. Long grew up in Vietnam. Here, he is talking about the Strategic Hamlet Program.

It created tremendous destruction to peasant life, especially in central Vietnam. People were sometimes moved great distances from their land and put in villages behind barbed-wire fences, moats and spikes...
It caused tremendous dislocation, even starvation. One day I entered a village by the name of Ka Rom where the highlanders had been re-grouped into a strategic hamlet. They [the villagers] said that two hundred people had starved to death in the past month. I knew they were telling the truth just by looking at them. Their hair was crinkled and brown, their skin was dark and flaky, and they smelled horrible.

Interpretation 1

From 'Ngo Dihn Diem and South Vietnam Reconsidered', an article by Philip E. Catton in *Triumph Revisited* (2010).

The Strategic Hamlet program [was] not only a Vietnamese initiative, but also an elaborate nation-building project – it was, in fact, the last and most ambitious of the regime's [Diem's government] plans for developing South Vietnam.

Interpretation 2

From 'The Failed Search for Victory', an article by Lawrence J. Bassett and Stephen E. Pelz in *Major Problems in the History of the Vietnam War* (1995).

Diem regained some favour with Washington by accepting another part of the Kennedy plan for Vietnam – strategic hamlets. Roger Hilsman [an official in Kennedy's government]… correctly concluded that the villages of South Vietnam willingly provided supplies and a great majority of recruits to the NFL [Vietcong]. He argued that the South Vietnamese government had to provide villagers with civic action programmes [schools, clinics and self-defence training] and physical security by creating fortified hamlets.

Exam-style question, Section B

Study Interpretations 1 and 2. They give different views about the reason for the Strategic Hamlets Program.

What is the main difference between these views?

Explain your answer, using detail from both interpretations. **4 marks**

Exam tip

When answering a question about how interpretations differ, be sure to quote details from both sources to support what you say, or you will lose marks.

Source F

A photograph showing Quang Duc, a Buddhist monk, who set light to himself in Saigon on 11 June 1963. He was protesting at Diem's persecution of Buddhists.

Diem's persecution of Buddhists increases

At the start of 1963, advisers were telling Kennedy that the Vietcong were being slowly defeated. However, on 2 January 1963, the ARVN lost the Battle of Ap Bac, despite outnumbering the Vietcong 5 to 1, having better weapons and having US air support. They also lost five US helicopters, three US advisers and 60 troops. Only three VC dead were found. While the US military tried to make Ap Bac sound like a victory, some of the US media reported it as a defeat. Worse followed. On 6 May, government troops fired on a Buddhist procession, leaving nine dead and 14 injured. In June, Buddhists were banned from flying flags for the Buddha's birthday.

On 11 June, having alerted the press the day before, Quang Duc, a Buddhist monk, set light to himself at a busy Saigon junction (see Source F). He burned to death. There was worldwide publicity. Just a month after

Kennedy had expressed shock at the photographs of police violence in Birmingham, Alabama, (see page 52) he was expressing shock at more horrifying images – this time caused by the government he supported in Vietnam.

The overthrow of Diem

Kennedy pressed Diem to make peace with the Buddhists. Instead, Diem increased the persecution. In August 1963, Diem's troops raided Buddhist temples. There were more killings. Kennedy reluctantly accepted that Diem would never run a democratic government and that his government was too unpopular to survive. The USA did not want to overthrow Diem publicly, but made it clear he no longer had US support. On 1 November, Diem was overthrown by ARVN generals. The USA had heard what the generals were planning and did not warn Diem. He was assassinated.

Kennedy's assassination

Kennedy said the US government had a responsibility to help the new South Vietnam government. He considered greater US military involvement, but stressed that his aims were:

- to influence the new government to act democratically
- to influence the new government to win over the people of South Vietnam
- to withdraw US advisers, and other forces as soon as possible.

On 22 November 1963, Kennedy was assassinated. Vice President Johnson became president. He had to work with the General Minh's new, unstable, government in South Vietnam. He hoped that only a limited amount of help would be needed before the USA could leave Vietnam. But, like Eisenhower and Kennedy, he wanted to be sure it was safe from communism first.

Activities

1. Make a flowchart showing how US involvement in Vietnam escalated up to 1963.
2. Draw a spider diagram to show the reasons for Diem's unpopularity.
3. Many Vietnamese said Diem was a 'US puppet'. In groups, make a list of points that support this argument and a list of points that do not. What is your conclusion?

Summary

- On 7 May 1954, French forces surrendered to the Vietminh at Dien Bien Phu.
- The Geneva Accords (21 July 1954) divided Vietnam temporarily along the 17th parallel and said elections should be held in July 1956.
- Diem took over in October 1955 and refused to hold elections in 1956. Vietnam remained divided.
- Diem hounded communists in South Vietnam. Fighting began.
- In 1959, North Vietnam began to send troops and equipment to South Vietnam.
- In 1960, the National Liberation Front was set up; resistance to Diem was more organised.
- On 2 January 1963, the communists won at Ap Bac.
- On 1 November 1963, Diem was assassinated.

Checkpoint

Strengthen

S1 Explain, or draw a diagram, to explain Eisenhower's domino theory.

S2 Explain one social, one political and one religious reason for Diem's unpopularity.

S3 List the key features of a 'strategic hamlet'. Write down what they were supposed to do.

Challenge

C1 Explain the steps by which the USA became increasingly involved in Vietnam between 1954 and 1963.

How confident do you feel about your answers to these questions? If you are not sure that you answered them well, try the activity on this page before having another go.

3.2 Escalation under Johnson

Learning outcomes
- Understand the increasing threat of the Vietcong.
- Understand how the Gulf of Tonkin incident led to greater US involvement in Vietnam.

Johnson had the same goals as Kennedy:

- setting up a government the South Vietnamese people wanted
- stopping communism; so keeping South Vietnam as a separate country
- stopping the war escalating and avoiding nuclear war.

However, his position was worse than Kennedy's in 1960. The Vietcong were stronger, the South Vietnamese government was weaker and the USA was more unpopular in South Vietnam.

The increasing threat of the Vietcong

Diem was gone, but the new government was even weaker. No clear leader emerged and various army generals struggled for power.

It was clear that South Vietnam would not survive without more US involvement. By this point, it only controlled 30% to 40% of South Vietnam.

- The ARVN was caught up in government struggles, rather than focusing on defeating the Vietcong. The ARVN had about 500,000 troops and control of the air. The VC had fewer than 100,000 (though numbers are hard to estimate), but were still putting the ARVN under pressure.
- North Vietnam sent increasing amounts of equipment and men along the Ho Chi Minh Trail. Between 1955 and 1963, China sent aid worth over $100 million. Much of it went south.
- The VC were getting stronger (see Figure 3.6). They attacked more often and they attacked more US targets (e.g. air force bases, such as Pleiku) as well as roads and bridges.

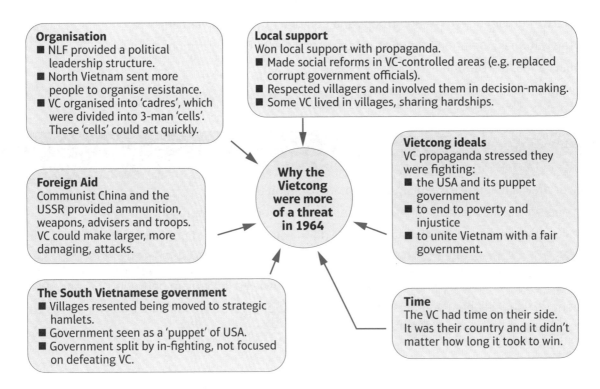

Figure 3.6 Why the Vietcong were an increasing threat in 1964.

Source A

From an interview given by Nguyen Tan Thanh, who joined the Vietcong in 1961, when he was 35. His village was visited by a VC propaganda group that was recruiting for the VC.

```
When I heard the cadres [communist
activists], I thought what they said was
correct. ... I knew that the rich oppressed
the poor. The poor had nothing to eat, and
they also had no freedom. We had to get rid
of the regime that allowed a few people to
use their money and authority to oppress
others. So I joined the Liberation Front
[NLF]. I followed the VC to fight for freedom
and prosperity for the country. I felt that
was right.
```

Source B

From an interview given by John Gilligan in 2003. He is talking about a visit to Vietnam when he was a member of the House of Representatives in 1965.

```
While we were in Saigon two American aircraft
got shot down trying to take out a bridge up
near Hanoi. The same day some guy on a bike
with six pounds of plastique [explosives]
took out a bridge down in the Mekong Delta.
We lost two planes and two pilots and failed
and the Viet Cong with a bicycle took out a
bridge. I began to think, jeez, this isn't
what we're used to. Of the dozen of us on
that trip, about nine of us came home opposed
to the war.
```

Exam-style question, Section B

Study Sources A and B. How useful are Sources A and B for an enquiry into the methods of the Vietcong? Explain your answer, using Sources A and B and your knowledge of the historical context.   **8 marks**

Exam tip

When considering how useful sources are, be sure to focus on the subject of the enquiry. Consider what aspects of the subject the sources discuss. Do not forget to consider the historical context.

The Gulf of Tonkin incident, 1964

Johnson continued to provide more advisers and more aid. By the end of 1964, there were over 20,000 advisers.

Johnson wanted Congress to authorise the use of US troops in Vietnam, but it was a presidential election year and he did not want to bring up issues that would divide Congress.

- Meanwhile, two US Navy ships, the *Maddox* and the *C. Turner Joy*, were ordered to make regular patrols in the Gulf of Tonkin (shown in Figure 3.2 on page 82) and along the North Vietnamese coast.
- At the same time, small US boats were secretly ferrying ARVN troops to carry out raids on North Vietnamese ships and territory.
- Eventually, angered by these ARVN attacks, the North Vietnamese struck in the Gulf of Tonkin.

On 2 August, the *Maddox* radar showed three North Vietnamese torpedo boats closing in. The captain called for air support. The North Vietnamese boats fired; the *Maddox* fired back and withdrew when US planes arrived.

On 4 August, during a bad storm, the *Maddox* and *C. Turner Joy* reported North Vietnamese torpedo boat attacks and claimed to have sunk two enemy boats. However, there was confusion as to what had really happened. Johnson was told of the incident, but was later told there may not have been an attack at all. Ignoring the confusion, Johnson ordered US planes to strike North Vietnamese targets in retaliation. Two US jets were shot down on this strike.

On 5 August, Johnson told Congress about the attack on the *Maddox* and *C. Turner Joy*. He asked Congress to give him the power to stop future attacks on US forces.

On 7 August, Congress passed the Gulf of Tonkin Resolution, with little opposition. It gave Johnson the power to take all necessary steps to stop attacks on US forces without consulting Congress, or officially declaring war. The powers given to Johnson included sending troops to Vietnam.

Key features of the incident

- There was certainly an attack by North Vietnamese boats on 2 August.

- At the start of the evening of 4 August, both the *Maddox* and the *C. Turner Joy* thought they were under attack and reported this.

- Johnson ordered airstrikes on North Vietnam, despite doubts over the attack.

- The Gulf of Tonkin Resolution was passed by Congress in the belief there had been two attacks.

- The Resolution allowed Johnson to do what he thought was needed, including the use of armed force, to defend South Vietnam and US forces there.

- The Resolution was not a declaration of war on North Vietnam, although it had the same effect.

Source C

Part of the Gulf of Tonkin Resolution passed on 7 August 1964. The first part refers to repeated attacks on US forces by the North Vietnamese.

... Congress approves and supports the determination of the President, as Commander in Chief, to take all necessary measures to repel any armed attack against the forces of the United States and to prevent further aggression.

... This resolution shall expire when the President shall determine that the peace and security of the area is reasonably assured... except that it may be terminated earlier by... Congress.

Figure 3.7 US involvement in 1964.

Source D

A photograph showing the front page of the *New York Times* for 5 August 1964. The Gulf of Tonkin Incident is the first headline – the second headline reports the discovery of the bodies of the Freedom Summer civil rights workers in Mississippi (see page 56).

Extend your knowledge

Were there North Vietnamese boats?

On the night of 4 August there was a bad storm, so the US captains had to rely on radar and sonar for their information. The radar of the *Maddox* was later found to have a fault, although that was not clear at the time. Both radar and sonar can be affected in storms where the sea is very rough, as it was that night. The North Vietnamese had definitely attacked on 2 August, so the captains of the *Maddox* and the *C. Turner Joy* were aware that there could be another attack at any time. Many people, on both ships, were convinced that they were under attack. The North Vietnamese denied that they attacked, and continued to do so after the war ended.

The North Vietnamese reaction

The Gulf of Tonkin Resolution gave Johnson the authority to escalate US military involvement in Vietnam to prevent further attacks on US forces, but he had not declared war. He did not want to declare war because this might lead to a larger conflict with the USSR and China. However, it looked like a declaration of war to the North Vietnamese. In response, they increased their involvement in South Vietnam.

- From November 1964 to February 1965, more and more people and supplies were sent south.

- The Vietcong were urged to target US bases.

- On 2 December 1964, fighting began at Binh Gia, just 40 miles south of Saigon. It lasted until 3 January 1965. Just as at Ap Bac, the VC won. Over 50 helicopters were destroyed or damaged and military equipment and prisoners were taken.

- On 7 February, the VC attacked the US airfield at Pleiku. They left nine dead, 128 wounded and 122 aircraft damaged or destroyed.

Activities ?

1 In groups, discuss the events of 4 August 1964 and what followed. Make notes on the following points:

   a what the crews of the *Maddox* and the *C. Turner Joy* thought was happening

   b what President Johnson was told

   c how President Johnson reacted and why

   d what Congress was told

   e how Congress reacted.

2 With a partner, consider the following question: 'Did President Johnson lie to Congress, and if so, why?' Write a couple of sentences explaining your conclusion.

3 Put yourself in President Johnson's shoes. Write a diary entry for the evening of 7 August, **after** Congress passed the Gulf of Tonkin Resolution, reflecting on your actions since 4 August.

Source E

A photograph showing a Chinese poster. It was printed in Beijing, China, in 1964, after the Gulf of Tonkin Resolution. It says: 'America's Aggression Towards the Democratic Republic of Vietnam is an Aggression Towards China'.

THINKING HISTORICALLY ▶ Interpretations (2b)

The importance of perspective

What we notice when we look at an historical source is shaped by our interests, questions and concepts. Historians are individuals too, and what they 'see' is shaped by what they are interested in and see as important. Historians also sometimes use different methods of investigating and make sense of sources in different ways.

Study Source E and the caption on page 93.

The photo shows a source that can be interpreted in many ways, depending on the questions asked and the interests and concepts that we bring to them.

1   Look closely at the image and the accompanying text. Discuss the following questions with a partner and write down your ideas.

   a   What might an art historian notice about the picture?

   b   What might a political historian notice about the picture?

   c   Explain how the two interpretations differ and why.

2   Sometimes historians look at history in great depth, but sometimes they are interested in getting more of an overview of what happened. Look at the image again.

   a   How would a historian interested in society in China in the 1960s study this poster? How much detail would they go into, and what might they compare it to?

   b   How would a historian interested in China's involvement in the Vietnam War study this poster? How much detail would they go into, and what might they compare it to?

   c   Explain how the scale that a historian is thinking about affects how they look at sources.

3   Answer the following question in a paragraph: How important are the interests, questions and concepts that historians bring to their study of the past in shaping their interpretations?

The situation in February 1965

By February 1965, US involvement in Vietnam was costing $2 million a day. After steady escalation, both the USA and North Vietnam were committed to a war neither really wanted.

- The USA had wanted South Vietnam to be a democratic nation that could defend itself.

- The North Vietnamese wanted the South Vietnamese to revolt and unite with North Vietnam.

Some of Johnson's advisers were wildly optimistic about how long fighting would last.

Spending
$700 million

Troops	Dead
184,300	1,928

Figure 3.8 US involvement in 1965.

Heavy bombing will make the North Vietnamese give in. — Military adviser

About 150,000 ground troops would win in a few weeks. — Political adviser

We need to go all out, bombs and troops, then they'll negotiate. — Political adviser

The war's pretty much won anyway. — Military adviser

Figure 3.9 Some arguments given to Johnson for escalation.

It was difficult for many Americans, politicians and the general public, to accept that a country as rich and powerful as the USA could not win against North Vietnam. However, all along there were people who argued that a government that was acceptable to most South Vietnamese had to be found and that the war was almost unwinnable. Eisenhower, Kennedy and Johnson all made speeches saying that the South Vietnamese needed to be won over, and that this had to be done by other Vietnamese. They admitted that this was vital to winning the war. But, the most important thing to the USA was to keep the South Vietnamese government in power, popular or not. So, step by step, they moved towards sending in troops to do that, because the ARVN could not.

Exam-style question, Section A

Explain why US involvement in Vietnam increased in the years 1963–65.

You may use the following in your answer:

* US advisers
* the Gulf of Tonkin Resolution

You **must** also use information of your own. **12 marks**

Exam tip

When answering this question, make sure you stick to the dates given in the question and include information of your own.

Activity

In pairs, write a memo for President Johnson, for a radio interview on Vietnam. Make sure he will be able to answer questions on:

a the situation in February 1965

b possible options for the future: the benefits and downsides.

Summary

* President Johnson did not want to send troops into Vietnam, but he was committed to keeping the South Vietnamese government in power.
* The South Vietnamese government was weaker after Diem's assassination.
* The Vietcong became more of a threat as North Vietnam sent more troops and supplies down the Ho Chi Minh Trail.
* The Gulf of Tonkin Incident led to the Gulf of Tonkin Resolution where Congress gave President Johnson the authority to commit troops to Vietnam, without declaring war.

Checkpoint

Strengthen

S1 Draw a flow diagram to show how US involvement in Vietnam escalated.

S2 List four reasons why the Vietcong were more of a threat in 1964 than in 1961.

S3 Write a short paragraph to explain why the North Vietnamese did not want to send troops into South Vietnam.

Challenge

C1 Give one military and one political reason to explain why Vietnam was important to the USA.

C2 Explain what was significant about the Gulf of Tonkin Incident.

How confident do you feel about your answers to these questions? If you are not sure that you answered them well, form a small group and plan your answers together. You could divide up the tasks so you each focus on investigating one thing before reporting back to your group.

The Americans, the North Vietnamese and the Vietcong had different views about Vietnam.

- The USA wanted to leave South Vietnam as soon as possible, while saving it from communism. Johnson wanted a limited war, involving sending as few troops as possible.
- The North Vietnamese and Vietcong wanted a united Vietnam. They were prepared to fight for as long as it took. Time was on their side.

Both sides had different levels of manpower and equipment, so fought in very different ways.

Vietcong guerrilla tactics

The Vietcong were less well armed than the South Vietnamese Army (ARVN), but they turned this into an advantage. They fought a guerrilla war, which put the ARVN at a disadvantage. The nature of guerrilla warfare meant that the VC were, for both ARVN and US troops, a shadowy enemy. Anyone could be a member of the VC – man, woman or child. The ARVN and US troops made little distinction between people who helped the VC by supplying food or information and those who were fully committed members of the VC. It was hard for US troops to tell their enemies from their allies. Figure 3.10 shows the theory of guerrilla warfare and how the Vietcong followed it. (The North Vietnamese troops that supported the VC in South Vietnam also used these tactics.)

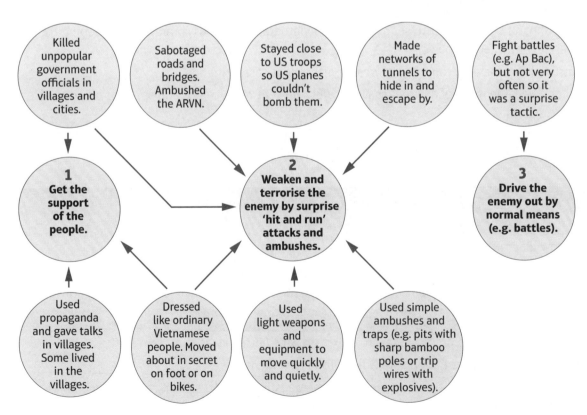

Figure 3.10 Vietcong guerrilla tactics. When people talk about 'guerrilla war' they usually mean a combination of parts 1 and 2 shown in the diagram.

Source A

From a letter written by Robert Ransom Jr. to his parents in April 1968. Ransom was wounded in an ambush on 3 May 1968 and died on 11 May. He was 23 years old.

I am now filled with both respect and hate for the VC and the Vietnamese. Respect because the enemy knows that he can't stand up to us in a fight due to our superior training, equipment and our vast arsenal of weapons. Yet he is able. Via his mines and booby traps, he can whittle our ranks down piecemeal until we cannot muster [raise] an effective fighting force. In the month that I have been with the company, we have lost 4 killed and about 30 wounded.

Source B

A part of a North Vietnamese propaganda poster from the Vietnam War. It had a caption saying: 'The Yankee [American] troops may well come, but they won't be able to move forward'.

Source C

From an interview with Duong Thanh Phong in 2003. He was a war photographer for the Vietcong.

Sometimes at sunset, near our jungle base, we'd move close to the edge of the rice fields to watch the people working. We could do that safely because the puppet troops [ARVN] didn't dare stay in the fields after dark. We often played with the buffalo boys [boys who minded the buffalo] and they leaked tidbits of information about the puppet soldiers — how many were in a nearby outpost, the number of weapons they had, or when they moved to another outpost. Those buffalo boys functioned as our messengers.

We also taught the children to rig booby traps and set land mines. They were responsible for letting the local people know where the explosives were hidden. In the evening, we'd unrig the traps for their safety.

Exam-style question, Section B

Study Sources A and B. How useful are Sources A and B for an enquiry into Vietcong tactics? Explain your answer, using Sources A and B and your knowledge of the historical context. **8 marks**

Exam tip

When considering how useful sources are, be sure to focus on the subject of the enquiry. Do not forget to consider the historical context and the purpose for which the source was created.

VC tunnels

The Vietminh had used tunnels to move around and shelter in during their war with the French. The Vietcong did the same thing, but their tunnels were much more complex. In the Cu Chi area, just 25 miles from Saigon, the VC built almost 100 miles of tunnels, on several levels. They connected many of the villages around Saigon, allowing the VC to move around easily. The Cu Chi tunnels contained hospitals, weapon and fuel storage areas and living space. Vietnamese people were smaller than most Americans; many tunnels were too small for most US troops. At first, US troops tried to destroy the tunnels by using 'tunnel rats' – troops who were small enough and went down to fight the VC or mine the tunnels to collapse them. Eventually, they just bulldozed over any tunnel entrances they found.

Extend your knowledge

Finding VC tunnels

The tunnels were hard to find, as they were often little more than a hole in the ground with a trapdoor covered by leaves. They were so hard to spot that one US division actually made a base camp on top of part of the Cu Chi complex and were attacked inside their security fencing, with no sign of a break-in.

What effect do you think such an attack might have on US troops?

Activity ?

In groups, discuss VC guerrilla tactics. Choose four words that you think best describe the effect that these tactics would have on US troops searching for VC in the jungle.

US tactics

From the start, most of the advisers in South Vietnam, especially those at the top, were part of the military. They thought in terms of battles, where capturing land, which side retreated and the number of dead were the most important outcomes. They did send troops into villages to try to build friendly relations, but most of their tactics in the war were destructive and only made

relations with the people of South Vietnam worse. They caused a lot of 'collateral damage' – unintended damage to villages, crops and civilians.

Operation Rolling Thunder

At the beginning of 1965, there were still no US ground troops in Vietnam, just the Green Berets and the air force crews. However, many 'advisers' wore uniform and some went with the ARVN on missions. Many Vietnamese felt that the US army was already in South Vietnam. However, the fact that there were no ground troops was significant in the USA. Johnson tried to force the North Vietnamese to negotiate peace without the USA sending in ground troops at all. In February 1965, he gave the go-ahead to Operation Rolling Thunder.

What was Rolling Thunder?

Rolling Thunder was a bombing campaign over North Vietnam. The military wanted immediate and heavy bombing all over North Vietnam, including Hanoi. However, at this point Johnson did not want to escalate the war rapidly, so he ignored the advice. Instead, Rolling Thunder began slowly, near the border with South Vietnam, and did not target Hanoi. Nor did it target Haiphong, the port where supplies from the USSR arrived in North Vietnam. It also had a 'no-bomb' area along the Chinese border. It targeted:

- the Ho Chi Minh Trail, to stop supplies being taken South
- what little industry there was in North Vietnam.

The planes dropped bombs but they also dropped:

- napalm: a slow-burning petrol mixture that sticks to the skin and can burn through to the bone
- pineapple bombs: canisters that explode and shoot pellets everywhere, like bullets.

Did Rolling Thunder work?

The first bombs were dropped on 2 March. Bombing stopped for Christmas 1965 and, in January 1966, the USA offered negotiating terms to the North Vietnamese. They were turned down. The bombing continued until the end of 1968. Johnson increased the number of targets that could be bombed, and the number of raids that flew. Figure 3.11 shows the effects of Rolling Thunder.

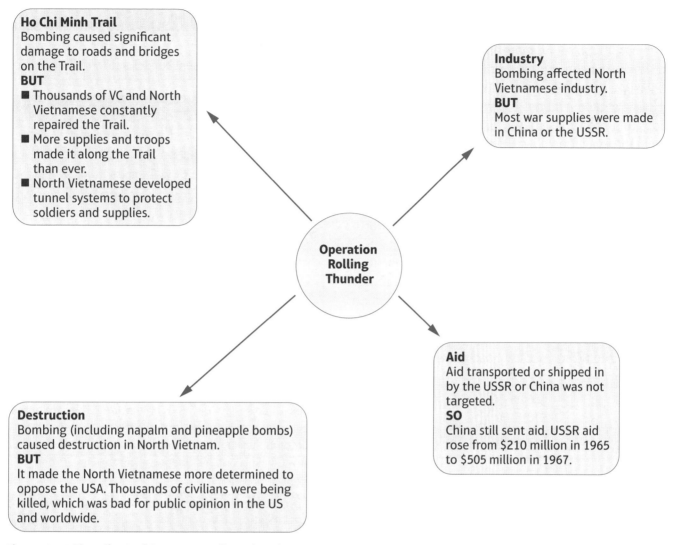

Ho Chi Minh Trail
Bombing caused significant damage to roads and bridges on the Trail.
BUT
- Thousands of VC and North Vietnamese constantly repaired the Trail.
- More supplies and troops made it along the Trail than ever.
- North Vietnamese developed tunnel systems to protect soldiers and supplies.

Industry
Bombing affected North Vietnamese industry.
BUT
Most war supplies were made in China or the USSR.

Operation Rolling Thunder

Destruction
Bombing (including napalm and pineapple bombs) caused destruction in North Vietnam.
BUT
It made the North Vietnamese more determined to oppose the USA. Thousands of civilians were being killed, which was bad for public opinion in the US and worldwide.

Aid
Aid transported or shipped in by the USSR or China was not targeted.
SO
China still sent aid. USSR aid rose from $210 million in 1965 to $505 million in 1967.

Figure 3.11 The effects of Operation Rolling Thunder.

Interpretation 1

From *The Vietnam War 1956–1975* (2014) by Andrew Wiest. He is discussing Operation Rolling Thunder.

The North's war supplies came, in the main, from its communist allies, who the American bombers could not reach. Although the US dropped over 643,000 tons of bombs on North Vietnam, the return on the investment was negligible [tiny]. Estimates by 1967 suggest that it cost the US $9.60 to inflict $1.00 worth of damage. In addition the fighter-bombers that carried out the bulk of the bombing stood only a 50 percent chance of surviving their one-year tour of duty.

Interpretation 2

From *The Vietnam War* (2007) by Mitchell K. Hall. He is discussing Operation Rolling Thunder.

During 1966 Rolling Thunder expanded to include North Vietnam's oil storage facilities, including those in the Hanoi and Haiphong areas, and destroyed 70 percent of the North's capacity. Sorties reached 108,000 in 1967, dropping 226,000 tons of explosives on North Vietnam. During that year the United States hit electrical, steel, and cement plants, factories, and targets near Hanoi, Haiphong and the Chinese border with an estimated damage of $340 million.

Sending in the troops

As the USA increased the amount of Rolling Thunder bombings, it also set up more aircraft bases in Vietnam. These were very obvious targets for the Vietnamese (as at Pleiku, see page 93). General Westmorland, who was in charge of US operations in Vietnam, asked for ground troops to protect these bases. This would be another step in the escalation of war. Between 8 and 10 March 1965, 3,500 marines landed at Danang. Up until this point, the only US fighting troops in Vietnam, apart from Green Berets and military advisers, were the air force.

As Operation Rolling Thunder continued to bomb North Vietnam, more and more ground forces were sent into South Vietnam (see table). Johnson used the draft* to get the greater number of troops needed. The draft was never popular and was a significant cause of opposition to the war in the USA.

US troop numbers in Vietnam	
1964	23,300
1965	184,300
1966	385,300
1967	485,600
1968	536,100

Key term

Draft*

Compulsory recruitment for service in military forces.

Activities ?

In pairs, use Figure 3.11, the information about Rolling Thunder and Interpretations 1 and 2 to do the activities.

1   What points would a US military adviser make in a press conference about Rolling Thunder in order to present it as a success?

2   What points would a North Vietnamese politician make in a press conference about Rolling Thunder into order to present it as a failure?

3   On balance, considering its aim, do you feel Rolling Thunder was a failure or a success?

Source D

A photograph showing Captain Vernon Gillespie of US Special Forces with his ARVN unit in 1964. They are burning down a supposed VC hideout. The photo was taken by a photographer for the US magazine *Life*. Other photographs show Gillespie and his troops talking to villagers and playing with children.

Search and destroy

The main US counter-insurgency tactic against the Vietcong was 'search and destroy' missions.

- Small units of US soldiers searched the jungle for VC camps and supplies. They then called up helicopters to bomb or spray chemicals on them. Although some ARVN troops took part, the aim was that the ARVN worked inside a protective shield of US troops.
- The missions were often on ground that the VC had already prepared with land mines and traps.
- Fighting occurred on these missions, but mainly 'hit and run' attacks by the VC, not full-scale battles.

Search and destroy missions show the problem with US military thinking. During the first wave of missions, the US killed about 1,100 VC; fewer than 100 US troops were killed. US troops found weapons and other supplies, and destroyed VC tunnels. They saw the missions as a victory. However, the VC were not counting bodies, or weapons. At the end of the missions, US and ARVN troops usually left the area, seeing their job as done. The VC then moved back in, and so they felt the US missions had failed. The VC were also quick to see that the missions failed on another level. US bombing and chemical spraying harmed ordinary villagers and their homes. This did not help the US win support from the villagers. Nor did the fact that the missions created about 4 million South Vietnamese refugees.

Operation Cedar Falls, 1967

Operation Cedar Falls is an example of how search and destroy tactics failed. Over 30,000 US and ARVN troops took part in this mission in the 'Iron Triangle', where the VC were strongest. Helicopters transported troops to the village of Ben Suc. Villagers were flown to refugee camps and the village was burned. Troops then moved across the Iron Triangle for three weeks, using the same tactics in all the villages. At the end of the operation there were 750 VC dead, and 450 US and ARVN dead. There were 3,500 refugees from the Ben Suc area alone. After US troops had cleared an area it became a 'free-fire zone' that could be bombed without warning at any time.

In many cases, villagers failed to understand this and returned to their homes in the free-fire zones. In other areas, villagers were given warnings of bombings, but the warnings were often in the form of dropped leaflets that not many villagers could read.

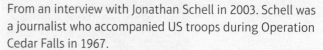

Source E

From an interview with Jonathan Schell in 2003. Schell was a journalist who accompanied US troops during Operation Cedar Falls in 1967.

```
You could say the operation came off
beautifully. It worked exactly as planned.
The helicopters flew in, moved the people out,
destroyed the village. Mission accomplished.
But to what end? Most of the reporting about
Operation Cedar Falls told you how many Viet
Cong were captured or killed, and those may
have been true facts. But they left out what
I believed was fundamental — that we were
destroying villages and throwing people off
their land. The unmistakable fact was that
the general population despised the United
States, and if they hadn't despised it before
we arrived, they soon did after we destroyed
the villages.
```

Source F

From *When Heaven and Earth Changed Places* (1989) by Le Ly Hayslip, who lived in a village in South Vietnam during the war. She is describing how the Vietcong used her village.

```
When the Viet Cong could not be found (they
spent most of their time, after all, hiding
in the caverns underground with entrances
hidden by cooking stoves, bushes, false
floors, or even underwater by flowing rivers
themselves), the Republican [ARVN] soldiers
took out their frustration on us: arresting
nearby farmers and beating or shooting them
on the spot, or carting anyone who looked
suspicious off to jail. As these actions
drove even more villagers to the Viet Cong
cause, more and more of our houses were
modified for Viet Cong use [given hiding
places].
```

Source G

A photograph showing troops taking villagers to helicopters to be flown to refugee camps during Operation Cedar Falls in 1967.

THINKING HISTORICALLY — Interpretations (4a)

The weight of evidence

Historians' interpretations are not simply their opinions. Interpretations are theories. In order for theories to be strong, they need to be backed up with convincing evidence. When you evaluate an interpretation, you should consider how strong the evidence is to support the conclusions it reaches.

Work in pairs. Read Source F. What does it tell you about the relationship between the villagers and the Vietcong? Read the three conclusions below, then answer the questions.

Conclusion 1

Villagers knew where the VC hid, but didn't tell the ARVN soldiers, so that shows support for the VC.

Conclusion 2

Not everyone in this village supported the VC at first, even if they knew other villagers did. Otherwise, the actions of the ARVN could not have driven more people to help the VC.

Conclusion 3

This village sounds like many villages. Some people gave more active help to the VC than others because, while everyone knew the VC were hiding there, at first only some homes were modified to hide them. But everyone knew about the underground caverns and hidden entrances and exits. ARVN actions affected the way people thought, because after the beatings and arrests, more people were actively involved in hiding the VC. So, the ARVN actions increased support for the VC.

1 Write out each conclusion and then use highlighter pens to colour code them. Use one colour for 'evidence', another colour for 'conclusions' and a third for language that shows 'reasoning' (e.g. "therefore", "so").

2 How do the conclusions differ in terms of the way that the evidence is used?

3 Put the conclusions in ranking order from the best to the worst. Explain your choice.

4 Consider what you know about support for the VC. For each conclusion, add any extra evidence you can think of that supports that conclusion.

5 Rank the conclusions again. Does the evidence you've added change which you think is the best?

6 Using evidence from the source and your own knowledge, write your own conclusion about the level of support for the VC in the villages. Remember to back up all your points by reasoning about the evidence.

Chemical warfare

Kennedy was the first president to agree the use of chemical weapons in the war. A variety of herbicides (each named after the colour of their container) were used to kill both the jungle plants and the crops in the farmland around the villages. This was to make the VC bases easier to find and also to deliberately kill crops in the sprayed areas, so that the villagers could not feed the VC. This defoliation programme was called Operation Ranch Hand. The first spraying was carried out on 10 August 1961.

Operation Ranch Hand

Between 1964 and 1970, over 24% of South Vietnam was sprayed with some kind of herbicide. Millions of Vietnamese, and also many US troops, were affected by Operation Ranch Hand.

- One plane could spray 300 acres in just four minutes.
- The herbicides were made up to 50% stronger than those used in the USA.
- Agent Blue, a fast acting herbicide, was used to kill crops.
- Agent Orange, a stronger herbicide, was used on the jungle forests.
- Over 3,000 villages were sprayed, in many cases without getting the villagers out first.

By 1970, there was clear proof that the herbicides used in Vietnam were a huge danger to health. During the war, the herbicides were made by a quicker process than normal, to make the huge amounts needed. This new process produced a poison that did not dissolve in water, so rain carried it into streams and rivers and affected the people who drank the water. The poison stayed in the soil, too, and affected crops for decades after replanting.

There was public outrage in the USA when the media made it clear that the chemicals the US was spraying were not only killing crops (so causing food shortages and starvation) but also causing many health problems, birth defects and deaths. The outrage increased when it became clear that US and ARVN troops were also affected. In October 1971, the Defense Department stopped the spraying. However, by then, a huge amount of damage had been done.

Extend your knowledge

The effects of the herbicides

The Vietnamese Red Cross estimates that up to three million Vietnamese suffered health problems from exposure to the herbicides. At least 150,000 children were born with health defects. The effects included a wide variety of cancers, skin diseases, heart diseases, lung diseases, and crippling bone diseases and defects.

Activities ?

1 In groups, think of three reasons why President Kennedy allowed the use of herbicides.

2 Write a paragraph explaining the problems caused by Operation Ranch Hand.

3 Explain one possible political reason why there was a time gap between knowing about the effects on people of the chemical herbicides and stopping the spraying.

Battles

There were few major battles in the Vietnam War. The Vietcong and the North Vietnamese Army avoided large battles, especially early in the war, so battles tended to be ones they chose to fight. The timeline shows the major battles. The most deadly (and the most important politically) was the Tet Offensive of 1968.

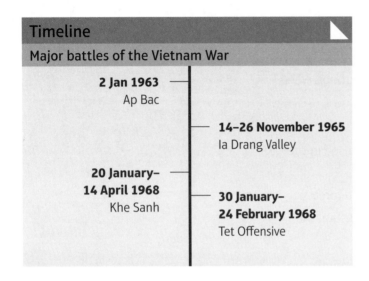

Timeline

Major battles of the Vietnam War

2 Jan 1963
Ap Bac

14–26 November 1965
Ia Drang Valley

**20 January–
14 April 1968**
Khe Sanh

**30 January–
24 February 1968**
Tet Offensive

The Tet Offensive, 1968

The North Vietnamese, working with the Vietcong, planned the Tet Offensive very carefully. It was a series of attacks on 26 cities and US bases in South Vietnam. The attacks began on Tet Lunar New Year, one of Vietnam's most important holidays. In 1968, this event was on 30 January. There was usually a ceasefire during Tet, so many ARVN were off duty for the holiday.

In the run up to the Tet Offensive, the North Vietnamese and VC did a number of things to try to catch the US and ARVN off guard.

- In late 1967, the North Vietnamese and VC attacked areas in South Vietnam just south of the demilitarised zone (DMZ) to lure US and ARVN troops away from cities and military bases.
- The North Vietnamese suggested it might be willing to negotiate for peace. This, along with recent North Vietnamese and VC losses, made the USA think they were ready to give in.

- On 20 January, North Vietnamese troops surrounded and attacked the US base at Khe Sanh near the DMZ. General Westmorland sent in 6,000 troops and bombers to defend it.

The key features and significance of Tet

When the Tet attacks were launched on 30 January, they began successfully. In Saigon, North Vietnamese troops and VC got into the US embassy, the Presidential Palace, ARVN headquarters, the radio station and the airport. The sight of VC in the US embassy was a huge shock for the American public, who had been told the US was winning the war. It was also a humiliation for the US government, even though the VC were soon captured. The old city of Hue was also captured – it took US and ARVN troops three weeks of fighting in the streets to win it back.

The nature of the Tet attacks and their scale was shocking to the US and ARVN.

- Unusually for the fighting in Vietnam, cities were attacked. South Vietnam's cities were regarded as the safest part of the country for the US and ARVN, but now they seemed vulnerable.
- The attacks were on a huge scale: 84,000 communist troops took part. This was a big change after years of 'hit and run' attacks.

US and ARVN troops managed to recapture most cities and bases quickly. Hue and Khe Sanh were the exceptions, but they were eventually recaptured. The North Vietnamese and VC expected the attacks to set off a South Vietnamese revolution, but this did not happen. They also suffered very heavy losses – the VC were almost wiped out. As a result, it could be argued that the communists had failed, but instead they had gained a huge propaganda victory. Despite the eventual US victory on the ground, the American public saw Tet as a humiliating defeat.

Figure 3.12 on page 105 shows the significance of the Tet Offensive to the various groups involved.

Interpretation 3

From *The Vietnam War 1956–1975* (2014) by Andrew Wiest.

The Tet Offensive... had been a total failure for the Communists. Of the 84,000 troops committed to Tet, nearly 58,000 had been killed, almost wiping out the Viet Cong as an effective fighting force... From this point, due to the demise of the Viet Cong the war... was controlled more directly from Hanoi. Also, the Communists had expected that the ARVN would crumble, but it had fought hard and well, indicating that South Vietnam... was something more than a lackey [puppet] state of the US.

Interpretation 4

From *No Sure Victory* (2011) by Gregory A. Daddis. He is discussing the reaction of the US public to the Tet Offensive, as shown by an opinion poll held by Gallup.

A March 10 Gallup poll found only 33 percent of Americans believed the United States was making progress in the war. For an increasingly isolated president, the collapse of congressional and public support forced painful decisions on the war's future conduct. Johnson approved only 10,500 additional troops for Westmorland and by late March conceded [agreed] to a suspension of air attacks over North Vietnam. When Johnson spoke to the American public on March 31 about his decision to deescalate the war in a bid for peace, he... [said] he would not seek or accept another term as president.

Spending

$26,266 million

Troops	Dead
536,100	16,899

Figure 3.13 US involvement in 1968.

USA

US politicians
- Growing anti-war feeling. Congress less willing to fund the war.
- Main reason for Johnson not running for president in 1968.

US Army
- Some feel they can win with more troops
- Others feel the ARVN did well, so US can leave.

US Public
- Feel cheated by US government saying war could end soon.
- Shocked by images of VC in US embassy compound.
- Huge rise in opposition to the war.

North Vietnam
- Heavy losses.
- VC allies almost wiped out.
- South Vietnamese did not revolt, as hoped.
  BUT
- Can rebuild forces.
- Can use Tet in their propaganda.
- Reaction in the USA against the war is a victory for them.

South Vietnam

Government
- Worried the US might leave too soon.
- Had some support from South Vietnamese people (no revolt).

People
- Unhappy with their government's failure to protect them.
- Attacks show that a communist takeover would be destructive.

Figure 3.12 The significance of the Tet Offensive to the USA, North Vietnam and South Vietnam.

Activity ?

In groups, prepare to debate the statement 'the Tet Offensive was a military defeat for the USA'. Remember, whichever side of the debate you are on, you need to consider what the other side will argue and how you can argue back.

Exam-style question, Section B

Suggest **one** reason why Interpretations 3 and 4 give different views about the success of the Tet Offensive from an American point of view. **4 marks**

Exam tip

When considering why interpretations differ, think about whether they are focusing on exactly the same aspect of the situation. Also, consider the sources they may have used to reach their judgement.

Summary

- The VC used guerrilla tactics and they blended in with the normal population.
- The VC had a lot of support and the tactics of the US and ARVN troops resulted in even more support for the VC.
- In February 1965, Johnson initiated Operation Rolling Thunder. The first ground troops arrived in Vietnam on 8 March 1965.
- US and ARVN troops ran ineffective search and destroy missions to root out the VC.
- Between 1964 and 1970, the USA sprayed about 24% of South Vietnam with harmful herbicides.
- The Tet Offensive of 1968 was a push by the communists for a revolution that would overthrow the South Vietnamese government. It failed and tens of thousands of communist fighters died.
- However, the US military had to accept that the end of the war was not close and that the communists had made significant progress before they were driven back.
- The Tet Offensive led to greater opposition to the war in the USA, from politicians and the general public. It was the main reason Johnson did not stand for re-election as president.

Checkpoint

Strengthen

S1 Choose what you think is the most important reason for the USA deciding to expand their military involvement and send troops into Vietnam. Explain your choice in a sentence.

S2 List the effects that search and destroy missions had on villagers in those areas.

S3 Think of four ways in which US tactics were likely to alienate the South Vietnamese.

S4 List three reasons why the Tet Offensive came as a shock to the US public.

Challenge

C1 Give one military, one cultural, and one political reason to explain why US and ARVN troops became increasingly unpopular from 1965.

C2 Why do you think the VC were able to survive in South Vietnam so successfully?

How confident do you feel about your answers to these questions? If you are not sure that you answered them well, reread the chapter, making notes as you go, then try them again.

Vietnam played a big part in the election of the next president, President Nixon. He promised to get the USA out of the war. Like earlier presidents, he did not want to leave the war if South Vietnam then became communist. However, he saw the growing opposition to US troops fighting in Vietnam. Nixon knew that people were angry that Johnson lied about the war. He promised to tell the truth and explain his policies to the public.

Nixon worked on several different approaches to the Vietnam War.

- **Official peace talks:** Five days after he became president, Nixon sent delegates to Paris to negotiate for peace with representatives from North and South Vietnam and the Vietcong. However, it became clear, as delegates argued over seating arrangements, that the talks would be long and difficult.

- **Secret peace talks:** In August 1969, Henry Kissinger of the USA began secret talks with Le Duc Tho of North Vietnam. Nixon did not tell the South Vietnamese or the American public about these talks.

- **Troop withdrawals:** In June 1969, Nixon lowered the maximum number of troops in Vietnam by 25,000. The USA began to withdraw troops on 14 July 1969.

- **ARVN training:** The military in Vietnam, now led by General Abrams, were told to focus on training ARVN (South Vietnamese) officers and troops.

- **Secret bombing of Cambodia:** On 15 March 1969, Nixon ordered the secret bombing of the parts of the Ho Chi Minh Trail that ran through Cambodia. Military orders and reports lied about bombing raids, because Nixon knew this expanding of the war would be very unpopular.

The Nixon Doctrine

On 25 July 1969, Nixon gave a speech outlining what came to be known as the Nixon Doctrine. It laid down what the role of the USA should be in Southeast Asian politics in the future. He said:

- the USA would honour any treaty commitments it had made
- the USA would help any ally against a nuclear threat
- the USA would provide aid and training against non-nuclear threats, but not troops; the country under threat had to provide its own ground troops.

Source A

A photograph showing the first troops leaving Vietnam under Nixon's withdrawal programme. It was taken on 14 July 1969.

Vietnamisation

'Vietnamisation' was the word used for the application of the Nixon Doctrine to Vietnam. The USA was to withdraw troops, but without looking like they had been defeated and without South Vietnam becoming communist. Vietnamisation shifted the responsibility for fighting, and so the casualties, to the ARVN. It was similar to US policy before Johnson sent in troops. Johnson had always wanted to return to a situation where the USA provided money and advice, but not troops.

Key features of Vietnamisation

- US troops were to withdraw.
- The ARVN was to provide its own officers.
- The US was still to provide training and equipment.
- The US withdrawal would be done 'with honour' – not leaving South Vietnam at the mercy of North Vietnam and the VC.
- South Vietnam would remain a separate country and not become communist.

Partial success

Vietnamisation succeeded in its most basic aim – there were fewer US troops in Vietnam and fewer US deaths (see the table on the left). However, many people did not see this as a success. Some felt US troops were being withdrawn too soon. Some US military advisers wanted to send in more troops after the Tet Offensive – they predicted a real chance of beating the North Vietnamese and the VC. On the other hand, many opponents of the war saw the US withdrawal as too slow.

Reactions to Vietnamisation

Most US citizens welcomed the fact that US troops would start to be withdrawn, while US generals and the South Vietnamese worried that the ARVN were not ready to fight alone. The communists saw Vietnamisation as a chance to gain the upper hand in the war.

ARVN and US Troop numbers and deaths		
	1968	1970
ARVN troops	820,000	970,000
US troops	536,000	335,000
ARVN deaths	28,000	24,000
US deaths	16,000	6,000

Spending
$18,536 million

Troops	Dead
334,600	6,173

Figure 3.14 US involvement in 1970.

Figure 3.15 How various groups reacted to Vietnamisation.

Source B

From a speech made by President Nixon on 3 November 1969. In this speech, he urged support for his policies and said that 'the silent majority' of Americans supported him.

In July, on my visit to Vietnam, I changed General Abrams' orders so that they were consistent with the objectives of our new [Vietnamisation] policies. Under the new orders, the primary mission of our troops is to enable the South Vietnamese forces to assume the full responsibility for the security of South Vietnam.

Our air operations have been reduced by over 20 percent.

... By December 15, over 60,000 men will have been withdrawn from South Vietnam including 20 percent of all of our combat forces.

The South Vietnamese have continued to gain in strength. As a result they have been able to take over combat responsibilities from our American troops.

Interpretation 1

From *Military Aspects of the Vietnam Conflict* (2000) by Walter L. Hixson.

During the war, many American officials viewed Vietnamization positively. On April 17, 1971, Nixon declared, "Vietnamization has succeeded." The military shared this positive position. In a 1974 survey of all generals in the United States Army who had served in Vietnam, 58 percent agreed that the Vietnamization program was soundly conceived [well thought out], and 36 percent conditionally [partially] agreed. Only 6 percent disagreed. In the same study, 73 percent of the generals stated that Vietnamization was so effective that it should have been implemented earlier.

Exam-style question, Section B

How far do you agree with Interpretation 1 about the success of Vietnamisation?

Explain your answer, using Interpretations 1 and 2 and your knowledge of the historical context.

16 marks

Interpretation 2

From *No Sure Victory* (2007) by Gregory A. Daddis.

Some MAVC [US advisers in Vietnam] and White House officials viewed Vietnamisation's progress with deep uncertainty. Despite a flurry of optimistic reports coming from Saigon at the end of 1969, the South Vietnamese armed forces had yet to be tested in a major battle without U.S. assistance. ... [As time passed] critical reports continued to question ARVN motivation and ability to stand against enemy attacks.

Source C

A cartoon published in 1972 with the caption: 'Now, as I was saying four years ago'. It shows Nixon campaigning for re-election. In 1968, Nixon had claimed he had a plan to end the war. This plan became Vietnamisation.

A 1972 Herblock Cartoon, © The Herb Block Foundation

Exam tip

You must make sure you refer to both interpretations in your answer or you will lose marks.

Activities ?

1 In pairs, draw a concept map of the key features of Vietnamisation.

2 Write a US newspaper headline to sum up these features.

3 Write a short paragraph to explain which feature you think was the most successful, based on the evidence you have so far.

Nixon expands the war

Cambodia, 1970

Since 1969, the USA had been secretly bombing the Ho Chi Minh Trail in Cambodia. Its ruler, Prince Sihanouk, was neutral in the Vietnam War. He let the Trail operate, but also let US and ARVN troops attack it.

In March 1970, pro-American General Lon Nol took over in Cambodia and told the North Vietnamese to leave. The North Vietnamese joined forces with Cambodian communist guerrillas (the Khmer Rouge) and supported Sihanouk by attacking the Nol government. US generals urged Nixon to invade Cambodia to support Nol and save Cambodia from communism. He agreed. About 50,000 ARVN and 30,000 US troops invaded. However, Nixon knew invading Cambodia would create public outrage in the USA – that was why he had kept the bombing secret. He said US troops could only go 19 miles across the border and had to be out by 30 June. He also went on television to explain why troops were going into Cambodia.

Source D

From Nixon's speech to the American people on 30 April 1970 about the invasion of Cambodia.

A majority of the American people, a majority of you listening to me, are for the withdrawal of our forces from Vietnam. The action I have taken tonight is indispensable for the continuing success of that withdrawal program.

A majority of the American people want to end this war rather than to have it drag on interminably. The action I have taken tonight will serve that purpose.

A majority of the American people want to keep the casualties of our brave men in Vietnam at an absolute minimum. The action I take tonight is essential if we are to accomplish that goal.

Source E

A photograph showing Nixon's televised announcement of the invasion of Cambodia in 1970.

The results of the invasion

- Significant damage was done to the Ho Chi Minh Trail. Hundreds of acres of jungle were destroyed. Weapons and supplies were captured from the hiding places built along the Trail.

- About 11,000 communists were killed and Nol's government was kept in power.

- Communist bases and other supply networks were destroyed.

However:

- The communists pulled back to safe places deep inside Cambodia. Although the ARVN were not limited to 19 miles inside the country, they still could not invade too far, or they would be cut off from US support.

- Damage to the Ho Chi Minh Trail did not stop the North Vietnamese getting into South Vietnam. They simply used the sections of the trail that were in the neighbouring country of Laos.

- There was huge public outcry in the USA. There were many protests, especially on university campuses.
- Congress was furious and cancelled the Gulf of Tonkin Resolution (see page 91). They also called for less funding for war and faster troop withdrawals from Vietnam.

Laos, 1971

Like South Vietnam, there were several groups struggling for power in Laos, including a number of communist groups. North Vietnam and the USSR supported the communists, while the USA 'advised' their opponents. As North Vietnam used the Laotian Ho Chi Minh Trail more, the South Vietnamese government pushed for an attack on Laos. After much argument, the USA agreed to provide air support for an ARVN invasion of about 21,000 troops.

The North Vietnamese heard of the planned invasion. They could not lose bases and the Trail in Laos, so decided to fight a battle for the first time since the Tet Offensive. They gathered about 36,000 troops and tanks. The ARVN took the city of Tchepone, with US air support, but then communist troops attacked. The fighting was bloody and the ARVN fled, leaving weapons and equipment behind. Despite US air cover, they had high casualties. The invasion raised serious doubts about Vietnamisation. The Trail and North Vietnamese bases remained secure, but there was still a struggle for political power in Laos.

The Easter Offensive 1972

Operations in both Cambodia and Laos had ended with no decisive victory. The USA continued to withdraw troops, despite the ARVN's failure in Laos. The peace negotiations, secret and public, dragged on, but showed little signs of reaching an agreement. The North Vietnamese, encouraged by Laos, planned a huge attack on South Vietnam directly attacking ARVN troops. On 30 March, nearly 120,000 North Vietnamese troops crossed the border into South Vietnam and attacked in three different places. VC and other guerrilla groups joined in. Shortly before the attack, the USA had said an invasion was not a serious possibility. The attack was a surprise and was very successful at first, but the ARVN, with US air support, eventually pushed the North Vietnamese back.

Timeline

Cambodia and Laos

15 March 1969 Nixon authorises secret bombing of Cambodia

29 April 1970 First ARVN and US troops into Cambodia

30 April 1970 Nixon's televised broadcast on Cambodia

30 June 1970 US troops leave Cambodia

8 February 1971 First ARVN troops invade Laos

6 March 1971 ARVN troops take Tchepone

10 March 1971 ARVN flee back to South Vietnam, huge number of lives and weapons lost

Bombing North Vietnam, 1972

In response to the Easter Offensive, the USA launched Operation Linebacker on 6 April 1972. This involved heavy bombing of North Vietnam. Unlike Rolling Thunder, Linebacker did not set any restrictions on targets. Both Hanoi and Haiphong were bombed. Nixon also ordered mines to be dropped in Haiphong harbour and blockades to keep ships from China and the USSR from reaching North Vietnam. Linebacker:

- almost wiped out the North Vietnamese war industry
- severely disrupted supplies from the USSR and China
- destroyed radio stations and other communication networks
- led to China and the USSR urging the North Vietnamese to reach a peace settlement.

Activity **?**

Debate the pros and cons of bombing North Vietnam after the Easter Offensive. Consider the effect of Operation Linebacker in your debate.

Figure 3.16 US involvement in 1972.

Why did Vietnamisation fail?

In the end, Vietnamisation failed. The North Vietnamese eventually took Saigon and Vietnam was united under a communist government. Why did Vietnamisation fail?

US troops

Knowing they would soon be going home, US troops no longer saw themselves as fighting to win. They had criticised ARVN troops for avoiding battles with the VC – now they did the same thing themselves. Some officers who tried to force troops to go into action were 'fragged' – killed by their own men. Cases of fragging rose from 96 in 1969 to 209 in 1970. Cases of drug use rose, too. Marijuana use was high, but in 1971, heroin use grew out of control. The army said about 35,000 soldiers were heroin addicts.

> ### Extend your knowledge
>
> **Avoiding battle**
>
> In June 1971, retired Colonel Robert D. Heinl wrote an article for *Armed Forces Journal* about the problems in the US military in Vietnam. He said drug-taking was shockingly common, as was avoiding combat and fragging. He suggested that this was partly because many drafted soldiers were young, undereducated and unwilling soldiers. This article came just a few months after Nixon told a group of newly-graduated officers they would have to realise that the soldiers under their command were not necessarily going to be disciplined, patriotic and ready to fight.
>
> What effect do you think this type of reaction would have on the soldiers left in Vietnam?

The ARVN

The ARVN became more effective and began to provide its own officers. However, it had problems.

- It did not have enough soldiers, despite conscription*. In 1971, over half of South Vietnamese men aged 15 to 49 were in the ARVN.
- Desertion* was common. In 1969, 123,000 men deserted, and this rose to 150,500 men in 1971. About 24,000 of the deserters in 1971 left to help on their local farmland and came back after the rice harvest. The rest did not.
- Many officers were reluctant to lead their troops into battle. Some officers did not want to admit their troops were struggling in combat, so they did not call for more military support until it was too late.
- There was a lot of corruption in the ARVN. For example, appointments of high-ranking officers were appointed for political reasons, not skill.
- Corruption made it hard to know troop numbers. Some officers falsified the number of men under their command (as it affected their pay). Others took bribes to record soldiers as present when they were not.
- Significant amounts of military supplies, such as petrol, were stolen and sold off.

> ### Key terms
>
> **Conscription***
>
> Compulsory military service.
>
> **Desertion***
>
> Leaving the army without permission.

Training and equipment

- The US supplied training and equipment. However, over time, Congress restricted funding.

- Because of the need for South Vietnamese officers, training was often hurried. The aim was to have South Vietnamese training the troops. However, the newly-trained officers were needed in the war, not in training. In 1971, about 75% of officers had less than a year's experience.

- US equipment had manuals in English. Many ARVN could not read English. English lessons were set up, but the troop shortages meant few had time for them.

Economic and political problems in South Vietnam

The USA withdrew troops despite knowing that the ARVN could not protect South Vietnam. The departure of US personnel also set off an economic crisis and 300,000 South Vietnamese lost their jobs. Many billions of dollars of US aid also stopped.

The government in Saigon fell because it was weak, politically and militarily. Politically, its members competed for power rather than running the country. It was also corrupt and lacked support among the South Vietnamese. Many South Vietnamese hated the government because they saw it as a puppet government for the US. However, even those South Vietnamese who did not hate the USA found little worth supporting in the government. Militarily, the ARVN could not hold out against the North Vietnamese, despite efforts to increase its size and efficiency.

Source F

From a 2003 interview with Judith Coburn, a reporter in Vietnam. Here, she is talking about the ARVN.

The early seventies was also the period of "Vietnamisation" when American troops were being withdrawn and the South Vietnamese Army was supposedly doing a larger and larger share of the fighting. You hear some Americans say that all the South Vietnamese troops were cowards and all the officers were corrupt. I don't subscribe to that. There were some very competent South Vietnamese officers and some serious fighting units. But for the most part it is true that the Vietnamese Army was a paper tiger. They were not loyal to the government — which they knew was corrupt and installed by the U.S. — and most ARVN grunts [ordinary soldiers] were there simply because they got drafted and would go to prison if they didn't fight.

Source G

A photograph showing US marines keeping South Vietnamese out of the US embassy, in the last few days before the fall of Saigon in April 1975.

Figure 3.17 US involvement in 1975.

Leaving Vietnam

From June 1972, North Vietnam and the USA were under increasing pressure to make peace. The American public and North Vietnam's communist allies were all pushing for this. Only South Vietnam, feeling increasing left out of the negotiations and abandoned by the USA, refused to sign the peace agreement of October 1972 (see Chapter 4). Nixon brought in huge amounts of military equipment and supplies, and promised continued support for South Vietnam. On 27 January 1973, the Paris Agreement was signed by the USA, North Vietnam, South Vietnam and the Provisional Revolutionary Government (created by communists in South Vietnam). It set up a ceasefire and a timetable for peaceful reunification of Vietnam. Very few people believed that it would do anything other than provide a ceasefire while the Americans withdrew.

The South Vietnamese government refused to negotiate with the communists in the months that followed the Paris Peace Agreement. Eventually, in March 1975, the North Vietnamese Army swept through South Vietnam. Congress refused to provide more aid to the South. The last Americans in Saigon left in a hasty scramble, and their final departure was anything but 'honourable'. With the fall of Saigon, Vietnam became a united, communist, country.

Summary

- Nixon was elected as president largely because of his promise to get US troops out of Vietnam.
- His 'Nixon Doctrine' was to help countries in Southeast Asia fight communism, but not to commit troops.
- He started withdrawing troops in 1969, shifting responsibility for fighting to the ARVN, in a process called Vietnamisation.
- Nixon also negotiated for peace and conducted secret bombing raids hoping to end the war.
- Events in Cambodia and Laos led to Nixon extending the war into those countries.
- The Easter Offensive led to Nixon launching Operation Linebacker, the unrestricted bombing of North Vietnam.

Checkpoint

Strengthen

S1 Sum up in a paragraph why Vietnamisation failed.

S2 In a sentence, explain why the bombing of Cambodia produced such an extreme reaction in the USA.

Challenge

C1 Explain the significance of the Nixon Doctrine on US policy towards Vietnam.

C2 Explain why Nixon ordered the bombing of North Vietnam in 1972.

How confident do you feel about your answers to these questions? If you are not sure that you answered them well, form a group with other students, discuss the answers and then record your conclusions.

Recall quiz

1 Who fought at Dien Bien Phu?

2 What was Eisenhower's domino theory?

3 What was a strategic hamlet?

4 What happened as a result of the Gulf of Tonkin Incident?

5 Who were the VC and what tactics did they use?

6 What was Operation Rolling Thunder?

7 Which president first sent ground troops to Vietnam?

8 When was the Tet Offensive?

9 What was Vietnamisation?

10 Which neighbours of Vietnam were bombed in 1970 and 1971?

In the exam you will be asked how useful contemporary sources are for an enquiry. Copy and complete the table below. Support what you say with your own knowledge if it helps you to make your point.

Sources	Enquiry	Ways they are useful
B and C on page 83	Eisenhower's views on supporting the South Vietnamese government	
C on page 92 and E on page 93	The significance of the Gulf of Tonkin Incident	
A and C on page 97	The advantages the VC had over US troops	
F on page 101 and G on page 102	The effects of search and destroy tactics	

In the exam you will be asked about how historians' interpretations can differ. To find out why interpretations give different impressions you need to ask:

- Are they thinking about the same aspect of the topic?
- Might they have used different sources (look carefully at both sources on your paper, as well as the interpretations; the sources will have been carefully chosen to help you)?

Interpretations	Enquiry	How they differ	Why they might differ
1 and 2 on page 87	The effect of the strategic hamlets policy		
3 and 4 page 105	The outcome of the Tet Offensive		

Writing historically: explaining and evaluating

You need to think about the purpose of your writing to help you structure it and choose how you express your ideas.

Learning outcomes

By the end of this lesson, you will understand how to:
- use the key features of explanatory and analytical writing
- structure your writing to ensure you explain or evaluate effectively.

Definitions

Explain: to make an idea clear using relevant facts, details and examples.

Evaluate: to examine two or more points of view closely and carefully in order to make a judgement or come to a conclusion.

What are the similarities and differences in writing to **explain** and writing to **evaluate**?

Compare these two exam-style questions (note Question B has been adapted to make reference to Interpretation 2):

Question A

> Explain why US involvement in Vietnam increased in the years 1963–65.
> **(12 marks)**

Question B

> How far do you agree with Interpretation 1 (see page 109) about the success of Vietnamisation?
>
> Explain your answer using Interpretations 1 and 2 (see page 109) and your knowledge of the historical context. **(16 marks)**

1. Look at the statements below. Which apply to Question A, which to Question B and which to both? This type of question:

   a. asks you to write to explain.

   b. asks you to evaluate.

   c. asks you to consider arguments for and against a point of view and reach a conclusion.

   d. requires you to explain how and why an event happened or a situation came about.

   e. requires you to provide evidence and examples to support your ideas.

   f. requires you to link all your ideas to key points.

   g. requires you to explain at least one sequence of events and their consequences.

   h. requires you to consider what contributed to a situation or event.

   i. requires you to link and develop your ideas logically to form a line of reasoning.

   j. requires you to demonstrate good knowledge and understanding of the features or characteristics of the historical period.

   k. requires you to explore how and why a series of circumstances, events or actions led to a particular outcome.

2. Look at your answers to Question 1. What are the key differences between questions that ask you to 'explain' and questions that ask you 'how far do you agree'?

How can I structure writing to explain and writing to evaluate?

3. Answers to 'explain why' questions often follow this structure: 1st point; 2nd point; 3rd point; Summary of causes and effects that led to a specific outcome.

The starts of some sentences have been written out below in answer to Question A.
Put the sentences in the order in which you think they should appear.

> a. It was hard for Americans to accept that the powerful USA could not win against North Vietnam and so, step by step, they moved closer to committing US troops.
>
> b. North Vietnamese retaliation led to the Gulf of Tonkin Resolution...
>
> c. Although Congress had not authorised the deployment of US troops, US ships...
>
> d. The Resolution looked to the North Vietnamese to be a declaration of war...
>
> e. By February 1965, US involvement in Vietnam was costing...

4. Now look at the plan below for an answer to an exam-style question that asks you to evaluate. Remember, in the exam you would need to refer to both interpretations in the question.

1st point to support the interpretation	a. Firstly, the number of US troops in Vietnam...
2nd point to support the interpretation	b. As a result, the number of US casualties...
Signal a turning point in the argument	c. However, Interpretation 1 only considers the view of 'many American officials'...
1st point to contradict the interpretation	d. Some Military advisers felt that troops were withdrawn too soon...
2nd point to contradict the interpretation	e. The communists saw it as a chance to gain the upper hand...
Conclusion: a judgement directly responding to the interpretation	f. So there are different ways to assess 'success'. Interpretation 1 is correct as far as one of these ways is concerned...

5. Look at these exam-style questions:

> Explain why tactics used by the civil rights movement changed in the years 1960–63. **(12 marks)**
>
> How far do you agree with Interpretation 1 (see page 69) about the impact of the Black Power movement?
>
> Explain your answer using Interpretations 1 and 2 (see page 69) and your knowledge of the historical context. **(16 marks)**

Plan an answer to each one, using the same structures as the responses above. Write the first sentence of each paragraph.

04 | Reactions to US involvement in the Vietnam War, 1964–75

In 1970, this unarmed student was shot dead by US soldiers on a university campus in Ohio. He was shot because of the Vietnam War. Three more students were shot and killed, and nine others were wounded. This chapter explains how the USA came to be at war with itself over the war in Vietnam.

Learning outcomes

In this chapter, you will study:

- reasons for growing opposition to the war from students, politicians, the media and the public
- the effect of the My Lai Massacre and the Kent State University shootings
- reasons for support for the war
- the peace negotiations and Paris Peace Agreement
- the cost of the war to the USA
- reasons for US failure in Vietnam, including the strengths of North Vietnam, the weaknesses of the US armed forces and strategy, and opposition to the war in the USA.

4.1 Opposition to the war

Initial reactions to the war

Before 1965, there was broad support for US involvement in Vietnam, although some anti-war groups spoke out against it from the start. Once Johnson escalated US military involvement in the period 1965–68, the media and the public quickly became more concerned. Opposition came from people of every race, class, age and religious belief. Here are some examples.

- Martin Luther King criticised the war privately from 1965. From 1967, he marched and spoke at anti-war protests. Some civil rights activists felt this lost support for the civil rights cause.
- On 2 November 1965, Norman Morrison, a Quaker, burned himself to death outside the Pentagon (US military headquarters), deliberately copying Buddhist monks who had done the same in Vietnam (see page 88). A week later, Roger Allan La Porte, a Catholic, did the same outside the UN building in New York.
- Wayne Morse, Senator for Oregon, spoke against the war even before 1965. He gave the only speech in the Senate against the Gulf of Tonkin Resolution.
- In 1967, some Vietnam veterans formed Vietnam Veterans Against the War. They spoke at demonstrations and meetings, and they handed in their medals. They collected evidence about the misconduct of the war, including the regular murder of civilians.

Measuring public opinion

Public opinion about Vietnam can be measured in various ways.

- **Opinion polls*:** the most regular were Gallup polls. They were run regularly and covered a variety of questions about Vietnam. Some questions were asked often, showing the movement of public feeling on a specific issue (see Figure 4.1).
- **Politicians:** who tend to react when an issue is significant enough to affect votes. As a result, their views might be a useful measure of public opinion.

- **Demonstrations:** their size, who took part in them, and the specific issues they targeted showed the opinion of the public towards the war. Counter-demonstrations* by people with opposing views can be a useful measure of public opinion too.

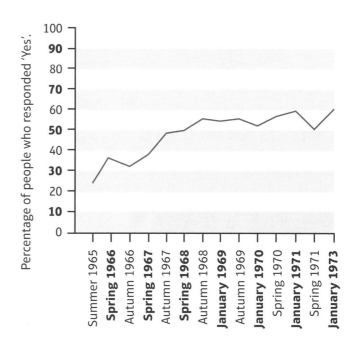

Figure 4.1 Results of a Gallup poll held in the period 1965–73. Participants were asked: 'Did the US make a mistake sending troops into Vietnam?' The graph shows the percentage of people who responded 'Yes'.

Extend your knowledge

Opinion Polls

Opinion polls can show both expected and unexpected opinions. In August 1965, a Gallup poll of 3,525 people of all ages and sexes across the USA were asked about Vietnam. The poll showed that:

- 187 people favoured sending more troops and invading North Vietnam; 3,338 were against

- 1,179 people would be more inclined to vote for a politician who would push for peace negotiations; 1,336 would be less likely to do so

- when given the age range 17 to over 26, most people said 20 year-olds should be drafted for Vietnam first.

Key term

Counter-culture*

Refusing to live by the cultural rules of your society. For the USA at the time, this was following the accepted rules for success: work hard, earn and spend wages, and obey the government.

Reasons for growing opposition to the war

As more and more troops were sent to Vietnam, opposition to the war grew. Short-term factors, such as events in Vietnam (e.g. the Tet Offensive), or presidential policy changes (e.g. invading Cambodia) triggered opposition. So did more long-term factors, such as the rising death toll, the loss (or serious injury) of family members or the length of the war. The cost of the war (paid for from taxes) became an increasingly important factor as the cost of US involvement rose. Some black Americans, such as the Black Panthers, opposed the war, saying they would not fight for a country where they faced racism on a daily basis. Mohammad Ali also refused, for the same reason (see page 75). Other factors affecting the growth of opposition were: the student movement; the draft and media representation of the war. Figure 4.2 shows significant reasons given for opposing the war.

The student movement

In 1950, there were just 2.2 million students in the USA. This rose to 5.9 million in 1965 and 8.5 million in 1970. A significant number of these students rejected the values of their parents' generation and wanted social change. These students became part of a 'counter-culture'* movement in American society. Not all students were part of this, and some supported the war. Many more simply focused on their studies and, while they may not have approved of the war, were not part of the student movement.

Students used similar methods to civil rights campaigners. They held sit-ins, boycotts and protest demonstrations and marches. They also went on strike, refusing to go to classes. Vietnam protesters often burned their draft cards (as did non-student protesters). As the 1960s progressed, student demonstrations became more organised, more radical, bigger and more violent. They also affected other anti-war demonstrations. Anti-war protesters, just like civil rights protesters, became caught up in a growing spiral of violence. Student protest got media attention, even if they represented a minority of students. This was probably because the protesters were largely white and middle class.

Opponents of the war included pacifists, parents of soldiers and students.

Figure 4.2 Different people had different reasons for opposing the war. Opposition to the war came from many parts of society. Pacifists, some parents of soldiers (and other military personnel) and students were vocal opponents.

Students for a Democratic Society

Students for a Democratic Society (SDS), set up in 1960, was one of the most significant student groups. By 1965, it had 3,000 members and groups on over 80 US college campuses. In October 1965, SDS gave its first statement against the war. SDS and other radical groups angered many people because they not only opposed the war, but also supported the North Vietnamese. Some carried banners with pictures of communists, such as the Cuban leader, Fidel Castro. As the war went on, student protesters often chanted slogans that shocked many, such as "Hey, hey, LBJ [President Johnson], how many kids did you kill today?"

Source A

A photograph showing an anti-Vietnam War demonstration in San Francisco in 1967. 'Uncle Sam' means 'the USA'. The man whose photo is on the red banner is Fidel Castro, leader of communist Cuba.

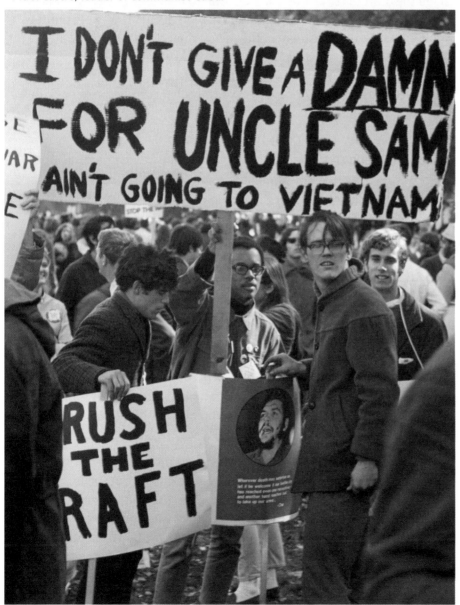

Source B

From the Students for a Democratic Society (SDS) Guide to Conscientious Objection, October 1965.

We feel that the war is immoral at its root, that it is fought alongside a regime with no claim to represent its people, and that it is foreclosing [cutting off] the hope of making America a decent and truly democratic society. The commitment of the SDS, and of the whole generation we represent, is clear: we are anxious to build villages; we refuse to burn them. We are anxious to help and to change our country; we refuse to destroy someone else's country. We are anxious to advance the cause of democracy; we do not believe that cause can be advanced by torture and terror.

Exam-style question, Section B

Study Sources A and B. How useful are Sources A and B for an enquiry into reasons for opposition to the Vietnam War? Explain your answer, using Sources A and B and your knowledge of the historical context. **8 marks**

Exam tip

When considering how useful sources are, be sure to focus on the subject of the enquiry. Consider what aspects of this are shown in the sources. Do not forget to consider the historical context.

Source C

From *The Strength Not to Fight* (1993), a book of interviews with Conscientious Objectors compiled by James W. Tollefson. He chose to leave all his interviewees anonymous. This interviewee is talking about working for the SDS in Boston.

Kids were brought in on buses from outlying areas, up to a forty-mile radius, for their physicals [to see if they were fit enough to do military service]. I would go out to the pickup points, mingle with the guys, and find every opportunity to talk about refusing induction and resisting the draft. At first, in '65 and '66, the mood was pretty tense. I had to try to keep a low enough profile not to get thrown off the bus, and then, after the bus arrived at the physical I had to sneak away. By 1968, everything had changed, and I got a sympathetic response from most guys on the bus.

Key term

Conscientious objector (CO)*

A person whose religious beliefs mean they will not fight. In 1966, the US military extended this to include beliefs such as Buddhism (not then seen as a religion). In 1970, they extended it to those who had any moral objections.

Activity

Sort the reasons for being against the war shown in Figure 4.2 on page 120 into military, social, personal and economic reasons.

The draft

The draft was compulsory service in the military forces. Those selected for the draft were sent draft cards, telling them where and when to report. Men were drafted from the age of 18. They took a basic training course, and then could be called up at any time to fight. Few people over 26 were ever drafted for Vietnam. The draft created even more opposition to the war, as many people felt it was unfair. People argued that the draftees were too young and not well enough trained, increasing the chances of them being killed. They also argued that poor families, black and white, were least able to avoid the draft by the various methods outlined below.

The draft system was changed in 1969 to a lottery system. All men born between 1944 and 1950 were given a random number, according to their date of birth. Each time more soldiers were needed, a number was drawn for the next draft year. This mixed up the ages and the fact it was random made the draft fairer. During the war, over 26 million men were eligible for the draft. Of the 2.6 million who served in Vietnam, 650,000 were draftees. Another million draftees were in the military but did not go to Vietnam.

Avoiding the draft

There were ways to delay, or even avoid (by being classified 'exempt'), being drafted.

- College students could delay being drafted until they graduated.
- Clergymen and students training to work in the Church were exempt.
- Some workers in the government, farming or industry were exempt.
- Those who could prove that their joining up would be a 'hardship' for their families (e.g. if they were the only wage earner in a family) were exempt.
- The only son of a family was exempt.
- The physically and mentally unfit were exempt.
- Conscientious objectors* (COs) could avoid fighting, but often had to do other war work (such as working in a weapon-making factory). If they refused to do this, they went to prison. During the war, about 300,000 young men applied as COs. 170,000 were exempted.
- Studying or working abroad. This was mainly an option for those whose families could afford to organise it for them.
- Leaving the USA illegally, or going into hiding in the USA. It is difficult to give an exact number of the people who did this, but it is estimated to be around 40–50,000.

Anti-war activists published pamphlets and set up 'clinics' to give advice on how to avoid the draft. They showed people how to fill out the form to apply for exemption as a CO, or explained the various exemptions to them. Others went further (see Source C). They made contact with young men who had been drafted and tried to persuade them to become COs or to otherwise avoid the draft. About three million young men served in Vietnam. About 15 million avoided being drafted. Most of those delayed being sent (e.g. by staying in college) or were legally exempt.

The media

The Vietnam War was the first war that was widely watched on television and where reporters were regularly allowed to travel with the troops into the war zone and were not censored.

The living room war

Ordinary Americans saw news footage and documentaries about the war. They also saw news reports of anti-war protests, such as the 100,000-strong protest on 21 October 1967 in Washington. Television showed Americans the war in uncomfortable detail and made them think about it. This came just when many Americans, not just students, were beginning to lose faith in their government. It was becoming clear that the government was keeping information from them, even lying to them. In 1968, the government claimed the Tet Offensive as a success, but CBS television news reporter Walter Cronkite came back from Vietnam and told the public that Tet was, at best, a stalemate and that the war looked unwinnable. Many Americans believed Cronkite, not the US government.

Source D

An image from a CBS report on the Vietnam War, broadcast on 5 August 1965. The journalist, Morley Safer, reported that the soldiers spoke no Vietnamese and set light to the houses in the village of Cam Ne without checking if there were people inside.

Interpretation 1

From *The Uncensored War* (1986), by Daniel C. Hallin.

There was… conflict and ill feeling between the media and government over Vietnam. In 1962 and 1963, the Kennedy administration made an effort to discredit the young Saigon press corps, which was often at odds with the generals and ambassadors running the war. In 1965, as American troops were committed to what was in effect the first televised war… , CBS enraged Lyndon Johnson by showing American marines setting fire to the thatched huts of Cam Ne [a Vietnamese village] with Zippo [cigarette] lighters.

Interpretation 2

From *A Bright Shining Lie* (1988), by Neil Sheeham. He is talking about reporting the early years of the war.

In the post-war period [after the Second World War] the American press remained the most vigorous on earth, but where foreign affairs was concerned the reporting… was weighted towards furthering the anti-Communist crusade. … The reporters of the period [the early 1960s] were not accustomed to thinking of their military leaders and diplomats as deluded men, and the military leaders and diplomats were not accustomed to reporters who said they were consistently wrong.

Exam-style question, Section B

Suggest **one** reason why Interpretations 1 and 2 give different views about the media's relationship with the US government. **4 marks**

Exam tip

When considering why interpretations differ, think about the sources historians may have used to reach their judgement.

The My Lai Massacre, 1968

On 16 March 1968, US troops went into action, as they thought, against the VC (Vietcong). Charlie Company were sent to the village of My Lai, briefed that they would come under VC fire. This did not happen, there were only women, children and old men in the village. Despite this, over the next four hours, the troops, led by Lieutenant Calley, killed all the people and animals. They even stopped for lunch. An army war photographer with them, Sergeant Ron Haeberle, took photos. They later said they had been ordered to kill everyone in the village. What happened next reinforced the American people's belief that they should believe the media about Vietnam, not the government.

> **Immediately after the massacre**
> Military announce a successful mission:
> - My Lai VC base destroyed and 128 VC killed.
> - Soldiers and a helicopter pilot who were there, report the massacre to army officers.
> - Chiefs from nearby villages also report to the army the massacre of hundreds of civilians.

> The army organised a cover-up. After a quick investigation it announced 20 accidental civilian deaths during the mission.

> One soldier, Ron Rindenhour, collected eyewitness evidence about the massacre. In April 1969, he sent it to key US politicians, to expose the cover-up.

> A new enquiry began. On 15 July 1970, it reported that the army had covered up what really happened at My Lai.

> On 5 September 1970, Lieutenant Calley was charged with murder. This was the first the public heard of the massacre.

> On 13 November 1970, 35 different newspapers reported the massacre. Reporters collected eyewitness testimony that over 500 civilians had been killed.

Figure 4.3 Events following My Lai.

At first, the public were not sure what to believe. The evidence was confusing and contradictory. Two military enquiries began. The Criminal Investigations Division (CID) conducted an investigation into what happened and the Peers Enquiry looked into whether the army had organised a cover-up. On 5 December, the photos of the photographer in My Lai were shown on CBS News. It was no longer possible to deny the killing of a significant number of civilians. There was a huge public outcry at the massacre itself and at the cover-up.

The CID found that 347 civilians were killed and that 35 members of Charlie Company should be prosecuted. The Peers Enquiry found that Calley, while ordering the massacre, was following the orders of his superiors and that the massacre was known about and covered up at a high level, including generals.

Calley's trial, 1970–71

The public had been horrified by My Lai. The various investigations all said the army had covered up the massacre, yet high-ranking officers were never charged. Criminal charges were brought against 18 officers, but only Lieutenant Calley was brought to a military trial. On 29 March 1971, he was convicted of killing 22 civilians and sentenced to life imprisonment.

Many people thought it was unfair for Calley to be the only one to stand trial, as he had been acting under orders. They felt the army was making him take the blame for more senior officers. However, others felt that 'acting under orders' was not a reasonable excuse for what he ordered his men to do.

On 3 April, President Nixon promised to review Calley's case himself. He also ruled that, while Calley's appeal was heard, Calley should be confined at his US military base, not in prison. On appeal, Calley's sentence was reduced to 20 years. He was released after three and a half years under house arrest on his military base.

Source E

A photograph taken by Sergeant Ron Haeberle in My Lai on 16 March 1968. It shows some of the civilians that were killed by US troops.

Source G

From a 2016 interview with Hilary Crain, who was in her early twenties and living in California at the time of Lieutenant Calley's trial.

For me, hearing about My Lai was a blow like hearing about the assassination of Kennedy, or that of Martin Luther King. It was a loss of innocence and there was a lot of press attention to the massacre and the trial, and a lot of public horror. There was a very strong anti-war movement in California at the time and My Lai added to the anger. People were appalled that although Calley was given a life sentence he only spent three years under house arrest. He was the officer in charge. He gave the order to kill babies and toddlers who couldn't possibly be Vietcong. There was a strong feeling here that he should have served a far longer term, if not life, in prison.

Source F

Results of a poll of 1,600 people across the USA in April 1971.

65% disagreed with Calley's life sentence

77% felt that the soldiers were only following orders

77% felt that Calley was being used to take the blame for more senior officers

58% felt that Nixon's reaction to the sentence was reasonable.

THINKING HISTORICALLY ▶ **Evidence (4a&b)**

The weight of evidence

One useful idea to have in mind when interpreting historical sources is 'consistency' (whether or not sources support each other). If a number of sources appear to suggest the same conclusion about the past, then we might feel more confident about accepting this conclusion.

However, we should also consider the nature of the sources and the reasons why sources might seem to disagree.

Sources F and G could be used by a historian to build up a picture of public reaction in the USA to the Calley trial.

1   Explain how Sources F and G differ in what they show about reactions to the Calley trial.

2   How can the difference between the sources be explained? Why do they suggest different things? Write down as many reasons as you can.

Discuss the following in groups:

3   Suppose a historian had ten more accounts that agreed broadly with Source F and only four that agreed with Source G. Would this mean that Source F was nearer to the truth? Explain your answer.

4   What else should we consider, apart from 'the balance of the evidence', when drawing conclusions from sources such as these?

The Kent State shootings

On 4 May 1970, Ohio National guardsmen shot dead four unarmed students during a protest on the Kent State University campus against the Vietnam War. Two of the dead were not even protesters, just students who were moving between classes. Nine more students were wounded.

Events leading up to the shootings

The shootings came four days after Nixon's announcement of US troops being sent into Cambodia. On Friday 1 May, a group of students decided to bury a copy of the US Constitution as a protest. One of them, who had fought in Vietnam, decided to bury his discharge papers, too. About 500 students took part in the protest. Events then spiralled out of control.

- That evening there was fighting between pro-war and anti-war groups.
- The next day (2 May) there were several demonstrations.
- In the evening of 2 May the Officer Training Corps building on campus (many US campuses had an army officer training programme) was burned down; there were now over 1,000 demonstrators.
- The mayor declared an emergency and 900 members of the National Guard arrived with rifles and tear gas.
- On 3 May, there were several demonstrations, broken up by the National Guard with tear gas.
- On 4 May, officials banned a demonstration planned for 12 a.m. About 2,000 people ignored the ban.
- The National Guard could not break up the demonstration with tear gas and students threw empty gas canisters and bricks at them. Then the National Guard fired into the crowd.

The public were horrified by the Kent State shootings, mainly because it involved white, middle-class students. Two weeks later, in contrast to this, two black students were shot during anti-war protests at Jackson State University, a predominantly black university. There was very little publicity. Public reaction over the Mississippi murders of 1964 (see page 56) followed a similar pattern. There was horror over the Mississippi shootings (where the dead included white middle-class CORE activists). However, the regular murder of black men in Mississippi had produced far less reaction.

Extend your knowledge

Protest songs

People involved in the civil rights movement sang particular songs to show unity. So did opponents of the war. Famous singers, such as Joan Baez and Bob Dylan, wrote songs for both groups and attended protests for both. The Kent State shootings inspired films, plays, poetry and dozens of songs. The most famous, *Ohio* by Neil Young, was written after he read an article about the shooting, that used John Filo's photos. The song was banned on several radio stations.

Why do you think songs can be a powerful protest tool?

Source H

A photograph showing the body of Jeffrey Miller, moments after he was shot at Kent State University on 4 May 1970. It was one of a series of photographs taken by John Filo, a photography student. The photographs were published worldwide.

Political opposition

Political opposition in Congress grew as the war went on, reflecting changes in public opinion. The Tet Offensive led many who had previously supported the war to change their minds. Those who pushed for an end to the war were called 'doves' after the symbol of peace. Those that were pro-war were called 'hawks'. Figure 4.4 shows the most significant reasons why some politicians opposed the war.

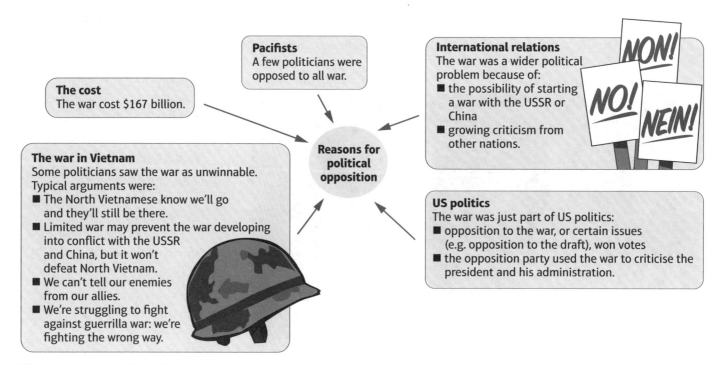

Figure 4.4 Reasons for political opposition to the war.

Opposition in Congress

Opposition in Congress was significant. Wars cost money. Presidents have to get Congress to pass laws to raise taxes and other funds for a war. With Vietnam, this situation led to yet more lies about the war. Just before the Gulf of Tonkin incident, Congress asked Johnson about the cost of the war. Congress was told that, if the war lasted until the summer of 1967, it would cost under $10 billion. The real estimated cost was $20 billion.

The invasion of Cambodia led to a rise in opposition to the war in Congress. On 24 June 1970, it repealed the Gulf of Tonkin Resolution, which had given presidents the power to make decisions about the war without consulting Congress. In June, it also set a limit on the funding for US troops in Cambodia, giving 30 June as the cut-off point for any involvement in Cambodia. Finally, it set the date for the final withdrawals of troops as the end of 1971. After the Paris Peace Accords (see page 140), Congress refused to give as much funding to the South Vietnamese government as Nixon had promised. This lack of support quickened the collapse of the South Vietnamese government.

Interpretation 3

From *Richard Nixon* (2004), written by historian Robert Mason. He is discussing Nixon's Vietnamisation policy.

Dissent found voice in Congress. Antiwar sentiment grew there not only among Democrats [Nixon was a Republican]… but also among some Republicans. In September 1969, Charles Goodell, the junior Republican senator from New York, announced his intention to introduce a disengagement bill that threatened to cut off congressional funding for the war unless Nixon brought all troops home.

Worldwide opposition

The media reported on the Vietnam War and civil rights at the same time. At home and abroad, US police and troops were shown using violence against civilians.

Americans saw the USA as representing freedom and democracy, as the only nation able to stand up to communism. They expected worldwide respect. It was a shock to find that many people saw them as supporting a corrupt regime and fighting a war with a shockingly high civilian death toll. Moreover, publicity over the treatment of civil rights protestors meant that the USSR and China could easily criticise the USA.

There were regular demonstrations against the war in Vietnam in many countries from 1965, but events such as My Lai sparked off bigger protests. One of the most shocking images of the war (Source I) set off worldwide demonstrations against the war the following day.

Source I

A photograph showing Vietnamese children running away from their village, which has just been bombed with napalm on 8 June 1972. Kim, the 9-year-old girl in the middle, tore off her burning clothes. The boy in front, her brother, was blinded in one eye by the napalm.

Extend your knowledge

What happened next?

The three children on the left of Source I are from the Phan family, the two on the right are their cousins. Nick Ut, the photographer who took the photo, was only 19. He took the children to the hospital. The doctors refused to treat Kim at first, saying that she would probably not survive, but Ut made them treat her. She did survive.

At first, the newspaper did not want to print the photo, because Kim was naked. Then the *New York Times* decided to use the photos. The next day there were anti-war protests all over the world.

What does this tell you about the role of the press in covering wars?

Activities ?

1   List three ways in which US actions over civil rights and in Vietnam might be viewed in the same way by the rest of the world.

2   Give two ways in which the world might see US actions in Vietnam as different to US actions over civil rights.

3   'The USA treated Vietnam like a colony'. In groups, discuss the evidence for and against this interpretation of the war in Vietnam. Decide how far you support the view on a scale of 1 to 10, with 1 being 'don't support much' and 10 being 'fully support'.

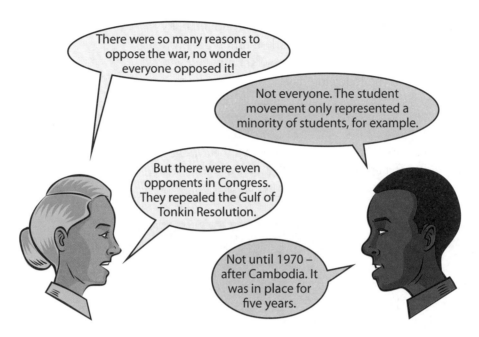

Figure 4.5 Assessing opposition to the war.

Summary

- Opposition to the war grew as the war went on due to increased US troop involvement, increasing cost and the rising death toll. It came from every level of society and involved people of all ages, races and religious beliefs.
- The student protest movement, which protested about various aspects of American society including civil rights, became increasingly extreme in its methods and increasingly opposed to Vietnam.
- The draft was a significant issue for opponents of the war.
- The media influenced opposition to the war in terms of what it reported and how it reported these events.
- Incidents such as My Lai were a shock to the American public not just because of the event itself, but also because of the military cover-up and the example made of Lieutenant Calley.
- The Kent State shootings provided shocking images of troops on a US university campus fighting with, and killing, students.

Checkpoint

Strengthen

S1 List five reasons why opposition to the war increased.

S2 Write a paragraph to explain what horrified the public about My Lai.

S3 Why were the Kent State shootings so shocking to people?

Challenge

C1 Explain how the public could be horrified at My Lai and yet be angry at the sentencing of Lieutenant Calley.

How confident do you feel about your answers to these questions? If you are not sure that you answered them well, spend a few minutes planning your answers and try the questions again.

4.2 Support for the war

Support for the war, just like opposition to it, came from a wide range of people, including students. One journalist remarked that you could go from a pro-war rally to an anti-war rally and the rallies looked the same. They had similar types of people, waving the American flag and holding banners urging support for US troops. It was only when you looked at other banners that it became clear which side the rally was supporting.

Figure 4.6 shows common reasons why 'hawks' (see page 127) supported the war. The most significant reason was probably the fear of communism.

Fear of communism

Immediately after the Second World War, Cold War fears in the USA had led to the 'Red Scare'*. People who were seen as communists were hounded out of jobs, even homes, and put in prison. The Red Scare had lessened by 1954, but fear of communist takeovers abroad was strong. Vietnam was one of several Cold War flashpoints – points where the Cold War might become the Third World War. This explains why the US government wanted only a limited war in Vietnam (see page 84). Eisenhower's domino theory applied to the flashpoints, too. However, the US did not want to escalate the war in Vietnam to the point of starting a war with the USSR.

Supporters of the war included some ex-soldiers and Vietnam War veterans, anti-communists and construction workers.

Figure 4.6 Reasons for supporting the Vietnam War. Support for the war came from many parts of society. For example, some ex-soldiers and Vietnam War veterans, anti-communists and construction workers ('hard hats') patriotically supported the war.

Source A

From a letter written by Richard E. Marks, a US Marine serving in Vietnam, to his mother on 12 December 1965. He headed it his 'Last Will and Testament', and told her what to do with his possessions. He was killed two months after he wrote the letter. He was 19 years old.

I don't like being over here [in Vietnam], but I am doing a job that must be done — I am fighting an *inevitable* enemy that must be fought — now or later. I am fighting to protect and maintain what I believe in and what I want to live in — a democratic society. If I am killed while carrying out this mission, I want no one to cry or mourn for me. I want people to hold their heads high and be proud of me for the job I did.

Source B

From a letter written by a US soldier in Vietnam, Jack S. Swender, to his aunt and uncle on 20 September 1965. He was killed on 18 December 1965, aged 22. Kincaid, Humbolt, Blue Mound and Kansas City are all in America.

Some people wonder why Americans are in Vietnam. The way I see the situation, I would rather fight to stop communism in South Vietnam than in Kincaid, Humbolt, Blue Mound, or Kansas City, and that is just about what it would end up being. Except for the fact that by that time I would be old and gray and my children would be fighting the war. The price for victory is high when life cannot be replaced, but I think it is far better to fight and die for freedom than to live under oppression and fear.

Source C

A photograph showing a pro-war demonstration in Boston in 1969. Many different groups were there, including students from the university.

Patriots and 'hard hats'

Supporters of the war came from many social groups, just as opponents of the war did. They had different reasons for supporting the war.

Patriotism

Patriotism is the love of, and loyalty to, one's country. Many Americans, across all classes, were fiercely patriotic. Many were taught, at home and at school, to obey authority and to be patriotic. This meant that when the government said that they had to take part in the Vietnam War to fight against communism, they accepted this and did so willingly. To not fight would be seen as letting the country down and betraying what it stood for. Once the USA was in the war, patriotism drove many people to support the war so that the USA did not look as if it was giving in to a communist country. This, many people felt, would mean the USA would 'lose face' and would be made to seem less powerful in the world.

Interpretation 1

From *American Protestants and the Debate over the Vietnam War* (2014), written by George Bogaski. He is discussing how the religious beliefs of extreme protestant groups affected their attitude to the war.

During the first half of the Vietnam War [their] faith guided their response to the war. They did not support the war simply out of political commitments. … [In their view] the war sought to stop Communists who sought religious, not political domination. Faced with the consequences of Communist success, Christians and the church had an obligation to see America through to victory.

Interpretation 2

From *Richard Nixon and the Quest for a New Majority* (2004), written by historian Robert Mason. He is discussing support for Nixon and the 'hard hat' riot.

In July [1970] the White House received a private poll showing popular approval for Nixon's Vietnam policy while revealing disapproval of his performance in all other policy areas. … Only days after a demonstration in Washington against the administration's Cambodian action… a crowd mostly of construction workers marched on Wall Street to show their opposition to young activists. … The march was not unique, and it inspired similar rallies in Buffalo, San Diego, and Pittsburg.

Activities ?

1 In groups, discuss why the following factors might make a person oppose communism and so support the war in Vietnam:
   a believing in an elected government
   b believing in building your own business and making it successful
   c believing that your country should be protected from outside threats.

2 Write a slogan of no more than six words to sum up the reasons why the author of Source B wants to fight.

3 How useful are Sources A and C for an enquiry about reasons for supporting the war? Which of them would you use if you could only use one?

The 'hard hat' riot, 1970

'Hard hats' was a nickname for construction workers (who need to wear protective clothing). After the Kent State University shooting, there were demonstrations all over the country in protest at the shooting and in sympathy with the families of the dead students.

- At a New York protest on 8 May 1970, construction workers charged out during their lunch break, wearing hard hats, and beat up protesters.

- They broke through a police line to get to protesters. The police did little to stop the beatings.

- The rioters moved on to City Hall, where the mayor had agreed to allow the American flag to fly at half-mast for the dead students. They protested against this action, saying the mayor, John Lindsay, was not tough enough on anti-war protesters and communists.

- On 20 May, the riot leader, Peter J. Brennan, led a pro-war rally outside City Hall, New York.

Extend your knowledge

Benefiting from the riot

The leader of the 'hard hat' riot, Peter J. Brennan, was treated like a hero by some New Yorkers. On 20 May, he led a pro-war rally in New York, which involved about 60,000 people. As well as supporting the war, the rally criticised the policies of New York mayor John Lindsay. Two days later, Nixon invited Brennan and 22 other pro-war union leaders to the White House. When Nixon was re-elected in 1972 he made Brennan his Secretary of Labor in the White House Administration.

Does Brennan's experience mean that all workers supported the war?

Activities ?

1 In groups, discuss what Source D shows you about support for the war.

2 Why do you think the demonstrators are carrying so many flags?

3 Compare Source D to Source C on page 132. Are the people shown similar or different? Think of at least three reasons for your answer.

Source D

A photograph showing the pro-war demonstration led by Peter J. Brennan on 20 May 1970.

The 'silent majority'

On 3 November 1969, Nixon made a televised speech about policy in Vietnam (see Source E for an extract). In it he appealed for the support of the group he called 'the great silent majority'. These were, he implied, Americans who mainly supported his policies, but did not actively campaign either for or against the war.

The idea was remarkably successful.

- A poll carried out over the next few days showed 77% of people supported Nixon's policy in Vietnam.
- Over 50,000 telegrams and 30,000 letters of support flowed into the White House.
- Later polls showed that many people considered they were part of the silent majority.
- One significant effect of the level of public approval for the speech was that both the House of Representatives and the Senate passed resolutions approving of Nixon's conduct of the war.

The reaction to the 'silent majority' speech showed support for the war when Nixon badly needed it. He was trying to get the North Vietnamese to the negotiating table. The support meant he could tell North Vietnam that, despite the anti-war movement's demonstrations and protests, he had support where it mattered – the general public and money-providing Congress. This meant that the USA was well placed to hold out for a gradual withdrawal and an 'honorable peace' – a phrase he had been using since May 1968.

Source E

From the 'silent majority' speech made by President Nixon on 3 November 1969, outlining his plans for the Vietnam War.

In San Francisco a few weeks ago, I saw demonstrators carrying signs reading: "Lose in Vietnam, bring the boys home."

Well, one of the strengths of our free society is that any American has a right to reach that conclusion and to advocate that point of view. But as President of the United States, I would be untrue to my oath of office if I allowed the policy of this Nation to be dictated by the minority who hold that point of view and who try to impose it on the Nation by mounting demonstrations in the street. ...

And so tonight — to you, the great silent majority of my fellow Americans — I ask for your support.

Source F

From a letter written to President Nixon after his 3 November 1969 speech. The letter, from Gerald B. Spinn of North Carolina, explains why he supports Nixon's policies.

(1) Immediate total abandonment [of Vietnam] at this time would, in effect, amount to surrender and would announce to the entire world that the United States of America was either unable or unwilling to fulfil its treaty commitments;

(2) The importance of winning a just peace in Vietnam far exceeds the necessity to appease and placate the [anti-war activists]... ;

(3) Although I personally feel that all of Vietnam is not worth one single American life... the inescapable fact remains that the repulsion of Communist agression (sic) is the primary issue at stake and that freedom cannot be compromised at any price;

and (4) If the Communist agressors (sic) are permitted to [conquer] Vietnam and (ultimately) all of Southeast Asia, what is to stop them from broadening their goals to include the entire world? If [anti-war activists] have their way, even the United States of America will ultimately fall to Communist aggression. And if that happens, letters like this one will not be permitted and writers like me will probably all be lined up and executed promptly.

Activities ?

1 In groups, list three ways in which Nixon's 'silent majority' speech proved to be a success.

2 How useful are Sources F and G for an enquiry into:

   a the success of Nixon's speech

   b the importance Nixon attached to public support

   c support for the Vietnam War?

3 What can Sources F and G tell you about opposition to the war?

Interpretation 3

From *Richard Nixon* (2004), written by historian Robert Mason. He is discussing the impact of Nixon's 'silent majority' speech.

The 'silent majority' speech both managed to provide Nixon with an extension of general public support for his foreign policy and seemed to identify a coherent group that sympathised with the administration's policies. In the long as well as the short term, public reaction to the speech was positive. White House polls revealed repeatedly that many Americans considered themselves members of the silent majority, who mostly supported Nixon's policies.

Source G

A photograph showing Nixon holding up a telegram with hundreds of signatures of support on top of more telegrams delivered on 4 November 1969, after his 'silent majority' speech. About 30,000 letters of support followed.

Political Support

White House administrations expected the support of their party when they were in power. One of the things the military complained about was that Democrats who had been 'hawks' under Johnson (because he was a Democrat) became 'doves' as soon as Nixon (a Republican) came to power. The fact that they were now the party in opposition to the president seemed to encourage them to do this. However, this was balanced against the fact that no politician wanted the USA to look as if it had been defeated by communist North Vietnam. Those who wanted to end the war did not want South Vietnam to become communist. Political support (and opposition) was complicated, because politicians wanted different things all at the same time. They wanted to end the war, they wanted to do what would make them popular (and win votes and power) and they did not want the USA to lose face.

Support in Congress

Support for the war in Congress did shift over time. So, the Gulf of Tonkin Resolution (1964) was passed unanimously in the House of Representatives and with only two votes against in the Senate. This clear support of increased US involvement of the war was made partly as a reaction to the supposed attack on US ships. It was also passed because Congress had no idea how much had really been spent in supporting the South Vietnamese government up to that point.

As time passed, Congress generally became less favourable to the war, but kept on funding it – even though it knew the real cost of the war. There were two main reasons for this:

- the military kept assuring the government that victory was close

- they did not want the USA (a rich and powerful country) to be beaten by North Vietnam.

Reactions in Congress shifted after events such as the Tet Offensive, or speeches such as Nixon's 'silent majority' speech. Congress was also influenced by public opinion. Simply put, it was more likely to express anti-war sentiments if there had recently been a large, peaceful anti-war demonstration. However, when anti-war demonstrations became violent, Congress tended to shift towards being pro-war. After 1970, Congress put restrictions on how money for the war could be spent – but it still funded the war.

Summary

- People supported the Vietnam War due to patriotism, fear of communism and, a desire not to lose.
- Levels of support changed during the war, depending on the cost and events.
- 'Hard hats' were construction workers and the phrase came to represent working class support for the war.
- On 3 November 1969, Nixon made a speech about the war in which he used the phrase 'silent majority' to refer to the millions of Americans who did not demonstrate for or against the war, but who generally supported his policies. The speech won Nixon a lot of support.
- Johnson and Nixon managed to gain the support of enough people in Congress to keep funding for the war until 1970.

Checkpoint

Strengthen

S1 Explain one way that the student movement sparked support for the war.

S2 List at least three reasons why Americans supported the war.

S3 Draw a flow diagram to show how the fear of communism led to support for the war in Vietnam.

S4 Write a short definition of Nixon's 'silent majority'.

Challenge

C1 Give one political and one social reason why some Americans supported the war. Explain your choices.

C2 Explain what was significant about Nixon's 'silent majority' speech.

How confident do you feel about your answers to these questions? If you are not sure that you answered them well, read section 4.2 again with a partner and make notes on what you find. Work together to answer the questions.

4.3 The war ends

On 6 April 1965, President Johnson explained his reasons for starting the Rolling Thunder bombing of North Vietnam (see page 98). He also said the USA wanted peace and would negotiate at any time, but said an independent South Vietnam must be part of any peace settlement. The North Vietnamese responded on 8 April, saying the reunification of Vietnam (as in the Geneva Accords) must be part of any settlement.

Negotiations up to 1972

A peace settlement seemed impossible. There were several false starts. The Tet Offensive of 1968 shook both sides (see page 104) and they agreed to talks. However, when these began (in Paris in 1968) all sides just restated their arguments. The USA wanted South Vietnam to be independent and non-communist. North Vietnam wanted Vietnam reunified as one country; and expected a communist government to be elected. Once Nixon became president he wanted to end the war as quickly as possible, as he had promised to do when elected in 1968.

There were huge barriers to agreement:

- whether to unite Vietnam
- how to unite Vietnam
- who governed South Vietnam: the government the USA supported, or the National Liberation Front (see page 86) – now renamed the Provisional Revolutionary Government
- troop withdrawals from South Vietnam on both sides.

Secret talks

The Paris peace talks, despite Nixon's attempts at real negotiations, went nowhere. So, Nixon held talks with both China and the USSR, hoping to end the Cold War. As a result, the North Vietnamese, fearing an end to aid from these countries, agreed to secret peace talks in 1970. The South Vietnamese government did not know about these talks. The USA was considering abandoning the South Vietnamese government, led by President Thieu, if they could get an agreement on an independent South Vietnam. The North Vietnamese had made it clear that they would not accept any government led by Thieu.

Source A

A British cartoon showing the problems Nixon faced during the US peace proposals in 1969. President Thieu was the leader of the South Vietnamese government, 1967–75.

Moving towards restarting talks, 1970–72

Nixon felt the USA had to seem willing to negotiate but should also be strong enough not to be pushed to accept unfavourable peace terms. From 1970, he kept pressure on North Vietnam to agree peace by:

- continuing official negotiations
- continuing secret negotiations
- continuing the process of Vietnamisation
- continuing fighting and bombing
- continuing meetings with the USSR and China, negotiating an end to the Cold War.

The most significant problem Nixon's actions created for the North Vietnamese was the possibility of losing the support of China and the USSR, who had begun to press them to make peace. However, the USA was also under increasing pressure. Congress was cutting funding and opposition to the war was rising. People were tired of the war, and the amount of time it was taking to bring the troops home.

In 1972, the North Vietnamese launched their Easter Offensive (see page 111), their first big attack since Tet. It was a shock to the US government that they were strong enough to launch this attack, even if it failed. It, and the US bombing that followed, showed both sides that the war could drag on for years. Figure 4.7 shows the reasons to return to the peace talks.

Talks, 1972–73

On 8 October 1972, the USA and North Vietnam produced an agreement at the official Paris talks, agreed in their secret meetings. Thieu refused to sign. He was furious that the agreement that he had no part in making was being forced on him. The North Vietnamese accused the US of using South Vietnam's refusal to back out of the agreement. The talks broke up with the agreement unsigned and an increased lack of trust on all sides.

Once more, Nixon tried several things to press for the peace talks to restart.

Figure 4.7 Reasons to negotiate. Some of the reasons apply to just the USA or North Vietnam, but others apply to both.

- The USA resumed heavy bombing of North Vietnam.
- Nixon persuaded President Thieu to come to the talks by promising an immediate delivery of weapons, supplies and aid, as well as yearly supplies after that.
- Nixon encouraged China and the USSR to press the North Vietnamese to reach an agreement.

The talks began again on 8 January 1973.

Activities ?

1 In groups, list the reasons each side had for negotiating for peace, under the headings: 'USA', 'North Vietnamese' and 'Both'.

2 The South Vietnamese government wanted peace too. Discuss with a partner why it might be concerned about peace talks and any peace settlement. List at least three reasons.

3 Make a list of at least two 'pros' and two 'cons' for the South Vietnamese of a peace settlement where the US would leave having set up a new, non-communist government.

Exam-style question, Section A

Explain why the US and North Vietnamese governments' attitudes to peace changed in the years 1969–73.

You may use the following in your answer:

- US public opinion
- President Nixon

You **must** also use information of your own. **12 marks**

Exam tip

When answering a question like this you should plan your answer carefully. In your plan, you could include notes on both bulleted points in the question, linking them to reasons, but you must also include an idea of your own.

The Paris Peace Accords

The Paris Peace Accords, signed by the USA, North Vietnam, South Vietnam and the Provisional Revolutionary Government, agreed:

- All countries to accept Vietnam as a single country. Reunification to be by negotiation and agreement, with no outside interference. New government to be elected with international supervision.
- A ceasefire to begin, kept by everyone, including both South Vietnam 'governments' (President Thieu's government and the Provisional Revolutionary Government).
- The armies of both South Vietnam 'governments' to remain, but no more US aid to ARVN.
- US troops, equipment and advisers to be withdrawn and military bases to be dismantled within 60 days.
- The US government could not interfere in Vietnamese politics, militarily or otherwise.

- Prisoners of war and captured equipment on both sides to be exchanged within 60 days.
- The USA to give aid for reconstruction, in North and South Vietnam.

Significance of the Paris Peace Accords

The Paris Peace Accords gave the USA a way to leave the war. However, the North Vietnamese and South Vietnamese both saw 'the peace' as a brief ceasefire while the Americans withdrew.

- **The USA:** By 23 March 1973 there were, officially, only 150 US Marines in South Vietnam, guarding the US embassy. However, about 10,000 US military personnel had become civilian advisers, and were still in Vietnam. Congress cut military funding and aid sent to South Vietnam was well below what Nixon had promised. This left the ARVN badly supplied.
- **The South Vietnamese:** The economy of South Vietnam collapsed partly due to the large reduction in US aid and the loss of income when the Americans left. Thieu did not make the government more democratic or replace corrupt officials in the villages, so the VC were soon strong in the villages again. Thieu's policy was not to negotiate or work with communists (either the North Vietnamese or the Provisional Revolutionary Government). Meanwhile North Vietnam's policy was to achieve a united, communist Vietnam.
- **The North Vietnamese:** North Vietnam became impatient with Thieu's refusal to negotiate. They sent troops and supplies down the Ho Chi Minh Trail and launched a new attack in December 1974. The ARVN could not cope. Despite US assurances of help if South Vietnam was invaded, Congress did nothing but allow funding to evacuate US citizens. The fall of Saigon, on 30 April 1975, came much sooner than expected.

Extend your knowledge

Impact in South Vietnam of the loss of US money
When the US troops left, about 300,000 South Vietnamese lost their jobs. South Vietnam was about $300 million worse off after their departure. At the same time, the aid that the South Vietnamese government was getting from the USA fell from $2.3 billion to $1 billion a year. The food shortages caused prices to rise, while unemployment levels meant many people could not afford to pay for even basic needs.

The cost of the war for the USA

The Vietnam War hit the USA hard, in terms of money and lives. The financial cost was not just how much money was spent on the war. It was the fact that this money could not be spent on solving problems in the USA (e.g. improving the lives of poor black Americans in inner-city ghettos). President Johnson had made plans for new benefits and projects to improve the lives of the poorest Americans, which he called 'the Great Society'. This lost out on funding as his administration used the money to pay for the war. Figure 4.8 shows you the cost of the war.

The war hit the USA in other ways too.

- It affected the way that Americans saw themselves. They had lost a war to a much less industrialised and less wealthy country and had both fought the war and left South Vietnam in ways that made them feel ashamed.
- It contributed to the growing lack of trust between Americans and their government, military and the police. These had also been significant factors in the civil rights movement.
- The extremes of the reaction to the war sharply divided US society. Not only were many Americans less trusting of their government, they were also less trusting of each other.
- Returning soldiers also had a significant impact.

Returning soldiers

Many of those who fought in Vietnam remembered the welcome for returning soldiers in 1945. People shook their hand, bought them a drink, or refused to let them pay for a meal. Many of those returning from Vietnam had a very different reception. Most of those who had served in the Second World War returned all at once, at the end of a war that had been won. The draft meant that soldiers were coming back from Vietnam after their tour of duty, all through the war. Many came home during the war, when opposition to it was significant. Some managed to return to normal life and make a success of it. Others did not. They found it hard to cope with what they had been through and the situation they faced on their return.

- There were few large parades welcoming them home.
- There was a lot of hostility. Veterans were beaten up, spat on, accused of killing innocent people and discriminated against when looking for work.
- At the time there was very little understanding, or acceptance, of post-traumatic shock in the military or the government, so few were given free counselling. During and immediately after the Vietnam War the suicide rate for veterans was almost twice that of men of a similar age who had not fought in the war. The exact number of veteran suicides is impossible to find, but estimates range from thousands to hundreds of thousands.

Activities ?

1. Draw up a list of the cost of the war to the USA under the headings: 'political'; 'military'; 'social' and 'economic'.
2. Draw a poster to advertise a coming home parade for Vietnam veterans. It needs to give, as briefly as possible, reasons for having the parade.
3. Draw a poster to advertise a counter-demonstration against the parade. It needs to give, as briefly as possible, reasons for having the counter-demonstration.

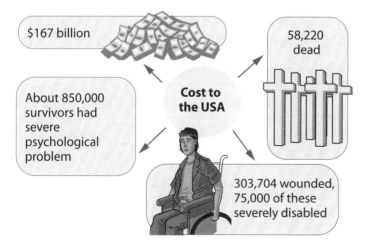

$167 billion

About 850,000 survivors had severe psychological problem

Cost to the USA

58,220 dead

303,704 wounded, 75,000 of these severely disabled

Figure 4.8 The cost of the war in lives and dollars.

The USA and the world

The US government was hit hard by the Vietnam War, and not only in its relationship with its people.

- It felt it had lost face abroad. It had entered the war to keep South Vietnam free from communism. By the end of 1975, all of Vietnam was communist.

- The gradual cooling off of the Cold War meant many politicians felt that the USA should, in future, be very careful not to get involved in conflict in other countries.

- In 1954, many people abroad had seen the USA as a country to respect due to its government, its wealth and the unity of its people. By 1975, many saw the USA as anything but united. Government actions over civil rights and the Vietnam War meant the government was less respected.

Source C

From an interview with Helen Tennant Hegelheimer in 2003. She worked on the planes that took the troops to Vietnam and brought them back.

And they came home to a world that was very different, even just twelve months later. Flying in, some guys asked, "How bad are the antiwar demonstrations?" That's the hardest question I've had to answer in my life. I'd say, "They're bad." There were often protesters at the gates outside Travis [the air force base where they landed]. I had to tell these boys that had just served their country to get out of their country's uniform as soon as they could. If they weren't wearing their uniform then maybe they wouldn't be targeted by the protestors.

Source B

A photograph showing a protest by veterans in opposition to a 'Home with Honor' parade in New York, to celebrate those who had served in the war.

Extend your knowledge

Nixon and the Cold War

Nixon was very anti-communist in his early career. However, by 1972 he was beginning to see the benefits of improved relations with China and the USSR. One of these benefits would be that they would encourage the North Vietnamese to negotiate for peace – which they did. Nixon visited China in 1972 and established friendly relations, opening the way for trade between the USA and China. He visited the USSR in 1972, 1973 and 1974, each time negotiating over the reduction of nuclear weapons and establishing friendly relations.

While these meetings helped to end the war in Vietnam, what effect do you think they might have had on the American public's opinion in terms of why troops were in Vietnam in the first place?

Summary

- The aims of North Vietnamese and the USA were so different that it made peace negotiations very difficult.
- Peace negotiations began in Paris in January 1969. Secret peace negotiations began in August 1969: these negotiations did not involve the South Vietnamese government.
- On 8 October 1972, the USA and North Vietnam produced a peace agreement that both were prepared to sign. The South Vietnamese refused to sign it.
- On 27 January 1973, the Paris Peace Accords were signed. US troops left shortly after.
- The peace fell apart as South Vietnam refused to negotiate with communists. The North Vietnamese invaded and took over, capturing Saigon on 30 April 1975.
- The war left the USA $167 billion poorer. Over 58,000 soldiers had died and many of the war veterans who returned had physical disabilities and/or psychological problems.
- The USA had lost a war for the first time, and lost much international respect.

Checkpoint

Strengthen

S1 Explain why negotiating peace was so difficult for the USA and the North Vietnamese.

S2 List the main terms of the Paris Peace Accords.

S3 Draw a flow diagram to show how the Peace Accords fell apart.

S4 Write a paragraph explaining what you think was the most significant cost of the war to the USA and why.

Challenge

C1 Give one military, one economic and one political problem that the USA left behind in South Vietnam that encouraged the North Vietnamese to invade in 1975. Explain your choices.

C2 Why do you think the South Vietnamese government did not negotiate with the North Vietnamese when the USA left? Explain your answer.

How confident do you feel about your answers to these questions? If you are not sure that you answered them well, form a group with other students, discuss the answers and then record your conclusions. Your teacher can give you some hints.

4.4 Why did the USA fail in Vietnam?

The USA lost the Vietnam War. It failed in its aim to keep South Vietnam as a separate, non-communist country. The reasons for this failure can be found in factors related to the USA, the South Vietnamese, the North Vietnamese and the Vietcong. Figure 4.9 shows the some of the main reasons for US failure.

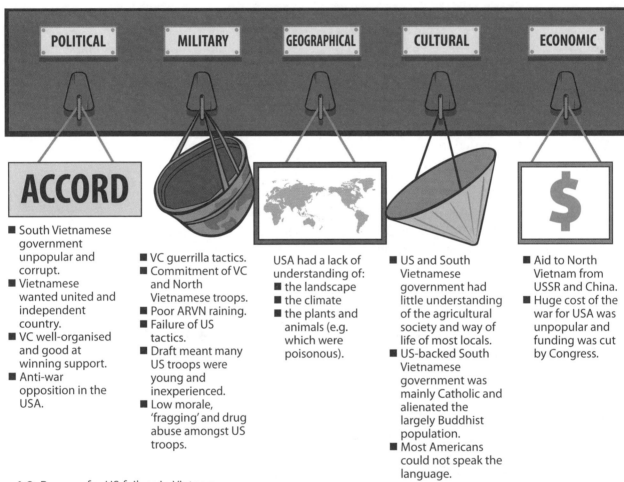

POLITICAL

ACCORD

- South Vietnamese government unpopular and corrupt.
- Vietnamese wanted united and independent country.
- VC well-organised and good at winning support.
- Anti-war opposition in the USA.

MILITARY

- VC guerrilla tactics.
- Commitment of VC and North Vietnamese troops.
- Poor ARVN raining.
- Failure of US tactics.
- Draft meant many US troops were young and inexperienced.
- Low morale, 'fragging' and drug abuse amongst US troops.

GEOGRAPHICAL

USA had a lack of understanding of:
- the landscape
- the climate
- the plants and animals (e.g. which were poisonous).

CULTURAL

- US and South Vietnamese government had little understanding of the agricultural society and way of life of most locals.
- US-backed South Vietnamese government was mainly Catholic and alienated the largely Buddhist population.
- Most Americans could not speak the language.

ECONOMIC

- Aid to North Vietnam from USSR and China.
- Huge cost of the war for USA was unpopular and funding was cut by Congress.

Figure 4.9 Reasons for US failure in Vietnam.

Activities

It will help to think back across all you have learned in Chapters 3 and 4 for these activities.

1   Under two headings, 'North Vietnam' and 'USA', list reasons from Figure 4.9 according to whether you think the reason shows the strength of North Vietnam or a weakness of the USA (some could be included in both).

2   Choose the reason you think was the most significant for the success of North Vietnam. Underline it and write down why you think it was the most significant.

3   Choose the reason that the USA would most easily have been able to change. Underline it and write down how you think the USA may have been able to change it.

The strengths of North Vietnam

The North Vietnamese understood both their own strengths and the weaknesses of the USA. North Vietnam's biggest strength was political, although familiarity with the geography and culture of South Vietnam were vital too.

Geographical and cultural strengths

North Vietnam and South Vietnam had been one country and many people on both sides wanted them to become one country again. This proximity gave them several advantages.

- The North Vietnamese understood the landscape, the climate and the language of the South.

- Those who had fought the French as Vietminh knew the location of tunnel systems that could be used and enlarged.

- A significant number of those who left North Vietnam to fight in the South were South Vietnamese who had moved north after the 1954 Geneva Accords. Many still had family and other contacts there.

Political and economic

Public opposition was not an option in North Vietnam. The government was committed to a unified Vietnam. If this meant war then the country was committed to war. So were its people – or at least they had to behave as if they were. North Vietnam had other political advantages.

- The Vietcong were already established in South Vietnam. North Vietnam could supply the VC and work with them. The VC were very organised, politically and socially (see page 90).

- North Vietnam had financial help from China and the USSR. They sent over $3 billion in aid (much of it in weapons and equipment) to North Vietnam between 1954 and 1967. Also, both Laos and Cambodia allowed the Ho Chi Minh Trail to operate in their countries. Without the trail, the North Vietnamese could not have moved people and equipment into South Vietnam as easily.

Military

Both the North Vietnamese troops and their VC allies were used to fighting in jungle conditions. They both used guerrilla tactics and fought small skirmishes to inflict

Source A

A photograph showing young children being trained to fight by the Vietcong in June 1968.

casualties on the US and ARVN troops, but sometimes they fought larger battles. There is more on VC guerrilla tactics on pages 96–98, but Figure 4.10 points out the crucial role of the North Vietnamese army in the war.

GUERILLA TACTICS
The VC were well-organised and experienced in guerrilla fighting. They built up a system of tunnels and bases stocked with guns, explosives and bikes to move around quickly and fight. The VC also gained the support of villagers.

BUT
The North Vietnamese, were supplied by China and the USSR. The North Vietnamese army brought a lot of these supplies south on the Ho Chi Minh Trail.

AND
After the Tet Offensive (1968), the VC were badly weakened. North Vietnamese troops did most of the fighting for the rest of the war.

REMEMBER
The war was eventually won by an invasion by North Vietnamese troops – not guerrilla fighting.

Figure 4.10 The vital role played by the North Vietnamese army.

Activities ?

1   In groups, consider the strengths of the North Vietnamese. Which of these could most easily become a weakness, and how?

2   If the strength you have chosen did become a weakness, how likely, on a scale of 1 to 10 (with 1 as 'least likely') do you think a US victory would be?

3   Your answer to Question 2 is a judgement reached by interpreting what you know. Write a paragraph to explain how an interpretation is different from a fact.

The weaknesses of the USA

Geographical and cultural

The USA was a long way from Vietnam. Americans were foreigners, fighting in a strange country. Some had the same racist attitudes towards the Vietnamese as opponents of the civil rights campaigns in the USA had towards black Americans. Americans in Vietnam also had disadvantages that they did not work hard enough to overcome, or maybe did not even see as disadvantages. Most Americans in Vietnam:

- had very little grasp on what the country was like, including even the top military officials
- used interpreters (because they did not speak the language themselves) making it much harder to gain the trust and support of the South Vietnamese people
- did not understand that villagers would not want to leave their land and the places where their ancestors and family members were buried
- did not realise that many villagers could not read, which meant that it was pointless dropping leaflets that told them to move out from places due to be bombed.

Source B

A photograph showing US troops 'evacuating' a village before burning it, in 1965. The Vietnamese man has a label around his neck, showing where he is to be moved to.

Political and economic

The USA had very serious political and economic weaknesses, at home and abroad.

- The USA may have said they were in Vietnam to fight for democracy, but to many South Vietnamese they were just like the French. They were a foreign nation occupying the country and imposing their own ideas.
- The US-backed South Vietnamese government was unpopular and corrupt, whoever was in charge. At the start of the war, many members of the government, and officials in the cities and the villages, had worked for the French. This meant they were unpopular with the local people.
- In the USA, there was significant opposition to the cost of the war. Congress supplied the funding that White House administrations needed to run the country. The military were always saying they needed more money to fight the war. By 1971, Congress was setting limits to the amount of money that could be spent on the war and the military ran short of equipment.

Military

Many historians argue that the assumptions and mistakes of the military were a significant reason for US failure. There were several reasons for this.

- The US military was convinced that the war could be won with more troops and by more bombing of North Vietnam, not by fighting a limited war.
- They measured success in the war in a way that made them seem more successful than they were. For example, they would measure the number of VC (or North Vietnamese troops) killed in an operation, or the number of VC bases (often villages) destroyed or cleared. They ignored the fact that the ARVN still did not control large areas of the South, destroyed bases were rebuilt and burning villages caused resentment.
- They had been told, from Kennedy's presidency on, to concentrate on counter-insurgency and on winning the support of the South Vietnamese people. However, working with the villagers was never done consistently enough to be effective.
- The draft meant that the troops on the ground were unusually young and inexperienced. Soldiers were drafted for a year and there was a constant turnover. This meant experienced soldiers returned home after a year to be replaced by inexperienced ones.
- The age and lack of experience of US troops, as well as their lack of training in guerrilla warfare, meant that morale dropped during the war. Once troop withdrawals started, many soldiers tried to avoid combat, while 'fragging' and drug abuse became a growing problem.

Extend your knowledge

Varying interpretations

Interpretations about losing the war vary a great deal, depending on the point of view of the person making the interpretation. Immediately after the fall of Saigon:

- Nixon blamed Congress, saying the South Vietnamese would have stayed in power if they had had the money he promised to get them when they signed the Paris Peace Accords.
- From 1965 onwards, the military blamed the various White House administrations for not giving them enough men and money, and for fighting a limited war.

Who might the South Vietnamese government have blamed?

Opposition to the war in the USA

Unlike North Vietnam, the USA was a democracy. Presidents and members of Congress needed public support to be elected. They had to face criticism in the media and from the public. The 1960s were a decade where protest and criticism of the government grew. For the first time, a significant number of people were saying that their elected government was not doing what they wanted. Indeed, both Vietnam and civil rights produced situations where the American public felt ashamed of the actions of their government, police and military.

The US government tried to ignore public opposition to the war. However, as opposition to the war grew it became almost impossible for the government to continue the war. It was the first war in which the USA had been involved where a large section of the US population did not accept the need for the war. Even worse, a growing number of people were actively against it. It was also the first war in which returning soldiers openly campaigned against it in large numbers and even returned their medals.

Interpretation 1

From *Triumph Forsaken as a Path to Setting the Record Straight* (2010) by Robert F. Turner.

A great deal of responsibility [for US failure in Vietnam], I believe, falls on President Johnson and especially Defense Secretary Robert S. McNamara, whose refusal to listen to the advice of their military and intelligence advisors led to horrible mismanagement of the conflict and the pursuit of an incredibly flawed strategy they should have realised would not maintain the support of the public.

Interpretation 2

From *The Vietnam War 1956–1975* (2014) by Andrew Wiest.

Tiny North Vietnam... could rely on billions of dollars worth of aid from the communist bloc [the USSR, China and their allies]. The aid included the very latest Soviet and Chinese weaponry, from the AK-47 infantry weapon or surface-to-air missiles, although not often in the quantities that the North Vietnamese desired.

Source C

A cartoon about opposition to the war in the USA. It was published in a British newspaper on 15 October 1969.

"No irresponsible demonstrators are going to tell me how to run the United States!"

Activities

1 In groups, consider the weaknesses of the USA. Which weakness does Source B show?

2 Which weakness does Source C show?

3 Explain which Source in this chapter you would use to show the weakness of the USA if you could only use one.

Interpretation 3

From *The Vietnam War* (2007), by Mitchell K. Hall. He is discussing the different aims of anti-war groups and who was part of them.

The military failed to utilise an effective strategy against the Vietnamese communists. It tried… fighting a war of attrition [trying to wear down the VC] instead of providing security to peasants. United States pacification efforts came too late or with too little emphasis. American tactics remained tied to heavy firepower rather than building better relationships at the village level.

THINKING HISTORICALLY ▸ Interpretations (2c/3a)

History as hypotheses

In science, you might have come across the idea of a hypothesis – a hypothesis is an idea that a scientist comes up with to explain what they can see happening. The scientist then tries to find evidence, through experiments, to find out whether their hypothesis is correct. Historians often work in a similar way, but look at sources to find their evidence, rather than doing experiments.

These three historians are thinking about the reasons for the failure of the USA in Vietnam.

Historian's interests	Historian's hypothesis	Evidence
Political historian: Interested in leaders, their views and actions and the effects these had on history.		
Economic historian: Interested in how economic conditions changed, and how this affected politics and society.		
Cultural historian: Interested in changes in how people think, what they read and listen to and their day-to-day lives.	The US government and military never understood the Vietnamese: neither the determination of the North Vietnamese, nor the culture of the South Vietnamese and their attachment to their villages.	

Work in groups of three.

1 Make a copy of the above table.

   a As a group, discuss the interests of each of the historians, and write a hypothesis that they might put forward based on their interests (the cultural historian has been done for you as an example).

   b Each person in the group should take on the role of one of the historians. For your historian, add at least three pieces of evidence into the table that support your hypothesis, based on the information and sources in this chapter.

   c For your historian, write a concluding paragraph, summing up your views on the reasons for the failure of the USA in Vietnam. Remember to restate your hypothesis and support it with your evidence.

2 Share your concluding paragraphs with the rest of the group and compare them.

   a Underline instances where different hypotheses use the same or similar evidence.

   b Look at each hypothesis in turn. Can you think of at least one piece of evidence that challenges each hypothesis? (Tip: you can start by looking at evidence for the other hypotheses being right!)

3 Discuss as a group: Is it possible to say which hypothesis is correct?

Activities

1. In groups, write down the letters of the Sources and Interpretation numbers in section 4.4. Next to each letter or number, write the reason for US failure in Vietnam that it supports.

2. Finish the sentences below about the failure of the US in Vietnam.
   a. It was the dedication of the VC because…
   b. It was the South Vietnamese government because…
   c. It was the Ho Chi Minh Trail because…

3. Are there any reasons missing from the sources and interpretations? Decide on a missing reason and choose a source from this chapter to support it. Share your reasons and the supporting evidence with a partner.

Summary

- The North Vietnamese had significant support from both China and the USSR.
- The North Vietnamese were also very committed and organised.
- The South Vietnamese government and US forces were unpopular.
- The USA's military tactics were ineffective.
- US public opinion worked against US involvement in the war.

Checkpoint

Strengthen

S1 Explain the role of the military in the failure of the USA in Vietnam.

S2 Explain why opposition to the war in the USA could be interpreted as both a North Vietnamese strength and a US weakness.

Challenge

C1 Give one cultural, one military and one geographical reason to explain why the North Vietnamese were in a strong position in the Vietnam War.

C2 List three arguments to support the statement: "The USA failed in Vietnam because of its own weaknesses".

How confident do you feel about your answers to these questions? If you are not sure that you answered them well, reread the sections on North Vietnam's strengths and the USA's weaknesses.

Recap: Reactions to US involvement in the Vietnam War, 1964–75

Recall quiz

1 Who were the SDS?
2 What was the draft?
3 What happened at My Lai in 1968?
4 Who was Lieutenant Calley?
5 What happened at Kent State University in 1970?
6 Who were the 'hard hats'?
7 Who asked for the support of the 'silent majority'?
8 What did the Paris Peace Accords say should happen to Vietnam?
9 How many US troops died in Vietnam?
10 When did the South Vietnamese government fall?

In the exam, you will be asked how useful contemporary sources are for an enquiry. Copy and complete the table below. Support what you say with your own knowledge if it helps you to make your point.

Sources	Enquiry	Ways they are useful
A and B on page 121	Opposition to the war	
E and G on page 125	The impact of My Lai	
A and C on page 132	Support for the war	
F on page 135 and G on page 136	The impact of the silent majority speech	

In the exam, you will be asked about how historians' interpretations can differ. To find out why interpretations give different impressions you need to ask:

- Are they thinking about the same aspect of the topic?
- Might they have used different sources (look carefully at both sources on your paper, as well as the interpretations; the sources will have been carefully chosen to help you)?

Interpretations	Enquiry	How they differ	Why they might differ
1 and 2 on page 123	Clash between the media and government over Vietnam		
1 and 2 on page 133	Working class feeling about the war		
2 on page 148 and 3 on page 149	Reason for US failure in Vietnam		

Explaining why historians' interpretations differ

In Paper 3, one question will ask you to suggest one reason why two interpretations give different views about an aspect of your study. To understand the reasons for difference you need to appreciate that historians writing about any society have to make choices and they have to make judgements. They choose what to concentrate on. They also come to views about the topics they research. Historians may be focusing on different aspects, using different sources, or reaching different conclusions on the same sources. These factors explain reasons for difference.

Historians focus on difference things

Interpretations of history are created by historians. Historians construct interpretations based on evidence from the past. Think of their role as similar to a house-builder: the evidence – the sources available - are the building blocks for their construction. Historians choose what enquiries to make of the materials available to them. No historian can write about the whole of history everywhere. What shapes the historian's work is what they want to explore and what they choose to focus on. Figure 1 below lists some of the choices they make:

Place	National History	Local History
Period	One century or more	One decade or less
Range	Overview	Depth
People	National Leaders	Ordinary people
Aspect	Political history	Social history

Figure 1 Some examples of historians' choices.

Figure 2 The historian's focus.

After choosing their focus, the historian must find evidence to pursue their enquiry. So, they will be looking for different things in order to answer different questions about the past.

Historians A and B below are both writing about the same school, but their focus is different. In looking at the history of a school, several different enquiries are possible, for example the focus could be on the building, the curriculum, students' achievements and so on. As you read the interpretations below, identify what the two historians are interested in - what have their enquiries focused on?

Historian A

The village school has been in continuous use since 1870. It continues to educate local children from the ages of 5–11. They are educated in the same building that was constructed in 1870. Its outward appearance has hardly changed. It was originally built of red brick, with white-painted wooden doors and the large windows that can still be seen today. The schoolroom windows, reaching almost to the high celling, were designed to give plenty of light, but with windowsills too high for students to be distracted by being able to see anything outside. Although a modern extension at the rear was added in the 1960s, the key features of the school building represent a remarkable degree of continuity in education in the locality.

Historian B

Education locally has changed in the period since 1870. Lessons in the 19th century focused almost entirely on the 3Rs of reading writing and arithmetic. There was much learning by heart and copying out of passages. By the 21st century, the wall displays and the students' exercise books show that science, history, geography, have all become important parts of the curriculum and with more emphasis on finding out and creativity. In terms of the curriculum, the degree of change in education since 1870 has been considerable.

Activity ?

Read each of the statements about Historians A and B below.

a The historians have different views about the amount of change in education in the village.

b One of the historians is wrong.

c One of the historians is biased.

d They are just giving different opinions.

e They have used different evidence.

f They have focused on different aspects.

g They are both correct in their conclusions.

h They have emphasised different things.

i They are looking for different things.

j The historians disagree.

k The historians do not disagree.

1 Make a list of each of the statements you agree with and another list of those that you do not agree with.

2 Explain why Historians A and B have different views about the extent to which education has changed in the village. Try to use words from the box below in your answer:

focus	*emphasis*	*aspect*	*evidence*	*conclusions*	*enquiry*	*interested*

Historians reach different conclusions from the evidence

Even when historians have the same focus and purpose – for example, even if they both seek to explain why the same thing happened – their conclusions may still be different. This is because the evidence from the past doesn't provide us with an answer: historians have to work out an answer from it – and often the evidence points in different directions. Then, the historians have to make judgments. Differences may arise because:

- they have given weight to different sources
- they have reached different conclusions on the same sources.

In a court of law, every member of the jury hears the same evidence, but they sometimes disagree about their verdict. It comes down to making judgments about what conclusions can be drawn from the evidence.

Activity ?

Study Interpretations 3 & 4 on page 105.

Which of the following reasons explains why the views in interpretations 3 and 4 are different? Make a list of all those that you think apply. You can add other reasons of your own if you wish.

a The historians are interested in different aspects of the topic.

b The historians have emphasised different things when giving their views.

c The evidence from the period points in different directions.

d The historians have reached conclusions by giving weight to different sources from the period.

Choose one reason you have listed and write one or two sentences to explain why you chose it. Remember to use the interpretations in your answer. Refer to sources from the period too, if you listed reason c or d.

Summary ◤

- What shapes the historian's work is which aspect of history the historian chooses to explore.
- Historians' judgments differ because the evidence can support different views. They may reach different conclusions because they have given weight to different sources or because they are looking at different aspects of the topic.

Preparing for your GCSE Paper 3 exam

Paper 3 overview

Your Paper 3 is in two sections that examine the Modern Depth Study. In Section A you answer a question on a source and one using your own knowledge. Section B is a case study using sources and interpretations of history and the four questions will be about the same issue. The paper is worth 30% of your History assessment.

History Paper 3	Modern Depth Study		Time 1 hour 20
Section A	Answer 2 questions	16 marks	20 minutes
Section B	Answer 4 questions	32 marks + 4 for SPaG	60 minutes

Modern Depth Option 33 The USA, 1954–75: conflict at home and abroad

Section A

You will answer Questions 1 and 2.

1 Give two things you can infer from Source A about... (4 marks)

Source A is included on the question paper. You should work out two inferences from it. An inference is something not directly stated in the source, but which you can support using details from it.

You have a table to complete for each inference: 'What I can infer…' and 'Details in the source that tell me this'. Allow five minutes to read the source and to write your answer. This question is only worth four marks and you should keep the answer brief and not try to put more information on extra lines.

2 Explain why... (12 marks)

This question asks you to explain the reasons why something happened. Allow 15 minutes to write your answer. You are given two information points as prompts to help you. You do not have to use the prompts and you will not lose marks by leaving them out. Always remember to add in a new point of your own as well: higher marks are gained by adding in a point in addition to the prompts.

You will be given at least two pages in the answer booklet for your answer. This does not mean you should try to fill all of the space. The front page of the exam paper tells you 'there may be more space than you need'. Aim to write an answer giving at least three explained reasons.

Section B

You will answer Question 3 (a), (b), (c) and (d). All four questions will be about the same issue. Question (a) will be based on contemporary sources (evidence from the period you are studying). Questions (b) (c) and (d) will be based on two historical interpretations.

3(a) How useful are Sources A and B for an enquiry into... (8 marks)

You are given two sources to evaluate. They are in a separate sources booklet so you can keep them in front of you while you write your answer. Allow 15 minutes for this question, to give yourself time to read both sources carefully. Make sure your answer deals with both sources and use your knowledge when you evaluate the source. You could use it, for example, to evaluate the accuracy or completeness of the evidence. You should make a judgement about the usefulness of each source, giving clear reasons. Only choose points which are directly relevant to the enquiry in the question. You should always take account of the provenance (the nature, origin and purpose) of the source when you think about the usefulness of the information it gives. How reliable is it?

3(b) Study Interpretations 1 and 2. They give different views about...

What is the main difference between these views? (4 marks)

Allow ten minutes for this question to give yourself time to read the extracts. Identify an overall difference rather than different pieces of information. For example, think about whether one is positive and the other negative. Then use details from both. The difference is… this is shown because Interpretation 1 says… but Interpretation 2 says…

3(c) Suggest one reason why Interpretations 1 and 2 give different views about... (4 marks)

Allow five minutes for this question. It does not need a long answer (it is only worth four marks) and you have already read the interpretations, but you will need to use both of the interpretations again and perhaps Sources B and C. Give a clear reason for the difference. One reason could be that the historians have chosen to give weight to different evidence. If you use this reason, you should use both Sources B and C to show that the evidence from the period differs. If you use other reasons, for example about what the historian is focusing on (see page 152) you will not need to use sources B and C.

3(d) How far do you agree with Interpretation [1 or 2] about...? (16 marks + 4 marks SPaG)

This question, including SPaG, is worth 20 marks – over one third of your marks for the whole of the Modern Depth Study. Make sure you have kept 30 minutes of the exam time to answer it and to check your spelling, punctuation and grammar. You will already have worked out the views in the interpretations for Question (b). Question (d) asks you how far you agree with the view in one. Plan your answer before you begin to write, and put your points in two columns: For and Against.

You should use points from the two interpretations and also use your own contextual knowledge. Think about it as if you were putting weight on each side to decide what your judgement is going to be for the conclusion. That way, your whole answer hangs together – it is coherent. Be clear about your reasons (your criteria) for your judgement.

In this question, four extra marks will be gained for good spelling punctuation and grammar. Use sentences, paragraphs, capital letters, commas and full stops, etc. Try also to use relevant specialist terms – for example, terms such as constitution, communism, legislation.

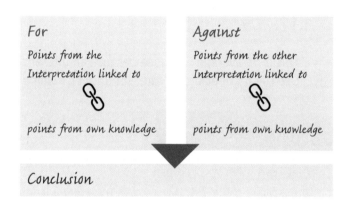

For
Points from the Interpretation linked to

🔗

points from own knowledge

Against
Points from the other Interpretation linked to

🔗

points from own knowledge

Conclusion

Paper 3, Section A: Question 1

Study Source E on page 27.
Give **two** things you can infer from Source E about integrating schools in the South in the 1950s.
Complete the table below to explain your answer.
(4 marks)

Study Source E on page 27.

Exam tip

Make two inferences and choose details from the source that directly support them. The examples below give only the first inference and support.

Average answer

What I can infer:
Some people didn't like the idea of integrated schools.

Details in the source that tell me this:
The girl is black and they are white.

The inference is correct, but the detail used does not explain how the picture shows some people's dislike of integration.

Verdict

This is an average response because an inference is made, but without accurate support.
Use the feedback to rewrite this answer, making as many improvements as you can.

Strong answer

What I can infer:
Some people didn't like the idea of integrated schools.

Details in the source that tell me this:
The white women crowded around Elizabeth Eckford look angry and they are yelling at her.

Details are given that support a correct inference.

Verdict

This is a strong response because an inference is made and supported from the source.

156

Paper 3, Section A: Question 2

Explain why the Montgomery Bus Boycott was a success.
You may use the following in your answer:

- Martin Luther King
- the media

You **must** also use information of your own. **(12 marks)**

Exam tip

Focus on explaining 'why'. Aim to give at least three clear reasons.

Average answer

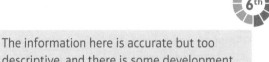

The Montgomery Bus Boycott was when the black people of Montgomery, Alabama, stopped riding the Montgomery buses to protest over the treatment of black passengers. They wanted to stop the segregation of black and white passengers into different parts of the buses. The leaders of the boycott included Martin Luther King, who had just become a pastor in Montgomery. To keep the boycott going they set up car pools, which was helpful.

As well as Martin Luther King's leadership, the boycott succeeded because of how many of the black people of Montgomery who usually went to work on the buses supported it. They supported it for about a year – that is a very long time and shows their determination and the bus company was losing money.

The publicity the boycott got in the media helped it to succeed. Because so many people heard about it, it strengthened everyone's determination who was involved and made them carry on and it may have actually helped convince people to make the anti-segregation court case.

The information here is accurate but too descriptive, and there is some development of the role of car pools, but most of it is not directly linked to an explanation of why the boycott was a success.

Relevant information is given here and is additional to the stimulus points. However, it should develop this further by explaining how the bus company's loss of money explains the success of the boycott.

Another reason for success is given here, but is not developed. It should expand on the impact of publicity. It could explain that the NAACP was providing the legal support for the case and how the NAACP usually only supported cases they thought they had a high chance of winning.

Verdict

This is an average answer because:

- information is accurate, showing some knowledge and understanding of the period, and adds a point additional to the stimulus (so it is not a weak answer)
- it does not analyse causes explicitly enough to be a strong answer
- there is some development of material, but the line of reasoning is not clear.

Use the feedback to rewrite this answer, making as many improvements as you can.

Paper 3, Section A: Question 2

Explain why the Montgomery Bus Boycott was a success. **(12 marks)**

Strong answer

The Montgomery Bus Boycott succeeded for a variety of reasons. It was well led and well-organised and got media attention but, most importantly, it was strongly supported by the black community that made up the majority of bus-users.

Strong leadership was important. The boycott went on for a long time, and it was important to keep people going. The leaders also had to be able to negotiate with the bus company and the mayor: King was important here because he was a newcomer who was also good at making speeches and negotiating.

Good organisation was vital on many levels. It was important to keep people informed of meetings. It was also important to organise alternative transport for those who lived too far away from their work to walk, or who could not walk for other reasons. At first this was done by taxis, but as the boycott went on there were car pools run by various churches and other groups. So these needed someone to organise drivers and times when they were running. People might have dropped out of the boycott if they found it too hard to get to work.

However, one of the key reasons for the boycott's success was the support of the black bus riders. Almost all of them stopped riding (which hurt the bus company financially, as black people were the majority of their passengers). More importantly, they kept on not riding, bringing lots of media publicity to the case, which also contributed to the success. Their determination encouraged the NAACP to bring the court case to desegregate the buses, which was not the first reason for the boycott. But once the case was brought the boycotters decided to carry on the boycott until buses were desegregated. Strong leadership set the boycotters off and kept them determined and good organisation supported them. However, their determination was probably the most significant element of all.

An introductory sentence is not strictly necessary, but shows understanding of context. Clear reasons are given in the second sentence to show focus on the question.

A slightly underdeveloped point. However, it is tied to the question and provides a valid reason.

The paragraph begins with a valid point, additional to those given as stimulus, provides specific information in support and ends with an explanation of its significance, tying the information to the question.

The paragraph begins with another valid point, additional to those in the stimulus (although the student has also chosen to incorporate the media stimulus). The point is effectively supported. Clear reasoning links it and other factors to the success of the boycott.

Verdict

This is a strong answer because:
- information is wide-ranging and precisely selected to support points that directly address the question
- the explanation is analytical and directed consistently at the question
- the line of reasoning is coherent and sustained.

Paper 3, Section B: Question 3a

Study Source B and Source C, and Interpretation 1 and Interpretation 2 on page 109.

How useful are Sources B and C for an enquiry into the extent to which Vietnamisation was a success? Explain your answer, using Sources B and C and your own knowledge of the historical context. **(8 marks)**

Exam tip

Consider the strengths and weaknesses of the evidence. Your evaluation must link to the enquiry and use contextual knowledge. Your reasons (criteria) for judgement should be clear. Include:

- what information is relevant and what you can infer from the source
- how the provenance (nature, origin, purpose) of each source affects its usefulness.

Average answer

7th

Source B is useful because it tells you how Vietnamisation was going when Nixon made this speech – for example, air operations were down 20% and over 60,000 US troops were out by 15 December. It also tells you that the South Vietnamese were doing more of the fighting – although it does not give numbers. You can tell that Nixon is providing a summing up of the situation for people, but you do need to be careful, because this is a speech by Nixon and it was his policy.

Source C is useful because it is a cartoon showing that there was more than one view of Vietnamisation. The cartoonist is showing why he thinks that Vietnamisation was not working that well. He is pointing out that by 1972 US troops still are not all out and soldiers are still being killed.

Source C is also useful because it shows that Vietnam was an important issue for people in 1972. Newspaper cartoons pick up things that are important to the public, they do not tend to comment on insignificant things. It does not tell you the number of people who agree or disagree with his point of view about the war – but it does tell you that there were different views about it.

> Some useful information is taken from the source and the answer begins to discuss the provenance of the source. However, the relevance of the fact it is Nixon's policy needs to be more clearly explained.

> Useful information is taken from the source and the answer makes an inference from the source ('that Vietnamisation was not working that well'), but doesn't explain why it is useful. This should be explained. There is the start of analysis of the provenance of the source, but this needs developing.

> This comment makes a valid inference from the cartoon. It would be stronger with more developed evaluation of how its provenance affects its utility.

Verdict

This is an average answer because:

- it has taken relevant information from both sources and shown some analysis by beginning to make an inference (so it is not a weak answer)
- it has added in relevant contextual knowledge and used it for some evaluation of both the sources, but this is not sufficiently developed
- it does not explain criteria for judgement clearly enough to be a strong answer. The evaluation using the provenance of the sources should be more developed.

Use the feedback to rewrite this answer, making as many improvements as you can.

Paper 3, Section B: Question 3a

How useful are Sources B and C for an enquiry into the extent to which Vietnamisation was a success? Explain your answer, using Sources B and C and your own knowledge of the historical context. **(8 marks)**

Strong answer

Source B gives Nixon's view of the effectiveness of Vietnamisation in a speech to the people about the Vietnam War in November 1969. He explains that army policy had changed to focus on getting the ARVN into a position to do most of the combat fighting. He goes on to emphasise the positive results – how Vietnamisation has meant that 60,000 troops have come home and reduced the air missions by 20%. In contrast he is vague about the ARVN, although he says they are in combat more. His speech seems to give useful, factual evidence that Vietnamisation is working in 1969.

> Good analysis of the evidence.

However, you have to consider that Vietnamisation is Nixon's policy. He wants public support for his policies in Vietnam, so he is hardly going to present evidence that he is failing. The fact that he does not produce statistics about the ARVN makes you wonder if those statistics are not very good. For example, in 1969, 123,000 men deserted from the ARVN. This rose to 150,500 in 1971.

> Good evaluation using own knowledge and taking provenance into account.

Source C is a cartoon from 1972. This is presidential election year (that's why 'secret election year plan...' is on the paper Nixon is holding) and the cartoonist is implying that Vietnamisation is not working because, since Nixon became president in 1968 (and almost immediately introduced Vietnamisation), 20,000 more American soldiers have died in Vietnam.

The source is also useful to show more than just the cartoonist's feeling about Vietnamisation because newspaper cartoons tend to pick up things that are important to the public. He has made the tombstone huge to show the number of deaths as a big issue. This also shows us that it was an issue in an election year (if it was not, then the cartoonist would focus on other issues). So, Source C certainly shows that Vietnamisation was not completely effective and we know that even by the end of 1972, over 750 more US soldiers had been killed and 24,000 still remained in Vietnam, which supports the cartoonist's view that Vietnamisation had not achieved its aim.

> Strengths and limitations of the source are shown and contextual knowledge is used in the evaluation, which also comments on the nature of the source.

Verdict

This is a strong answer because:
- it has analysed both sources, making inferences from them
- it has used contextual knowledge in the evaluation of both sources
- evaluation takes provenance into account and explains criteria clearly when making judgements.

Paper 3, Section B: Questions 3b–c

Study Interpretations 1 and 2 on page 109. They give different views about the extent to which Vietnamisation was a success.
What is the main difference between these views?
Explain your answer, using details from both interpretations.
(4 marks)

Exam tip

Remember to identify a main difference and then use details from both interpretations to support your answer.

Average answer

A main difference is that Interpretation 1 emphasises the view that Vietnamisation was a success. Interpretation 2 looks at the way it did less well, considering how the ARVN coped with Vietnamisation. Daddis suggests that there was a feeling that they could not cope without American troops.

A valid difference is identified, but no details are given from Interpretation 1.

Verdict

This is an average answer because it identifies a difference, with some detail from Interpretation 2, but it does not use detail from Interpretation 1 to support the difference. Use the feedback to rewrite this answer, making as many improvements as you can.

Suggest **one** reason why Interpretations 1 and 2 give different views about the extent to which Vietnamisation was a success. You may use Sources B and C (on page 109) to help explain your answer. **(4 marks)**

Exam tip

Give a clear reason. If you decide to use Sources B and C choose details from them to show that the historians may have given weight to different sources.

Average answer

The interpretations may differ because the historians have given weight to different sources. For example, Source B gives the statistics about 60,000 troops being withdrawn and 20% fewer air missions. That supports Interpretation 1, which emphasises how US officials and the military view the policy as successful.

A reason is given and Source B is used, but nothing is said about Interpretation 2.

Verdict

This is an average answer because it gives a reason for the different views with support from Source B, but it does not refer to Interpretation 2 and Source C has not been used. Use the feedback to rewrite this answer, making as many improvements as you can.

Paper 3, Section B: Questions 3b–c

Study Interpretations 1 and 2. They give different views about the extent to which Vietnamisation was a success.

What is the main difference between these views?

Explain your answer, using details from both interpretations. **(4 marks)**

Strong answer

A main difference is that Interpretation 1 is very positive about Vietnamisation. It emphasises the American view of the situation, discussing Nixon's view that it succeeded (given in 1971) and those who had served in Vietnam saying so too (including 70% of generals). Interpretation 2 emphasises the problems, not the successes. It shows that even Americans thought the ARVN were not going to be able to manage.

> Details from Interpretation 1 are used as well as those from Interpretation 2.

Verdict

This is a strong answer because it identifies a valid difference with support from both interpretations.

Suggest **one** reason why Interpretations 1 and 2 give different views about the extent to which Vietnamisation was a success.

You may use Sources B and C (from page 109) to help explain your answer. **(4 marks)**

Strong answer

The interpretations may differ because they have given weight to different sources. For example, Source B (Nixon's speech) is positive about Vietnamisation (which was his policy). This supports Interpretation 1, because it talks about official approval in the USA, including in the military, and it also talks about Nixon saying it was working in 1971.

Source C provides some support for Interpretation 2 in that it suggests there are problems with Vietnamisation. The cartoon is making the point that the troops are not all out yet, although it is focusing on the deaths. Interpretation 2 is underlining the problem with withdrawing: US advisers and military think the ARVN can't cope on its own. Daddis may have had sources about the ARVN and its problems that meant he decided to focus on that aspect of Vietnamisation.

> Details from Source B are used to show support for Interpretation 1 as well as details from Source C to support Interpretation 2.

Verdict

This is a strong answer because it gives a valid reason for the different views and supports it using both sources.

Paper 3, Section B: Question 3d

Up to 4 marks of the total for part (d) will be awarded for spelling, punctuation, grammar and use of specialist terminology.

How far do you agree with Interpretation 1 about the extent to which Vietnamisation was a success?

Explain your answer, using both interpretations and your knowledge of the historical context. **(20 marks)**

Exam tip

Be clear what view the author gives and then consider points for and against this view from both interpretations and your own knowledge. Make a judgement, giving reasons for your decision.

Average answer

Interpretation 1 says that many American officials were positive about Vietnamisation. They felt it was working and Nixon said it was in 1971. Interpretation 1 also points out that the military seemed to think it was working. The 1974 survey showed 73% of generals thought it was working so well it should have been brought in earlier.

From my own knowledge I know that Vietnamisation did get troops out of Vietnam, but slowly. However I also know that the ARVN was having trouble with counter-insurgency.

But Interpretation 1 does not consider the impact of Vietnamisation on the South Vietnamese army or whether they were going to be able to cope when the US troops left. It is only considering success from the point of view of the USA and the people there. Interpretation 2 suggests that Americans working with the ARVN knew that they were just not ready to manage alone.

So I do not agree with Interpretation 1. I am more likely to agree with Interpretation 2 that it was not working.

Relevant details are chosen from Interpretation 1 and own knowledge is included. But the knowledge is simply added on to the extract. The answer should explain clearly whether the information supports or challenges the view.

Relevant details are chosen to contrast Interpretation 1 with Interpretation 2 and own knowledge is added in. A judgement is given, but this is not well explained.

Verdict

This is an average answer because:

- it has chosen relevant details from both the interpretations and used contextual knowledge in the answer, so it is not a weak answer

- it does not explain criteria for judgement clearly enough to be a strong answer

- spelling is accurate and there is some use of specialist terms (counter-insurgency), but this is not wide-ranging and punctuation is limited to the use of full stops.

Use the feedback to rewrite this answer, making as many improvements as you can.

Paper 3, Section B: Question 3d

How far do you agree with Interpretation 1 about the extent to which Vietnamisation was a success? Explain your answer, using both interpretations and your knowledge of the historical context. **(20 marks)**

Strong answer

Interpretation 1's view is that many Americans were convinced that Vietnamisation was working, especially during the war. To back this up, he quotes a speech by Nixon in 1971, while US troops were still in the country, and a 1974 poll of generals who had served in Vietnam (when all troops were technically out of the country, but it was still at war). Over half of them thought Vietnamisation was 'soundly conceived'. Some were less positive, but only 6% disagreed. Even more suggestive of broad agreement is that 73% thought it had been such a success it should have been adopted earlier. However, Interpretation 2 suggests that many Americans thought the ARVN were clearly never going to cope without US backing. When you consider the US spent over $160 billion over the course of the Vietnam War you can see how that could be so.

> The extracts are analysed to show contrasting views and contextual knowledge is integrated.

Vietnamisation was Nixon's policy. It was his way of getting the US out of the war 'with honour' as he said. Therefore, he was bound to see it, or at least present it, as a success. The 1974 poll was of a very limited group, generals who had fought there. They also had an interest in saying it had been a success. So Interpretation 1 is using a very selective set of sources. It does not consider the situation in Vietnam, where the ARVN had always had a lot of support and training from US troops. Interpretation 2 points out that American advisers feared the ARVN would not be able to cope alone. If so, South Vietnam was likely to be taken over by North Vietnam and become communist. This would be a failure of Vietnamisation.

> A key issue is identified and there is good use of contextual knowledge to make a judgement.

It is possible to agree with both interpretations depending on the answer to the question "successful for whom?" Interpretation 1 deals with the views of Americans like Nixon and the generals, who were probably looking at it from an American point of view. They were considering the troops that came home, the saved costs, and the falling US death toll. From that point of view, you could call it a success. Interpretation 2, on the other hand, is considering the success of Vietnamisation from the other side. He explains that Americans, including the advisers in Vietnam, do not think the ARVN will do well. In terms of thinking about success for the South Vietnamese, the fact that, in 1975, the North Vietnamese invaded and took over South Vietnam make Vietnamisation a failure.

> A judgement is reached with clear reasons and both views are considered. Knowledge is very well used to support the judgement. Spelling, punctuation and grammar are good, too.

Verdict

This is a strong answer because:
- both interpretations are analysed and evaluated using own knowledge
- the line of reasoning is coherent and the judgement is appropriately justified with clear criteria
- SPaG demonstrates accuracy, effective control of meaning and the use of a wide range of specialist terms.

Answers to Recall Quiz questions

Chapter 1

1   Any answer similar to: 'Separating groups of people by race, religion or belief'

2   State laws enforcing segregation

3   Any answer similar to: 'It ruled that schools should be desegregated'

4   White people moving from integrated housing areas to all-white areas

5   Nine

6   A fourteen-year-old black child from Chicago, murdered by white people in 1955

7   Racist groups set up to fight to preserve segregation

8   President of the Women's Political Council in Montgomery, Alabama

9   Polite drivers; 'first come, first served' seating; black drivers on black routes

10 Any answer similar to: 'Southern politicians who were Democrats but did not support Democrat policies in favour of civil rights for black Americans'

Chapter 2

1   There was a sit-in to demand desegregation of the Woolworths lunch counter

2   Rode buses through the South to test desegregation of bus station facilities

3   James Meredith enrolling at the University of Mississippi

4   Bombingham

5   Washington

6   James Cheney, Michael Schwerner and Andrew Goodman

7   Nation of Islam

8   Member of SNCC; black power leader

9   1968 report on the causes of the ghetto riots in various cities

10 Martin Luther King

Chapter 3

1   French and Vietnamese (Vietminh) troops

2   If one country becomes communist, neighbouring countries will follow – like toppling dominoes

3   A village fortified against the Vietcong

4   The Gulf of Tonkin Resolution was passed

5   Communist resistance fighters in South Vietnam; guerrilla tactics

6   A limited bombing campaign of North Vietnam

7   President Kennedy

8   1968

9   South Vietnamese taking over the fighting, allowing US troop withdrawal

10 Cambodia, Laos

Chapter 4

1   Students for a Democratic Society, a student protest group

2   Enforced military service

3   A massacre of the villagers by US troops

4   The US officer in charge at My Lai

5   Four students killed and nine wounded by state troops

6   Construction workers

7   President Nixon

8   Reunification of Vietnam after fair elections

9   Over 58,000

10 30 April 1975

Index

Acknowledgements

Picture credits
The publisher would like to thank the following for their kind permission to reproduce their photographs:

(Key: b-bottom; c-centre; l-left; r-right; t-top)

1. A 1972 Herblock Cartoon The Herb Block Foundation: Library of Congress, Prints & Photographs Division, [reproduction number, e.g., [LC-00652238] 109; **Alamy Images:** Everett Collection Historical 33, 68, Granger, NYC 50, Pictorial Press Ltd 7l, 31, World History Archive 125; **Getty Images:** AFP 80, Afro Newspaper / Gado 7r, 18, 44, 53, Bettmann 27, 48, 84, 107, 110, 136, Buyenlarge 57, Carl De Souza 93, Carl Iwasaki / The LIFE Images Collection 22, CBS Photo Archive 123, Charlotte Observer 46, David Fenton 75, Dick Swanson 102, Dominique Berretty 146, Don Cravens 29, 34, 36, Hank Walker / The LIFE Picture Collection 12l, 12r, Hulton Archive / Stringer 60, Jill Freedman 142, John Filo 118, 127, Joseph Louw / The LIFE Images Collection 74, Larry Burrows 6, 79, 100, Leif Skoogfors / CORBIS 121, nik wheeler / Corbis 113, Photo 12 97, Robert Abbott Sengstacke 72, Santi Visalli 134, SLADE Paul 70, Spencer Grant 132, Stan Wayman 8, 9, ullstein bild 145; **Mary Evans Picture Library:** Photo Researchers 15; **Press Association Images:** AP 66, HENRY GRIFFIN / AP 63, MALCOLM BROWNE / AP 88, Nick UT / AP 129, Press Association Images 38; **Telegraph Media Group:** Nicholas Garland published in the Daily Telegraph on 09 Jun 1969, British Cartoon Archive, University of Kent, www.cartoons.ac.uk 138, Nicholas Garland published in the Daily Telegraph on 15 Oct 1969, British Cartoon Archive, University of Kent, www.cartoons.ac.uk 148; **The Herb Block Foundation:** A 1962 Herblock Cartoon 25; **TopFoto:** The Granger Collection 45, 92

Cover images: *Front:* **Bridgeman Art Library Ltd:** Private Collection

All other images © Pearson Education

Every effort has been made to trace the copyright holders and we apologise in advance for any unintentional omissions. We would be pleased to insert the appropriate acknowledgement in any subsequent edition of this publication.

Text
Extract on page 12 in Source C from Senator James Eastland United States Senate, 27/05/1954; Extract on page 13 in Source D from The Southern Oral History Program, interview with William Patrick Murphy by Sean Devereux, January 17, 1978 Interview B-0043, in the Southern Oral History Program Collection #4007, Southern Historical Collection, Wilson Library, University of North Carolina at Chapel Hill; Extract on page 14 in Interpretation 1 from *Grand Expectations, The United States, 1945-1974*, OUP (Patterson, JT 1996) p. 381,Oxford University Press with permission; Extract on page 20 Interpretation 2 from *Race and Racism in the United States: An Encyclopedia of the American Mosaic [4 Volumes*, ABC-CLIO (Editors Gallagher.C.A, Lippard.C.D 2014); Extract on page 20 in Interpretation 3 from *From Jim Crow to Civil Rights The Supreme Court and the Struggle for Racial Equality*, OUP (Klarman,MJ 2004) p.386, Oxford University Press with permission; Extract on page 24 in Source C from Freedom's Children by Ellen Levine, copyright © 1993 by Ellen Levine. Used by permission of G. P. Putnam's Sons Books for Young Readers, an imprint of Penguin Young Readers Group, a division of Penguin Random House LLC; Extract on page 25 in Interpretation 1 from *From Jim Crow to Civil Rights The Supreme Court and the Struggle for Racial Equality*, OUP (Klarman, MJ 2004) p.368, Oxford University Press with permission; Extract on page 27 in Source F from Interview with Daisy Bates by Elizabeth Jacoway, October 11, 1976, Interview G-0009, in the Southern Oral History Program Collection #4007, Southern Historical Collection, Wilson Library, University of North Carolina at Chapel Hill; Extract on page 28 in I nterpretation 3 from *We Ain't What We Ought to Be: The Black Struggle from Emancipation to Obama* by Stephen Tuck, Cambridge, Mass: The Belknap; Press of Harvard University Press, copyright © 2010 by Stephen Tuck; Extract on page 28 in Interpretation 4 from Retreat into Legalism: The Little Rock Desegregation Case in Historic Perspective, *PS: Political Science and Politics Journal* Vol. 30, No. 3, p.447 (David L Kirp 2000), © American Political Science Association, published by Cambridge University Press and with permission from the author Professor David Kirp; Extract on page 33 in Source C from Interview with John Lewis by Jack Bass, November 20, 1973, Interview A-0073, in the Southern Oral History Program Collection #4007, Southern Historical Collection, Wilson Library, University of North Carolina at Chapel Hill; Extract in Interpretation 1 on page 36 from To Walk in Dignity: the Montgomery Bus Boycott, *Magazine of History*, p.13 (Carson,C 2005), reproduced with permission of Organisation of American Historians, in the format Book via Copyright Clearance Center; Extract on page 37 in Interpretation 2 from *The American Civil Rights Movement; Readings and Interpretations*, McGraw-Hill/Dushkin (D'Angelo.R 2001) pp.267-8, McGraw-Hill Education; Extract on page 39 in Interpretation 3 from *Grand Expectations, The United States, 1945-1974*, OUP (Patterson,JT 1996) p.406, Oxford University Press with permission; Extract in Interpretation 4 on page 39 from *From Jim Crow to Civil Rights The Supreme Court and the Struggle for Racial Equality*, OUP (Klarman,MJ 2004) p.372, Oxford University Press with permission; Extract in Source C on page 47 from an interview given in 2015 by Samuel Jones, with permission from the interviewer Jane Shuter; Extract in Source D on page 47 from an interview given in 2015 by Julian Bond, with permission from the interviewer Jane Shuter; Extract on page 47 in Interpretation 1 from *We Ain't What We Ought to Be The black struggle from Emancipation to Obama*, by Stephen Tuck, Cambridge, Mass.: The Belknap; Press of Harvard University Press, Copyright © 2010 by Stephen Tuck; Extract on page 53 in Interpretation 1 from The Children's Crusade and the Role of Youth in the African American Freedom Struggle, *OAH Magazine of History*, 19, 1 (Martin Luther King, Jr), Oxford University Press on behalf of Organization of American Historians, reproduced with permission of Organization of American Historians in the format Book via Copyright Clearance Center; Extract in Source B on page 55 from 'I have a dream' speech, 28 August 1963 Dr. Martin Luther King Jr., reprinted by arrangement with The Heirs to the Estate of Martin Luther King Jr., c/o Writers House as agent for the proprietor New York, NY. © 1967 Dr. Martin Luther King Jr.© renewed 1995 Loretta Scott King; Extract in Source G on page 61 from Lyndon B. Johnson: "Remarks in the Capitol Rotunda at the Signing of the Voting Rights Act." August 6, 1965. Online by Gerhard Peters and John T. Woolley, The American Presidency Project; Extract in Source B on page 66 from Washington University Digital Gateway Texts Interview with David Dawley July 6,1989; Extract in Source E on page 68 from interview with Raney Norwood by

Bob Gilgor, January 9, 2001, Interview K-0556, in the Southern Oral History Program Collection #4007, Southern Historical Collection, Wilson Library, University of North Carolina at Chapel Hill; Extract in Interpretation 1 on page 69 from *The Civil Rights Movement*, Edinburgh University Press (Newman, M 2004) p.116-7; Extract in Interpretation 2 on page 69 from *We Ain't What We Ought to Be The black struggle from Emancipation to Obama*, by Stephen Tuck, Cambridge, Mass: The Belknap; Press of Harvard University Press, Copyright © 2010 by Stephen Tuck; Extract on page 73 in Source D from Interview with Albert Raby, Washington University Digital Gateway; Extract in Source E on page 73 from *Voices of Freedom: An Oral History of the Civil Rights Movement and from the 1950s through the 1980s* by Henry Hampton, copyright © 1990 by Blackside, Inc. Used and by permission of Bantam Books, an imprint of Random House, a division of Penguin Random House and LLC and The Random House Group. All rights reserved; Extract on page 76 in Interpretation 1 from The American Dream: from Reconstruction to Reagan by Wright, Esmond, reproduced with permission of Blackwell, in the format Book via Copyright Clearance Center; Extract on page 76 in Interpretation 2 from *The Civil Rights Movement*, Edinburgh University Press (Newman,M 2004) p.144; Extract on page 83 in Source B from 73 - The President's News Conference April 7, 1954, Dwight D. Eisenhower, American Presidency Project; Extract on page 83 in Source C from 306 - Letter to the President of the Council of Ministers of Viet-Nam Regarding Assistance for That Country. October 25, 1954, Dwight D. Eisenhower, American Presidency Project; Extract in Source E on Page 87, Source B on page 91, on page 97 in Source C, on page 101 in Source E, on page 113 in Source F and on page 142 in Source C from *Vietnam The Definitive Oral History, told from all sides* Ebury Press (Appy, CG) p.57,p.110, p.204, p.248, p.310, p.409, The Random House Group; Extract on page 87 in Interpretation 1 from *Triumph Revisited Historians Battle for the Vietnam War* Tylor and Francis Group LLC – Books (Philip E. Catton 2010) p.34, reproduced with permission of Routledge in the format Book via Copyright Clearance Center; Extract on page 87 in Interpretation 2 from *Kennedy's Quest for Victory: American Foreign Policy 1961-1963, ed Thomas G. Paterson, pp 223-225, 225-234, 237, 245 and 252*, OUP, Oxford University Press with permission; Extract on page 91 in Source A from *'Vietnam' A Portrait of Its People at War*, Tauris Parke Paperbacks (I.B. Tauris & Co Ltd) (Chanoff,D. & Van Toai,D. 2009) p.43, reproduced with permission of I.B. Tauris & Company Limited in the format Book via Copyright Clearance Center; Extract on page 99 in Interpretation 1 from *The Vietnam War 1956-1975*, Osprey Publishing (Weist, A 2002) p.27; Extract on page 101 in Source F from When Heaven & Earth Changed Places by Le Ly Hayslip, copyright ©; 1989 by Le Ly Hayslip and Charles Jay Wurts. Used by permission of Doubleday, an imprint of; the Knopf Doubleday Publishing Group, a division of Penguin Random House LLC. All rights; reserved; Extract on page 105 in Interpretation 3 from *The Vietnam War 1956-1975*, Osprey Publishing (Weist, A 2002) p.45; Extract on page 105 in Interpretation 4 from *No Sure Victory: Measuring U.S. Army Effectiveness and Progress in the Vietnam War*, OUP (Daddis, GA 2011) p.143, by permission of Oxford University Press, USA; Extract on page 109 in Source B from 425 - Address to the Nation on the War in Vietnam November 3, 1969, The American Presidency Project; Extract on page 109 in Interpretation 1 from *Military Aspects of the Vietnam Conflict 1956-1975*, Taylor & Francis (Hixson.WL 2000) p.291; Extract on page 109 in Interpretation 2 from *No Sure Victory: Measuring U.S. Army Effectiveness and Progress in the Vietnam War* OUP (Daddis, G.A.) p.178-9, By permission of Oxford University Press, USA; Extract on page 110 in Source D from 139 - Address to the Nation on the Situation in Southeast Asia. April 30, 1970, Richard Nixon The American Presidency Project; Extract on page 122 in Source C from *The Strength not to fight, a History of Conscientious objectors of the Vietnam War*, Little Brown and Co (Tollefson,J.W. 1993) p.104-105, Reprinted with the permission of Little Brown and Company. All rights reserved; Extract on page 123 in interpretation 1 from *The Uncensored War The Media & Vietnam*, University of California Press, Ltd London England (Hallin,D.C. 1989) p.6, with permission from Oxford University Press; Extract on page 123 in Interpretation 2 from *A Bright Shining Lie: John Paul Vann and America in Vietnam*, Random House (Sheehan,N 1988) p.315, The Random House Group and Penguin Random House LLC; Extract on page 125 in Source G from an interview given in 2015 by Hilary Crain, with permission from the interviewer Jane Shuter; Extract on page 128 in Interpretation 3 from *Richard Nixon and the Quest for a New Majority* by Robert Mason. Copyright © 2005 by the University of North; Carolina Press. Used by permission of the publisher; Extract on page 133 in Interpretation 1 from *American Protestants and the Debate over the Vietnam War*, Lexington Books (Bogaski, G. 2014) p.132, reproduced with permission of Lexington Books in the format Republish in a book via Copyright Clearance Center; Extract on page 133 in Interpretation 2 from *Richard Nixon and the Quest for a New Majority* by Robert Mason. Copyright © 2005 by the University of North; Extract on page 135 in Source E from 425 - Address to the Nation on the War in Vietnam November 3, 1969, The American Presidency Project; Extract in Interpretation 3 on page 136 from *Richard Nixon and the Quest for a New Majority* by Robert Mason.Copyright © 2005 by the University of North; Carolina Press. Used by permission of the publisher; Extract on page 148 in Interpretation 1 from *Triumph Forsaken as a Path to Setting the Record by Robert F. Turner in Triumph Revisited Historians Battle for the Vietnam War*, Routledge (Taylor & Francis) (ed Andrew Wiest and Michael J Doidge 2010) p.110; Extract on page 148 in Interpretation 2 from *The Vietnam War 1956-1975*, Osprey (Wiest,A. 2002) p.19.